Learning and Teaching in Social Work

Towards Reflective Practice

*of related int*erest

Handbook of Theory for Practice Teachers in Social Work
Edited by Joyce Lishman
ISBN 1-85302-098-2

Community Care Practice and the Law
Michael Mandelstam with Belinda Schwer
ISBN 1-85302-273-X

Performance Review and Quality in Social Care
Edited by Anne Connor and Stewart Black
ISBN 1-85302-017-6
Research Highlights in Social Work 20

Good Practice in Supervision
Statutory and Voluntary Organisations
Edited by Jacki Pritchard
ISBN 1-85302-279-9

Learning and Teaching in Social Work

Towards Reflective Practice

Edited by Margaret Yelloly and Mary Henkel

Jessica Kingsley Publishers
London and Bristol, Pennsylvania

First published in the United Kingdom in 1995 by
Jessica Kingsley Publishers Ltd
116 Pentonville Road
London N1 9JB, England
and
1900 Frost Road, Suite 101
Bristol, PA 19007, U S A

HV
11
L43

Library of Congress Cataloging in Publication Data
A CIP catalogue record for this book is available from the Library of Congress

British Library Cataloguing in Publication Data
A CIP catalogue record for this book is available from the British Library

ISBN 1-85302-237-3

Printed and Bound in Great Britain by
Biddles Ltd, Guildford and King's Lynn

For Anthea Hey

Contents

Part Three: Learning Processes and the Learning Environment

Introduction

This book addresses contemporary themes in professional education. While its genesis lies in the continuing education of social workers, the key issues which it addresses – the nature of knowledge for professional education, the contemporary emphasis on competence and learning outcomes, the changing models of professionalism, and the nature of the learning process itself – are common to all the helping professions.

The book was conceived as a joint enterprise between staff of the Department of Government at Brunel University and the Tavistock Clinic. At first sight, this might seem an improbable conjunction of two very different traditions, public policy and clinical, but it was the exploration and development of these two in the name of post-qualifying education in social work that formed the basis of the joint M.Phil. in Social Work course mounted by the University and the Clinic. Staff and students from the course are strongly represented among the authors of the book.

The conception, scope and authorship of the book extend well beyond that particular shared project but one of its starting points is a belief in what might emerge from a coming together of those traditions: not a neat integration but a celebration of the value of reflecting on and analysing experience; a conviction that institutions and policies are empty if they neglect the intersubjective worlds of individuals, and that understanding of those worlds must be brought to bear on welfare systems.

Both institutions are major players in post-qualifying education. The Department of Government at Brunel has for many years run a successful M.A. in Public and Social Administration, which attracts students from the health and personal social services, as well as from other sectors of the welfare state. More recently, it has established an M.Phil. in the Evaluation of Public Services, on which, again, students from the health and personal social services are highly represented. The Tavistock Clinic has been involved in the training of the caring professions since its inception in 1926, and its programmes provide for professional staff in a wide range of employment settings. The Clinic has an international reputation for its psychotherapeutic work and training; its trainees come from all over the world, and many of its programmes are common to many disciplines. Between them, the University and the Clinic offer a wide range of courses and workshops, some of them unassessed, others leading to further professional qualifications, for example, in child care practice, in psychotherapy, family therapy, policy, administration or research; many of these lead to a master's or doctoral degree.

The Tavistock Marital Studies Institute, some of whose staff have also contributed, is a separate but closely related organisation which has made a unique contribution to training and theoretical developments in social work over the years; many of its staff, like those of the Clinic, combine social work and psychotherapeutic practice and training.

The contributors share a common perspective on professional education and between them can draw on an extensive reservoir of social work practice and training experience. The book is intended to articulate and communicate something of that experience to a wider audience. It is not an academic treatise, nor a text on how to educate; rather it sets out to explore dilemmas, and to illuminate the pathways and pitfalls to professional growth and development from the standpoint of experienced educators who are also themselves engaged in the same process of continuing learning.

Sadly, Anthea Hey, who would have been a major contributor to the book, died while it was in the early stages. She was a key person in the Tavistock/Brunel collaboration (particularly the joint M.Phil. in Social Work) and we have greatly missed her unique combination of practice, research and teaching experience, her vision and her sharp intellect. Nevertheless, her ideas are strongly present in the book, and it is dedicated to her.

The book is mainly concerned with the post-qualifying level and is organised in three parts. The first concerns conceptual issues in social work education. It examines professional models, the purposes of advanced training, and epistemological questions. The second part incorporates a number of chapters which explore aspects of theory directly relevant to the social work practitioner; they are not intended to be comprehensive but focus on emerging perspectives influencing contemporary practice. The third part is in some ways the culmination, in that it relates earlier discussions directly to the real and actual experience of learning and teaching.

Psychodynamics and New Theories of Science

One of the most persistent themes of the book concerns the shifting and competing ideas about the nature of knowledge and how these impinge upon professional education and practice. Different facets of the debates between positivism and hermeneutics, modernism and postmodernism are present in a number of chapters. A further important source is psychodynamic thinking, in which the Tavistock Clinic's research and practice is firmly rooted. The epistemological basis of psychoanalysis has always been contentious. A brief review of the reverberations of contemporary debates in this field may therefore help to clarify its current status and set the scene.

Misconceptions continue to surround psychoanalysis and the psychodynamic social work tradition fuelled by it. In social work generally psychodynamic ideas appear to have little currency, and are probably regarded as somewhat old hat. The reasons for this curt dismissal are complex and to do in part with the nature of psychoanalysis itself and its scientific standing. But there is something about the psychoanalytic enterprise which arouses strong passions in both its proponents and its critics. Some practitioners have found a knowledge of conflict, ambivalence, anxiety and defence, and the concepts of transference and countertransference, essential tools in their understanding of the complex situations with which they work; others regard them as mistaken or unhelpful. Yet psychoanalysis is one of the major and most fertile intellectual traditions of our time, generating a huge literature and exciting the interest and enthusiasm of philosophers, students of literature, historians, anthropologists and sociologists. This sense of excitement is evident in the burgeoning of Masters' programmes in Psychoanalytic Studies in many of our universities, in the establishment of new journals such as Free Associations (which links psychoanalysis, politics and culture), and in the growth of conferences which bridge psychoanalysis and the contemporary social world. The vibrancy of the annual Psychoanalysis and the Public Sphere Conference at the University of East London is testimony to the relevance and resonance of newer thinking in psychoanalysis for those in a variety of disciplines and spheres of work. Such thinking draws particularly on the object relations tradition, and its central themes of identity and the emergence of the self. Here psychoanalysis can provide fresh insights into aspects of contemporary life, for example, psychoanalytic feminism, the psychodynamics of race, and the integration of psychoanalytic with other frames of reference in understanding culture, politics and art (Frosh 1991, Rustin 1991). The work of Mitchell (1974, 1984) and Sayers (1986), which illuminates the experience and the psychic world of women, illustrates this resonance, and provides rich seams for feminist social workers to mine. In the more practical sphere there has been a huge expansion of training in psychodynamic counselling. Yet mainstream social work seems largely untouched by this intellectual and practical resurgence.

Of course psychodynamic thinking is not in itself an adequate foundation for social work practice: its concepts arise out of and primarily relate to the clinical world of analytic therapy, and care has to be taken in using them in situations to which they were never designed to apply. The social worker who works with families, with groups, with local communities, often in conditions of extreme environmental deprivation and poverty, may need quite other theoretical frames to understand and tackle work problems. But just as one would not sensibly employ a psychoanalyst to run the economy, so one would not look to an economist for help with problems of interpersonal difficulty and emotional distress; and these are pervasive, not only for individuals and in families, but within the organisations in which we work and which so powerfully control our everyday experience. The common stance of the contributors to this book is that psychoanalysis is more than a revolutionary psychological and psychotherapeutic system; its particular perspectives can illuminate everyday dimensions of personal and social experience in a way which makes them less perplexing, painful and confusing, and more manageable.

The objections to psychoanalysis, particularly its status as a science, are well known and it is not our intention to revisit paths which are very well-trodden already (Eysenck 1985, Gellner 1985, Pearson *et al.* 1988, Yelloly 1980). However, it is important to note that more recent thinking on the nature of scientific knowledge, and the ways it is acquired, brings psychoanalysis much closer to other human sciences and their epistemologies. Bruner refers to an 'epistemological awakening' within the natural sciences, a fundamental re-evaluation which has led to a recognition of the uncertain nature of much of their data.

> It is not at all clear how one should characterize what is 'real' in nature and what is a construct, its 'facts' are subject to the perspective of the theory that drives the search for them. Indeed…we know now that facts are not found, but made. (1987 p.x)

All sciences are conceived and constructed in particular ways, within the parameters of a dominant paradigm; from time to time a paradigm shift occurs, allowing the process of knowledge creation to proceed along different lines. Such a shift radically changes the way in which 'facts' are perceived and interpreted.

Similar moves can be discerned in the social sciences, particularly that away from nineteenth century positivist models to qualitative or constructivist forms of inquiry which focus on meaning. The classical scientific model is based on the ontological assumption that there does exist a reality which can objectively be known; the tree is still there during the hours of darkness whether or not we observe it. The constructivist approach starts rather from the position that 'there is no reality except that created by people as they attempt to make sense of their surrounds' (Guba and Lincoln 1989); *all* reality is socially constructed. Social researchers, particularly anthropologists, have become increasingly aware of the difficulty of achieving objectivity in human affairs; furthermore, the very attempt to achieve it may cut researchers off from some of the most significant data available to them; their perceptions, responses, hunches and intentions. In studying human societies, behaviour is not merely observed, data collected and analysed from a position of externality; the researcher is part of the social world which is studied. The mind which analyses and interprets is itself constructed in particular ways; indeed, a shared perspective may be important in constructing, selecting and understanding the significance of the phenomena under study. From this point of view, the human mind and its activities are involved at every stage of the research process.

Such a shift in thinking throws a very different light on the traditional critiques of psychoanalysis as science, since its central theoretical propositions are, on this view, qualitatively no different from those of other human sciences; what does distinguish them is the greater difficulty of obtaining the evidence on which they are based. Freud himself saw psychoanalysis as essentially a natural science, and this was also the view of John Bowlby, who believed profoundly that psychoanalysis, as a body of theory, could move forward only on the basis of evaluating and testing 'real experience' (Bowlby 1980). These two positions seem fundamentally opposed. Yet neither appears fully satisfactory alone. The natural science stance pushes psychoanalysis in a more behavioural and less fully psychological direction; it acts like Procustes' bed, reducing the complexity and richness of psychoanalysis to something more narrow which can be handled by the limited scientific methods available. Those familiar with research on the effects of hospitalisation on children will know how difficult it is to capture the richness of the data by the kind of research methods which give primacy to questions of validity; indeed these methods may do violence to the phenomena by studying only what is measurable and quantifiable. In practice, recent work at the Tavistock, both in research and training, demonstrates an openness to and fertilisation by work developing within different paradigms, and examples are the relation of psychoanalysis to developmental psychology in the work of Stern (1985) referred to by Briggs, and the expanding theoretical horizons of family therapy outlined by Gorell Barnes, both in this book.

A distinction needs to be made between the theoretical foundations of psychoanalytic psychotherapy or social work, and its practice. In terms of the latter, Holmes (1993) maintains that 'although couched in the language of science, psychoanalytic psychotherapy has come increasingly to be seen as a hermeneutic discipline, more concerned with meanings than mechanisms, in which patient and therapist collaboratively develop a narrative about the patient's experience. Such objectification and coherence are in themselves therapeutic, irrespective of the validity or otherwise of the meanings that are found' (p.8).

However, the hermeneutic or constructivist position, concerned as it is with interpretation and with the construction of a coherent narrative, and not with causes, can end up on the shifting sands of extreme relativism, in which 'making sense' is all there is; the possibility of the rightness or wrongness (either of a theoretical proposition, or an interpretation) simply evaporates. Generalisations from particular instances or case studies cannot be made, either for the purposes of advancing knowledge, or for achieving practical ends such as improvements in social welfare. Taken to extremes there appears to be no way of distinguishing between different psychological or therapeutic systems, and no theoretical basis for the training of practitioners. Issues of validity become questions of coherence. An extreme hermeneutic position, therefore, seems to dispose rather effectively of any scientific claims psychoanalysis might have, and within a hermeneutic paradigm it is difficult to see on what established area of knowledge or expertise psychoanalysts can ground their special claims.

A hermeneutic view of therapy which is not linked to and integrally bound up with a core set of scientific theories cannot be defended as truly 'psychoanalytic'. While therapy is of necessity highly *individual* it is not *idiosyncratic*; individual experience is explicable in terms of the general theories of the mind from which psychoanalytic or psychodynamic therapies derive. The psychoanalytic enterprise can indeed be seen, in terms of the newer philosophies of science as scientific and a strong case for this is put by Rustin (1991). Clinical practice is however much more than this, and there is a dualism present within both psychoanalysis and social work, which mirrors the distinction between science and art; elements of both are involved in all professional activities (Bowlby 1979). The practice of therapy (or of social work) is essentially an informed clinical skill which has a scientific basis and is grounded in a general framework of scientific propositions, but is flexibly and individually used in therapy. The therapist is engaged in a dialectical encounter, in which psychodynamic knowledge is a strong element but not the only one. The epistemological process in the therapeutic encounter can be seen as akin to the research process, and this point of view has been persuasively put by Rustin (1991). An interpretation is not plucked out of the air, but is a construction which emerges (initially tentatively) over a period of time. It is framed on the basis of a number of indicators – repetitive behaviour on the part of the patient, interpretation of the symbolic language of dream and phantasy, imaginative guesswork, and the analyst's own counter-transference responses. Ultimately the test is whether it makes sense, and changes something. Thus psychoanalysis does encompass two very different kinds of theory-building: the general propositions of psychoanalysis, and the way that they operate in the individual case.

Clinical practice can be seen as analogous to music. There are laws of harmony, which the musician must follow; the act of musical creation or interpretation is grounded in and underpinned by accepted regularities which allows it to be heard and understood by the listener. But its precise form is in no way determined by these laws, and at some times they clearly do not apply, and a new musical language may be introduced. It is likely that the effective therapist, like the accomplished musician, combines an informed understanding of principles and theories with an intuitive gift which enables her to tune in to the experiences of troubled people. Knowledge, personal capacity, and the practice of the craft, can be identified as the central components in any professional education.

Education for Reflective Practice

We have thought it important to set the approaches to learning for practice developed in this book in the context of different models of professionalism. Those derived from empirical or behaviourist conceptions of practice lay relatively little emphasis on the learning process, whilst for others learning is an inherent and central characteristic (Jones and Joss). Yet even those who are process-oriented acknowledge that what actually happens in professional education is little studied or understood. As Eraut has observed:

> Apart from the limited though valuable literature on professional socialisation, we know very little about what is learned during the period of initial qualification... Still less is known about subsequent learning, how and why professionals learn to apply, disregard or modify their initial training immediately after qualification; and to what extent continuing on-the-job or even off-the-job learning contributes to their professional maturation, updating, promotion or reorientation. Yet without such knowledge, attempts to plan or evalu-

ate professional education are liable to be crude and misdirected. (1985)

Social work is seldom routine and involves working with people all of whom are unique, in situations which are complex, frequently messy and obscure, rarely easy to understand, and almost never amenable to standardised or prescribed responses. The outcomes of professional action are difficult to predict and there is disagreement as to the models of intervention and the relevance of the theories from which they derive. There does however seem to be considerable agreement on educational models which stress learning from experience, since these are congruent with the aims and objectives of social work practice. (Boud *et al.* 1986, Harris 1985, Winter and Maisch 1992). In social work training, experiential learning tends to take three forms: *learning by doing* in practice (Schon's 'practicum') which involves a cycle of action and reflection; *learning by observation and attention,* for example, through infant observation, institutional observation, and through videotapes; and *learning through reflection on the here and now,* whether it be in seminar groups, work with clients, or a staff group. This last form of learning involves the capacity to draw back in order to reflect on what is happening almost as it happens, and enables learning to take place in a way which allows thought-less action to become thought-ful.

The emphasis on the capacity to think is a further distinctive feature of the approaches described here. Thought and reflection are key ideas in professional education and are emphasised in the influential work of Schon (1987); his conception of the professional as 'reflective practitioner' is by no means unique to any institution or professional group, and has been taken up by occupations as diverse as nursing, teaching, social work and engineering. However, the connotation of 'thought' and reflective practice in much of this book is somewhat distinctive and requires explanation. It connotes more than cognitive activity, and draws on the work of Wilfred Bion on the nature of thinking, and the recognition of impediments to thought and their nature (1967). Bion's contribution is explored much more fully by Pietroni, but, in brief, his work on thinking principally refers to the unconscious and often primitive and unverbalised feelings aroused in the worker by the impact of work which is often intense, intimate, conflictual, and may have resonances with the worker's own internal world. The organisation of one's own time, and of one's agency, may be managed in such a way as to minimise the powerful and distressing impact of the work; indeed, sometimes the organisational structures themselves seem almost designed to keep pain at bay and to prevent thought. Many of the ideas here are owed to Isabel Menzies Lyth's classic paper on 'Institutional Defences Against Anxiety' (Menzies 1961) and her other later work, much of which still has relevance and significance for the creation of genuinely caring and personal work and learning environments. These ideas remain useful, particularly to illuminate the impact of stressful work such as child protection on the worker (Cooper 1992); Woodhouse and Pengelly (1991) have noted how difficult it is for professionals in such anxiety-producing work to remain open and responsive (rather than reactive); routinised responses and procedures (though an essential framework for action) can also lead to a rigidity which is inimical to the uniquely personal response needed in the caring professions.

An authentic and personal response cannot be achieved, we suggest, without thought, and without pondering upon the way that the world without is inextricably intertwined with the world within. We carry with us throughout life structures of meaning, assumptive worlds, which frame our experience, and enable us to interpret and articulate it, and to act. The organisational worlds we inhabit reflect that psychic world, the internal society of 'images and phantasies, conscious and unconscious, of other people, the self, and interpersonal relationships...' (Menzies Lyth 1989 p.35). Effective learning is therefore dependent, at least in part, on access to that world of feeling and phantasy, which allows structures of meaning to be recognised, and to be open to change, in a way which facilitates a different (and perhaps more constructive) professional response. Great emphasis is placed in this book on the learning environment, particularly on the need for space and for containment – another idea drawn from Bion, pointing to the need for a safe and secure space for learning. Technically, containment is 'the introjection of an object capable of understanding the infant's experience, and giving it meaning' (Hinshelwood 1991); as applied to the educational setting, and in particular to small learning groups (the essence of the approaches described here) high value is given to creating a space which is somewhat apart from the everyday world, where a reflective mode and a slower pace is promoted, and where it is permissible to allow vulnerability to surface (a view somewhat at odds with the dominant ideas of competence and 'mastery').

The Political Context of Social Work

Social work is one of the most political of all professions. Indeed, it has virtually no role, no identity outside the welfare institutions where it is located. These in turn are shaped and developed by government policies. The Central Council for Education and Training in Social Work (CCETSW) which controls qualification and training for social work, although formally a Quasi-autonomous Non-Governmental Organisation (or Quango) has very little independence; it is wholly government financed, and every word of its Strategic Plans is agreed with Ministers. Thus social work is deeply affected by dominant political ideas and its practitioners are seen as key instruments in the operationalisation of government policy, in community care for example. Social workers' daily activities reflect political intentions and are largely defined by them.

The political context has changed out of all recognition. The idea of collective provision on which the postwar welfare state and the profession of social work were built has lost cogency. There is an erosion of state welfare, and in its place a new pluralism and a shift to competitive market solutions, with the aim of extending choice and driving down costs. With these social strategies have come not only changes in the economics of welfare but new structures and a new management culture based on primary values of efficiency, effectiveness and value for money. These may collide with the person-centred ethos of social work, creating difficult professional and ethical dilemmas.

Professional education thus operates amidst radical external change: reappraisal of professionalism itself, of the place of professions in the structure of the labour market, of relationships between professions and the state and of the role of the state in the provision of welfare. The power of the professions to impose their conceptions of needs, priorities, requisite skills and good practice is being questioned. The idea that professions could be a medium through which the interests of individuals and groups, particularly those on the margins of society, could be reconciled with the needs of the state has lost credibility. Responsibility for welfare has shifted back to the individual and the market, as belief in the capacity of state institutions to accommodate either the scale of need or the degrees of difference in society has faded. At the same time concern with the social processes of exclusion and oppression has weakened.

The scale of these changes and the implications they have for educators and practitioners are the ever-present context for this book. But it is the intermeshing of the inner and outer worlds which is characteristic of the educational models drawn on here, and the central focus is on interaction and reflexivity.

References

Bion, W.R. (1967) A theory of thinking. In *Second Thoughts: Selected papers on Psychoanalysis*. London: Heinemann.

Boud, D., Keogh, R. and Walker, G. (1986) *What is Reflection in Learning*. London: Kogan Page.

Bowlby, J. (1979) Psychoanalysis as art and science. *International Review of Psycho-analysis*, Vol.6, 3–14.

Bowlby, J. (1980) Psychoanalysis as a natural science. *International Review of Psycho-analysis*, Vol.8, 243–56.

Bruner, J.S. (1987) Introduction to D. Spence *The Freudian Metaphor: Toward Paradigm Change in Psychoanalysis*. New York and London: W.W.Norton and Co.

Cooper, A. (1992) Anxiety and child protection work in two material systems. *Journal of Social Work Practice*, 6, 2, 117–128.

Eraut, M. (1985) Knowledge Creation and Knowledge Use in Professional Contexts, *Studies in Higher Education, 10*, 2, 117–133.

Eysenck, H. (1985) *The Decline and Fall of the Freudian Empire*. Harmonsworth: Penguin Books.

Frosh, S. (1991) *Identity Crisis: Modernity, Psychoanalysis and the Self*. London: Macmillan.

Gellner, E. (1985) *The Psychoanalytic Movement*. London: Paladin.

Guba, E.G. and Lincoln, Y.S. (1989) *Fourth Generation Evaluation*. New York: Sage.

Harris, R. (ed) (1985) *Educating Social Workers*. Leicester: Association of Teachers in Social Work Education.

Hinshelwood, R.D. (1991) *A Dictionary of Kleinian Thought*. London: Free Association Books.

Holmes, J. (1993) *John Bowlby and Attachment Theory*. London: Routledge.

Menzies, I. (1961) *The Functioning of Social Science Systems as a Defence Against Anxiety*. London: Tavistock Insititute of Human Relations.

Menzies, Lyth, I. (1989) *The Dynamics of the Social: Selected Essays, Vol. II*. London: Free Association Books.

Mitchell, J. (1974) *Psychoanalysis and Feminism*. London: Allen Lane.

Mitchell, J. (1984) *Women: The Longest Revolution*. London: Virago.

Pearson, G., Treseder, J. and Yelloly, M.A. (eds) (1988) *Social Work and the Legacy of Freud*. London: Macmillan.

Rustin, M.J. (1991) *The Good Society and the Inner World: Psychoanalysis, Politics and Culture*. London: Virago.

Sayers, Janet (1986) *Sexual Contradictions: Psychology, Psychoanalysis and Feminism*. London: Tavistock Publications.

Schon, D. (1987) *Educating the Reflective Practitioner*. MA: Jossey-Bass.

Stern, D. (1985) *The Interpersonal World of the Infant*. New York: Basic Books.

Winter, R. and Maisch, M. (1992) *Assessing Professional Competence: Final Report of the ASSET Programme*. Chelmsford: Anglia University and Essex County Council.

Woodhouse, D. and Pengelly, P. (1991) *Anxiety and the Dynamics of Collaboration*. Aberdeen: University Press.

Yelloly, M.A. (1980) *Social Work Theory and Psychoanalysis*. London: van Nostrand Reinhold.

Part One

Professional Education in Social Work

Chapter 1

Models of Professionalism

Sandra Jones and Richard Joss

Introduction

Jessup (1991) defines competence in connection with professions in a way which suggests a difference between professional and job-related competences:

> A person who is described as competent in an occupation or profession is considered to have a repertoire of skills, knowledge and understanding which he or she can apply in a range of contexts and organisations. To say that a person is competent in a 'job' on the other hand, may mean that their competence is limited to a particular role in a particular company.

This definition offers as key to this difference the general constructs of repertoire, contexts and organisations with an emphasis upon the transferability of a professional repertoire across practice contexts. It also suggests that although there may be both generic and specific differences in the kinds of knowledge, skills and understandings between professions, there is nevertheless an essential commonality in the nature of the competences they share. This commonality has been the focus of more recent work on professional competence and its constituent parts (Pearson 1984, Preston and Walker 1992) and is explored at a later point in this discussion. Behind this notion of essential commonality lies a further fundamental assumption about what constitutes 'a profession' and what makes it somehow different from other occupations.

The literature suggests that there are different approaches to the definition of what constitutes 'professions' and what might be their defining features. It is also possible to distinguish different models of professionalism, each of which is underpinned by a different combination of assumptions about the nature of professional work. These assumptions have implications for the way in which professional competence is defined and developed. Further, these differing models of professional practice may exist side by side within the same organisation. It follows then that any attempt to define the core competences of a particular form of professional work should take account of the relative effectiveness of the differing professional modes and their applicability in professional practice within a social and political context which is increasingly questioning the status, autonomy and accountability of the 'professions'.

This paper briefly summarises the different approaches to the definition of professions. Although much of this early work is quite well-known, and has been superseded by more recent analyses, many of the early concepts (such as the notion of esoteric knowledge) still influence current discussions without their source being adequately recognised. We then discuss the different models of professionalism which emerge from the literature and suggest a framework for identifying the professional competences associated with each model.

From this analysis we then argue that the most appropriate model of professionalism is one which emphasises the importance of experiential learning as the means by which professional competence is acquired and refined. This model is derived from the work of Gibbs (1988), Kolb (1984), Schon (1983,1987) and Winter (1991).

Defining the Professions

The meanings of the terms *profession* and *professionalism* provoke little controversy in everyday conversation. Most people have some notion of the difference between 'professions' and other occupations and indeed have, until recently, accorded people with professional status a considerable amount of deference and respect. However, a close examination of this difference has shown how difficult it is to find an agreed set of characteristics which distinguish the professions from other occupational areas. Much of the early academic interest in the professions was concerned with descriptive and analytic exercises which attempted to characterise some of the similarities and differences.

The trait approach

The early trait approach, for example, was based upon the idea that the description of professional structures would explain the nature of professions.

It assumed that there was an ideal type which represented the essence of professionalism and that the claims of an occupation to professional status should be assessed according to how closely it approached this ideal type. The classic statement of this approach was that of Greenwood (1965) who distinguished five attributes of a profession. These were *systematic theory, community sanction, authority,* an *ethical code* and a *professional culture.* All these were presumed to be grounded in an altruistic, vocational desire to serve the interests of the community.

However, even at a descriptive level it has proved impossible to isolate the common characteristics of professions. A review of twenty-one different studies (Millerson 1964) found that no single attribute was accepted by all of them though some were mentioned frequently. The approach also fails to account for the origin or development of professions.

The division of labour

Structural differentiation and the functional division of labour in society provide the second main approach to the definition of professions. The basis of structural-functional analyses is the special nature of the occupational function of the professions. A key assumption is that there is a naturally evolved social and biological fit between the characteristics of the professions and the nature and needs of society (with some authors arguing that professions fulfil, in a formalised manner, the traditional functions of family members in non-industrial societies). Professionalism is thus a method through which the knowledge available to society is developed and used for the service of the common good. This consensual, vocational service view is evident in the work of Durkheim (1957), Etzioni (1964) and Parsons (1951). Some of these accounts (e.g. Halmos 1970) also emphasise the role of professional ethics in promoting a sense of moral order.

As with the trait approach there is very little consensus about the common structural or functional elements of professions. Nor do these analyses provide significant insight into the process of professionalisation. There is another more serious drawback to both these approaches. This is that the idea of consensual, vocational service for the common good (through shared values and collaboration) is invalidated by the everyday experiences of conflicts of interest between professionals in different occupational areas.

Occupational control

An approach based on the idea of occupational control does provide an explanation for difficulties in collaboration. From this perspective, professionalisation is just one of many methods by which occupations seek to control their own area of work and as such professions are comparable to Trades Union and Guilds. The occupational control approach rests on a conflict, action, model of society in which competing groups struggle to secure their own interests.

The approach argues that there is no real difference between professions and other occupations save that a profession has become 'an occupation which has assumed a dominant position in the division of labour, so that it gains control over the determination of the substance of its own work' (Friedson 1973). As such, professions are no more than an ideological commitment to one specific form of occupational organisation, and professionalisation is the process by which some occupations attempt to secure greater control over their internal and external environments.

In this model, work is underpinned by exclusive knowledge. This knowledge is of an expert kind rather than service- or vocationally-based. It is held that professionals acquire power through using a variety of gatekeeping methods to ensure exclusive control of that knowledge.

These include limiting the right of entry to selected candidates, determining and providing the training, and 'licensing' members to practise. This power is exchanged for certain privileges such as autonomy (to control the content of work as well as members' behaviour), financial reward, and relative freedom from external accountability. Professional codes of ethics (often, though not always, formally stated) and other implicit controls, such as restricted entry and socialisation through training, are meant to ensure self-regulation. Together these restrictions maintain shared professional value sets, derived from the deep rules and meanings of the occupational culture. They are seen to be necessary for internal control.

The occupational control model predicts that where different professions have similar areas of work, the boundaries between them may overlap and result in conflict. This often expresses itself through the different value sets held by different professions, with each group claiming legitimacy for its own theoretical paradigms or methods of working. Proponents of this approach (see for example Huntingdon 1981) argue for the analysis of the structural and cultural characteristics of an occupation as a means of explaining professional work.

From Definitions to Practice

The difficulties in defining professions and professionalism through their characteristics led researchers to look more closely at the detailed processes of professional work. Up until this point, discussions had remained at a general level, describing the work as altruistic, vocational or service-oriented. It was also common to emphasise the importance of esoteric (and exclusive) knowledge.

The new era of 'value for money'

From the early 1980s onwards, the accountability of professionals for their work came under increasing scrutiny. With some irony we see that an occupational control definition treats the professions just like other occupations – legislation to limit the activities of the Trades Union has been paralleled by executive action to curb the autonomy of the professions and to make them more accountable across a whole range of previously inviolate occupations. Government inspired initiatives such as 'value for money' and 'effectiveness and efficiency' secured greater financial control over professional activity and, through this, more purchase over the substance of professional work.

The emphasis on evaluation, through the use of performance indicators as well as more formal modes of inspection (including audit) has reinforced this. Neave (1988), for example, has written persuasively about the 'Rise of the Evaluative State'. This has been coupled with a premium on consumerism and consumer power through quality of service and citizen's charter initiatives. Teachers, doctors, dentists, lawyers, social workers and the police have all been subjected to firmer limits on their professional discretion with a constant nibbling away at the edges of their professional autonomy. What is emerging is a new and external definition of professions. It is based upon the idea of consumer-led definitions of quality of service rather professionally-led definitions. This has led to conceptual shifts from professional definitions of 'needs' to user definitions of 'wants'.

Towards work-based definitions of professions

It is against this background that the emphasis has now moved towards defining professions in terms of what professionals actually do. As such, professional competence can be seen as a social and political phenomenon, and the competency movement as an extension of the trend towards greater executive control of the economic workplace. In this context it is no accident that the current dominant approach to competency should be firmly rooted in behaviourist, reductionist theories of individual performance, which were themselves derived from the Taylorist efficiency movement (Walker 1992). Defining competences, specifying the work to be done, measuring performance against specified criteria (and paying accordingly), combined with opening up the professional market-place, has further eroded professional autonomy.

On the nature of professional work

Here we return to Jessup's definition of professional competence and possible differences with other forms of work. The analysis by Winter (1991) also points to the broad and complex nature of professional competence. Throughout his authoritative account of the nature of professional competence, it is clear that assessments of competence involve complex judgements rather than 'a simple reading from a measurement scale' and that competence can only be inferred rather than observed. In other words professional competence is more than prescribed performance in a range of functions underpinned by knowledge and understanding.

The units and elements derived by functional analysis may provide a basis for inferring competent performance but cannot themselves explain what Schon (1983) has termed the 'artistry' of professional competence. We would argue that an occupationally derived classification of professional competence will do justice to this artistry only if it reflects what professionals actually do in practice. Whilst there may be a common process behind professional work (discussed later) it is apparent that what professionals do in their practice varies both across professions and within them. To understand this variation, and its implications for defining professional competence, we need a framework for examining models of professionalism.

Models of Professionalism

Although definitional approaches foundered on a lack of agreement about common features of professions, the shift in emphasis to professional performance, rather than characteristics of professions, has produced some consensus.

The role of uncertainty

One area of agreement is the ability to deal with the uncertainty that attaches to professional work. Although many situations are routine, the professional worker constantly has to deal with novel, indeed apparently unique, situations. He or she can exercise discretion to act in different ways (or not act at all) to resolve a situation. The exercise of this judgement is recognised as a fundamental aspect of professional practice and is considered by some analysts to be the essential commonality between professional groups (Pearson 1984, Schon 1983). A competence for judgement is offered as one of two elements of a theory of the nature of professional work argued for by Walker (1992a). The other element is held to be professional responsibility to continuously improve personal performance.

The role of knowledge

The nature and application of knowledge (and understanding) is still held to be a key dimension of professional work, though it is increasingly argued that single concepts of knowledge are inadequate. For example, Eraut (1992) distinguishes six different forms of knowledge which 'inform' professional practice. Walker (1992b) reports three constructions of knowledge which are related to professional performance developed by the Centre for Applied Research in Education. These are *content knowledge* construed as public bodies of theories, procedures and information; *knowledge as a cognitive process*; and the *practical knowledge* (often tacit) of the practising professional.

A knowledge base is required for all work but this approach argues that the difference lies in a particular dimension – the knowledge base's *theoretical orientation*. This refers to the presence or absence of a set of systematic underpinning theories in the knowledge base, their degree of sophistication and, importantly, the values attached to them. Again these vary between and within professional groups. Similarly, there is variation in the methods of application of knowledge, and in particular whether or not there is an implicit or explicit *practice theory* which governs this process. Practice theory allows the integration of theory with practice and puts an emphasis upon the professional values of practice.

The role of values

As was apparent from the discussion of definitional approaches, there is by no means one consistent value base shared by the professions – a fact which has been used to explain the conflict between different professional groups, particularly in situations where there is a shared 'client' base (as for example, between probation officers and the police). Differences include the deep rules and shared meanings which constitute an ethical code, which itself may or may not be formally stated. This value base includes 'informal' rules and meanings which derive from sub-cultures within an organisation. These may conflict with the formal position in the way they promote practices which would be unacceptable elsewhere – for example the way some professions treat women and members of the ethnic minorities.

Other key variables

Three other variables also help to explain these different models of professional work. The first two, *relations with client* and *self-image* are to some extent consequent upon the knowledge base, theoretical orientation, practice theory and values inherent in a professional context. Relations with client refers to the way in which the professional interacts with clients and the assumptions which inform that relationship. The emphasis placed in a practice theory on, for example, the process of working with clients could vary considerably between different professions.

Similarly with the professional's *self-image*. The way in which the professional views her/himself reflects the value base of the occupation and the cultural norms into which individuals are socialised through recruitment and training processes. This is reinforced by the nature of the knowledge base, theoretical orientation, and practice theory. The self-image has been shown to be a significant feature of professional performance (Jones and Levi 1983). Both the value base and self-image involve some incorporation and internalisation of cultural norms within professional work – an issue that has implications for the development of professional competence. As we shall see presently, holistic approaches deriving from the work of Neumann (1979), in contrast to the behaviourist competency movement referred to earlier, make specific allowance for the influence of culture and sub-cultures of an occupation or profession on the level of performance.

The final variable we explore here is the *method of professional development*. This refers to the methods by which professional knowledge and experience are acquired, developed and refined. Methods vary according to the relative emphasis placed upon learning by experience, learning from experience, and learning in formal academic settings. Some explanation of the distinction of 'learning by' experience and 'learning from' experience is pertinent here since the concepts are used later. *Learning by experience* implies a strong emphasis on learning-by-doing on a trial and error basis with very little building of models of practice. There is little opportunity for learning from the experience of other practitioners other than a workplace mentor.

Learning from experience can mean learning from one's own experience or that of other practitioners, either directly, or through the use of processed experience such as case-studies, simulations and so on. In other words, the experience does not have to be exclusively direct. Another distinguishing feature is that whatever the form of the experience, it will be coupled with built-in opportunities for reflection and the building, testing and refinement of models of practice through further experimentation. Methods of professional development are significant determinants of professional performance, rather than a consequence of it, and have far reaching implications for the continuing professional development of individual practitioners.

Using these dimensions it is possible to distinguish three main professional models from the literature and a further 'variant' which, whilst it shares most of the features of its 'parent', has emerged as a specific organisational response to external pressure. First, however, a word of caution. As with all models it is important to remember that these are 'ideal types' which only approximate to reality. Further, they do not form a continuum – indeed there is some overlap in their various different features. It is also the case that these models (or approximations of them) can exist side by side in an organisation, though there is usually a most often occurring or dominant form. The salient features of each of these models are discussed and summarised in Table 1.

PRACTICAL OR CRAFT PROFESSIONALISM

The self-image of the practical professional is one of a 'craftsman' (sic). The knowledge base is practical knowledge (know-how) generated from work situations. Often this cannot be articulated and exists as 'tacit knowledge'. There is little unique or esoteric knowledge. Practical professionals will draw from a variety of disciplines as and when required. As a result, the orientation is essentially a theoretical and based upon common sense. The practical professional denies the relevance of the prescriptive claims of theory.

The practice theory is implicit, based upon the concept of know-how, and upon trial and error in applications to new situations. Each new situation is treated as requiring a unique solution to be found and applied on the spot. The values are derived from the vocational nature of the work, the traditions of the occupational culture, and informal rules of practice. Relations with the client are based upon demonstrations of mastery in which the professional has exclusive control of the interaction.

Professional development in this approach is based on learning by experience ('by doing'), usually through a form of apprenticeship model (sitting by Nelly). It is informed by the belief that you can't learn the 'craft' by reading books and that 'theory' is irrelevant. There is often a period of initiation into the traditions of practice through a process of coaching. Essentially it is a social-constructivist approach to professional work.

There are similarities between this model and the 'implicit expertise' model proposed by Dreyfus (1980) and it is often found associated with the so-called minor, emergent, or quasi-professions. The main criticism of this form of professionalism is that the competences have an intuitive base and since they cannot be verbalised they cannot be taught in a systematic manner. It lacks a theory of the process by which professional knowledge and

Table 1

MODEL	SELF-IMAGE	THEORETICAL ORIENTATION	KNOWLEDGE BASE	PRACTICE THEORY	VALUE BASE	RELATIONS WITH CLIENT	PROFESSIONAL DEVELOPMENT	CRITIQUE
PRACTICAL PROFESSIONAL	CRAFTS(MAN)	Atheoretical, common sense – denies relevance of theory to practice.	Practical knowledge generated from work. No unique established base of esoteric knowledge. Tacit knowledge is predominant form.	Implicit expertise. Trial and error. 'Know how'.	Vocational traditions of culture and practice highly valued – organisation centred.	Exclusive control. Demonstration of mastery.	Apprenticeship mode. Can't be learned from books. Learning-by-doing without explicit reflection and abstraction. Initiation into traditions of practice through coaching.	Skill is intuitive – can't be verbalised or taught. Lacks theory of the process by which knowledge is deepened and refined.
TECHNICAL EXPERT	EXPERT	Espoused theories derived from systematic knowledge. Theories developed through scientific enquiry.	Esoteric knowledge is dominant form. Practitioner is sole possessor of relevant knowledge. Knowledge is that of rational experts.	Explicit and based upon techniques and expertise applied to problems. Rule governed inquiry. Fragmented rather than 'holistic' approach.	Technical rationality. 'Thinking like a professional'. Encourages differentiation and specialisms which are highly valued. Problem-centred rather than client-centred.	Objectivist approach. Expert expects/demands deference. Authority is secured through control; organisational 'needs' rather than client 'wants' are reference point.	Knowledge and academic theory valued, plus rules and guidance. Learning approaches often static and didactic	Relevance of process/interpersonal relations and dialogue denied. Relevance of clients' knowledge down-played or denied. Process skills 'bolted on' as extra dimension.
MANAGERIAL	EXPERT	As above, plus management theory which may be Populist and not rigorously scientific.	As above. Much knowledge concerned with resource management and issues of efficiency and effectiveness.	As above plus management techniques. May draw opportunistically on range of on social psychological theories - eg in interpersonal skills.	As above, but most managerial professionals not yet as highly valued as established professions (except within own peer groups).	As above plus authority relations with 'operative' colleagues.	As above. Increasingly strong emphasis put on academic or at least formal learning and qualifications eg MBAs and NCVQs.	Beginning to go way of Technical Experts but uneasily so. Tension exists between different models of professionalism. Problem is that development of practice theories may not keep pace with development of management theory.
OPERATIVE		'De-professionalised' by ever more prescriptive rules, regulations and guidance. Limits and boundaries set on professional discretion through managerial impositions, by increasingly hierarchical structures and by non-collaborative modes of decision making. Often result of external requirements on organisation to demonstrate accountability and increase customer satisfaction.						
REFLECTIVE PRACTITIONER	FACILITATOR	Espoused theories which include theories of social relations. Recognises there is no single right answer to most social problems.	Specialist knowledge can be esoteric but need not be. Knowledge becomes manifest in interactions with client. Uses all sources of knowledge available including relevant information from client.	Based on process and interpersonal theories-in-use. Congruence between espoused theories and theories in use. Constructivist view of the reality of practice. New rules created out of practice to make new sense out of uncertainty or unique and conflict-ridden situations.	Client-centred, socially constructed and holistic.	Collaborative, based on on-going dialogue, surfacing conflict, sharing meanings and a reflective contract with the client. Authority achieved through consensus.	Process of experiential learning by doing, observing, reflecting, conceptualising and experimenting. Knowledge becomes a process and not a product. Abstract conceptualisation leads to new models and principles to be tested and refined.	Schon's model only explicitly seen when experienced practitioners are coaching neophytes - not clear if professionals actually consistently operate in this way. Difficulties associated with identifying and defining cognitive competences.

understanding are deepened and refined since the learning is based upon trial and error. There is little systematic reflection or abstraction to different practice situations. By implication, since the specific competences which constitute practice cannot be verbalised, they cannot be disaggregated, specified or broken down into discrete elements. Nevertheless it remains an essentially behaviourist model of professional work. This may be seen by its emphasis on the visible output of work and its denial of cognitive processes, theoretical knowledge, and values and attitudes, through which this output is achieved.

TECHNICAL EXPERT PROFESSIONALISM

Here the self-image is one of being an 'expert' who has exclusive technical knowledge and expertise. There is invariably an esoteric body of formal content knowledge (construed as public bodies of theories, procedures and information); expert practitioners are seen as the sole possessors of the relevant knowledge. Further, this is the knowledge of rational experts. The notion of knowledge as a cognitive process rather than a product is rarely included within the knowledge base. The knowledge may easily be seen to be objective truth and in many ways can be regarded as 'value-free'.

The theoretical orientation is one of espoused theories derived from systematic knowledge which itself is the result of empiricist research. Practice theory is explicit and based upon the application of technique and expertise to problems. New problems are 'solved' through rule-governed inquiry. Problems are then broken down into smaller parts which can be dealt with by specialist experts. The practice theory rarely includes theories of inter-personal relations with the client.

The value base is one of technical rationality and there is a premium upon 'thinking like a professional' (through being detached and objective) and upon differentiation and specialisation. The value system is problem- rather than client-centred with primary allegiance to the discipline or subject area. Relations with the client are governed by an objectivist approach. The technical expert expects the deference due to his/her superior knowledge. He/she controls the interaction with the client and selects and imposes any solution to the problem independently of the client. This reinforces the idea of professionally-defined needs rather than clients' wants.

The process of professional development is one which values both academic knowledge and theory and where practitioners learn the rules, procedures and guidelines which constitute the techniques of practice. Initial learning tends to be away from practice environments, using didactic approaches with an emphasis on propositional rather than process knowledge. The relevance of process, interpersonal relations and dialogue is de-emphasised (either explicitly in the training environment, or through socialisation into the cultural mores) but process skills may be bolted on as 'sweeteners'. Essentially the model constitutes an empirical and behaviourist view of professional work. It encourages a fragmented, disaggregated approach to the definition of professional competence.

VARIANT: MANAGERIAL EXPERT PROFESSIONAL

This shares most of the features of the Expert Model but is a two-tier model where there are 'expert managers' and 'technical operatives'. The theoretical orientation of the managers includes 'management theory' and the practice theory includes 'management techniques'. *Relations with the client* are similar to the expert model but the managerial expert also has authority relations with 'operative' colleagues.

By way of contrast, the 'technical operative professionals' are increasingly de-skilled and de-professionalised by ever more prescriptive rules and regulations. These create pre-defined boundaries to professional discretion by increasing managerial control of work. This approach is often associated with increasingly hierarchical structures, non-collaborative decision-making and the introduction of organisation-wide management systems such as Management By Objectives (MBO). This is often the result of the perception that the organisation needs to demonstrate more explicit accountability and increase client satisfaction.

REFLECTIVE PRACTITIONER

The self-image here is one of a facilitator whose role is to help find an optimal course of action or solution to problems in an uncertain world. The model holds that there is no single right answer. There may be a range of solutions and courses of action which may vary from context to context, time to time, and from practitioner to practitioner. The theoretical orientation includes (and gives priority to) espoused theories of social relations as well as those from systematic knowledge. It recognises that theories may be incomplete or deficient.

The knowledge base may include special esoteric knowledge but need not do so. Knowledge is seen to manifest itself in, and be modified by, interactions with the client. The practitioner will use all sources of relevant knowledge including the client's. Practice theory is strongly developed and based upon process and interpersonal theories-in-use. There is relative congruence between the espoused theories and these theories-in-use. The constructivist view of the reality of practice means that new rules are created out of practice to make new sense of uncertainty. The value base derives from the centrality of the client to practice situations and interactions. Holistic approaches to problem analysis and problem solving are valued since they are said to exist within a socially-constructed reality and therefore cannot be treated separately from social, political and economic contexts.

The relationship with the 'client' is at the centre of professional practice. It is a collaborative on-going dialogue which is facilitated by, but not controlled by, the professional. She or he attempts to surface and resolve conflict, share meanings and build a reflective contract with the client. The professional does not expect deference due to superior knowledge but achieves authority through consensus.

Professional development occurs through a process of experiential learning from (rather than by) doing. Learning is through analysis by observing, reflecting, experimenting and conceptualising. Knowing becomes a process rather than a product. Abstract conceptualisation leads to new models and principles to be tested and refined. Central to this model of practice is the notion that professional competence is the product of a complex, shared and negotiated process which also involves responsibility for continuous professional growth and development.

Implications for Professional Competence

As discussed earlier, the current emphasis upon defining and specifying occupational competency can be attributed to a political and economic climate which has placed much emphasis on value for money and efficiency. Initially this was associated with a demand for greater general financial accountability, but increasingly that accountability is being extended to the substance of occupations, including professional work. One major consequence is that the dominant approach to defining and measuring occupational competence is behaviourist, emphasising as it does the output of professional work. In keeping with the behaviourist tradition the focus is directed at the individual practitioner.

Within this context, competent professional performance is viewed as a series of discrete elements of behaviour, each of which can be observed and measured. Competence is inferred and judged from observed behavioural outputs. Little account is taken of the processes by which outputs are generated or of the influence of other inputs including the organisational context of professional work. As described by Preston and Walker (1992) the 'apparent simplicity, intelligibility, and potential for comprehensive application' has led to this becoming the basic model for considering and assessing occupational competence.

This essentially reductionist and 'fragmentation' model may be contrasted with an alternative, *holistic* approach. As described by Walker (1992) it derives from the work of John Dewey and is consistent with contemporary learning theory in cognitive psychology. It acknowledges that competence is complex and as such cannot be conceived of as a series of discrete and seemingly independent elements. Holists argue that individual competences rarely appear solo but always combine in structured sets. The combination of the elements in these sets 'vary from time to time, place to place and practitioner to practitioner'.

Which of these elements are assembled into sets and how they are then further manipulated depends on *judgement*. The composition of sets will be modified in response to continuous feedback from the environment. These are then tested and refined through further experimentation and reflection on experience. The role of judgement in performance, based upon the formation of process knowledge, becomes central in a holistic approach. It allows for the many situations in professional work where there is a high degree of ambiguity and uncertainty.

Where the behaviourist model is essentially individualistic, the holistic perspective is wider. It recognises the influence of individual experience, but also takes account of group processes and the impact of organisational culture and values on the individual's professional performance. Culture, values and group norms have a continuous influence on the development of professional competences. The value base of a profession both frames individual practice and becomes embedded in it.

The implications are considerable. Both the 'practical' and 'technical expert' models of professionalism have a behaviourist pedigree. The practical professional, for example, puts a premium on performance and achieving mastery through trial and error, evoking echoes of stimulus-response-reinforcement learning theory. The sole knowledge base is tacit (content knowledge and process knowledge are discounted) and, although difficult to break down in behaviourist terms, behavioural output forms the major source of inferred competence.

Similarly, the technical expert is an empirically-based behavioural model of professionalism. Technical rationalism actually involves fragmentation and reductionism. Indeed, expert (as contrasted with novice) competence is often manifest in a professional system of relevant specialists who each deal with their own 'solvable part' of a problem. The process of professional development values academic knowledge, theory and technique. It is technique which allows knowledge and theory to be applied, and through these, competence to be inferred.

The professional development process also emphasises individual detachment and objectivity. It is underpinned by a value base which discounts the relevance of personal experience, background or organisational context. So, although it is an individualistic model, it nevertheless denies the influence of individual characteristics and attitudes on developing and demonstrating competence.

In contrast, the reflective practitioner is essentially a holistic model in which occupational competence cannot be distinguished in principle from competence in the knowledge base, values, attitudes and philosophy of the occupation. As such it is not only concerned with the outcomes of professional practice but the cognitive processes by which these are developed and demonstrated.

Central to this form of professional practice is the view that all participants are whole persons who each bring their own background, values and culture to the specific context of professional practice. Professional competence involves forming judgements through a process of negotiating shared meanings. It is here that elements of knowledge, values, cognitive and behavioural competences combine into structured sets which are dependent on the judgements made in specific contexts. The model is highly appropriate where questions of equity and non-oppressive and non-discriminatory behaviour are paramount.

Developing Competence and Reflective Practice

The holistic approach to competence is embodied in the reflective practitioner model of professionalism and, as described earlier, it is grounded in experiential learning theory. The cycle of experiential learning, (Figure 1 below), was first described by Kolb (1974) and has been developed by Gibbs (1988) and Schon (1987):

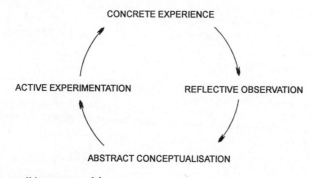

Figure 1: Kolb's 1974 model

In essence, individuals 'reflect' on their experience; construct new 'theories of action' by abstract conceptualisation; 'experiment' with these in practice; and then re-enter the cycle of reflection, developing practice on each iteration of the cycle. Although helpful in describing the cognitive process, the model is not explicit about the relationships between inputs, processes and outputs. Our view would be that there could be both inputs and outputs at each stage of the cycle. The inputs and outputs could include cognitive, affective and behavioural components. The practitioner may enter the cycle at any stage – reflecting in the bath upon displaced water is the classic example of reflecting, abstracting and theorising!

Outputs can include new analyses, models of action, forms of knowledge, and changes in a value base. These outputs are not always observable and it may be a considerable time before changes in what we have called an individual's 'cognitive stance' become manifest. Note, too, that the net effect of changes to this 'cognitive stance' might be to decide *not* to act in certain situations. A judgement of this sort is the most difficult for an output-competence model to handle since it is not observable. This takes the enquirer into the world of cognitive competences.

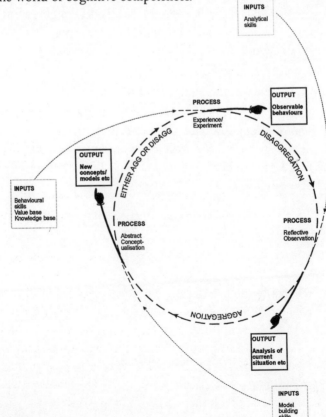

Figure 2: Inputs, process and outputs in our learning cycle

Figure 2 extends the learning cycle by including these inputs and outputs. It can be seen that we have combined Kolb's Experimentation and Experience stages in order to simplify the model, although it is, in reality, a good deal more complex.

The model hypothesises that the cognitive processes of disaggregation and aggregation may both occur during each iteration of the cycle. Typically, disaggregation will happen when the worker is reflecting on experience, and aggregation will happen when moving from reflection to abstract conceptualisation. After that, either process may occur depending on what the worker wants to do in the next phase of experimentation. She or he may want to test out one particular aspect of the previous phase, or a fully integrated solution.

We may now speculate about the different kinds of competences involved in professional development based upon this extended learning cycle. For example, it is possible to begin building a matrix of competences which the reflective practitioner can draw upon to assemble holistic structured sets with which to inform the exercise of professional discretion. An initial analysis of the three kinds of competences involved at each stage of the learning cycle is presented in Table 2:

Table 2: A Matrix of competences for professional work

Stage	Input Competences	Process Competences	Output Competences
Experience/Experimentation	Behavioural skills Practical/tacit knowledge Values/beliefs Theories of action	Interpersonal/Interaction skills	Observable behaviours
Reflective Observation	Analytical/reflective skills Content knowledge	Analytical skills Integrative skills Process knowledge Means generation	Solution analysis Conflict resolution New forms of knowledge New values/beliefs
Abstract Conceptualisation	Knowledge of models and model building	Model building skills Ability to integrate experience and reflection	Theories of action New models New forms of knowledge Potential interventions

As described earlier, traditional models of competence focus on output of observable behaviours. This is supported in functional analysis by 'underpinning knowledge and understanding' but this aspect may well only play a minor role when there is ample evidence of competent behavioural outputs. Our concern is that outputs have little explanatory power when, for example, competent performance is *not* being achieved. It is here that one needs to be able to delve into an individual's ability to integrate personal and external knowledge, values, and skills effectively; to handle the resulting processes, and to construct new models of her or his working world.

As implied by our description of the reflective practice approach, we believe that one cannot consider knowledge separately from understanding, or from the values implied by selective acquisition and use of different forms of knowledge, or from the context in which knowledge is being applied. Knowledge is never complete, and is constantly being modified through practice and reflection. It is the understanding, and the integration of theoretical developments with practice theory and practice itself, that are important for competent professional practice.

Table 2 makes it clear that this requires detailed consideration of the other boxes in the table – particularly the middle column. If a rigorous competence approach has been applied and, even worse, training has been conducted within an output model – for example a 'Systems Approach to Training' – then information about, and understanding of, the process necessary to support individuals in their personal development may well not be available.

There are clear difficulties in writing competences for cognitive processes in the context of traditional output competence models. These should not be minimised but we believe it is essential that further research into the specification and measurement of cognitive and process competences should be pursued. If we are not able to define more accurately the measures by which professional competence can be judged, we will surely see the gradual de-professionalisation of those working in a range of both public and private service arenas.

References

Cave, E. and McKeown, P. (1993) 'Managerial effectiveness: the identification of need', in *Management Education and Development*, Vol 24, 2, pp.122–137.

Dreyfus, S. and Dreyfus, H.A (1980) *A Five Stage Model of Mental Activities Involved in Directed Skill Acquisition*. Berkeley: University of California.

Durkheim, E. (1957) *Professional Ethics and Civic Morals*. London: Routledge and Kegan Paul.

Elliot

Eraut, M. (1992) 'Developing the Professional Knowledge Base: a process perspective on professional training and effectiveness'. In R.A. Barnet (ed) *Learning to Effect*. London: SRHE.

Etzioni, A. (1964) *Modern Organisations*. Englewood Cliffs, New Jersey: Prentice Hall.

Friedson, E. (1973) *The Professions and their Prospects*. London: Sage.

Gibbs, G. (1988) *Learning by Doing*. London: Further Education Unit.

Greenwood, E. (1965) 'Attributes of a Profession'. In M. Zald (ed) *Social Welfare Institutions*. London: Wiley.

Halmos, P. (1970) *The Personal Service Society*. London: Constable.

Huntingdon, J. (1981) *Social Work and General Medical Practice: Collaboration or Conflict?* London: George Allen and Unwin.

Jessup, G. (1991) *Outcomes: NVQs and the Emerging Model of Education and Training.* London: The Falmer Press.

Jones, S. and Levi, M. (1983) 'The Police and the Majority: the Neglect of the Obvious', in *The Police Journal*, Vol 41, No. 4.

Kolb, D.A. (1984) *Experiential Learning.* Englewood Cliffs, New Jersey: Prentice Hall.

Millerson, G. (1964) *The Qualifying Associations, A Study in Professionalisation.* London: Routledge and Kegan Paul.

Neave, G. (1988) On the Cultivation of Quality, Efficiency, and Enterprise: An Overview of Recent Trends in Higher Education in Europe, 1968–1988. *European Journal of Education*, Vol.23, 1–2.

Neumann, W. (1979) 'Educational responses to the Concern for Proficiency'. In G. Grant *et al. On Competence: A Critical Analysis of Competence-Based Reforms in Higher Education.* San Francisco: Jossey-Bass.

Parsons, T. (1951) *The Social System.* London: Routledge and Kegan Paul.

Pearson, H.T. (1984) 'Competence: A Normative Analysis'. In E.C. Short (ed) *Competence: Inquiries into its Meaning and Acquisition in Educational Settings.* Lanham, New York and London: University of America Press.

Preston, B. and Walker, J.C. (1992) *Competency based standards in the professions and higher education.* Centre for Research in Professional Education, University of Canberra.

Schon, D.A. (1983) *The Reflective Practitioner.* New York: Basic Books.

Schon, D.A. (1987) *Educating the Reflective Practitioner.* San Francisco: Jossey Bass.

Walker, J.C. (1992a) *The History and Philosophy of the Competency Movement in Australia.* Centre for Research in Professional Education, University of Canberra.

Walker, J.C. (1992b) *Standards and Partnerships in Teaching and Teacher Education: USA and UK Experience.* University of Canberra: Centre for Research in Professional Education.

Winter, R. (1991) *Competence and the Idea of Professionalism.* ASSET Programme Conference Paper No. 1, Danbury Park, Chelmsford.

Chapter 2

The Nature and Aims of Professional Education for Social Workers

A Postmodern Perspective

Marilyn Pietroni

Introduction: The Irony of this Theme

It is difficult in the UK in 1994 to consider the nature and aims of professional education in relation to social care without a sense of irony. The corporate languages of management, evaluation and cost-effectiveness are already superseding the former languages of the social care professions. In the case of social work, they have done so with little opposition since social workers have at best been somewhat uneasy with what is experienced as the elitism of professional status and, at worst, have attacked the idea of individual excellence with which it was felt to be linked. It would not be going too far to describe both the term social work, and the ideas that it represents, as 'under erasure' in the Derridean sense (1976, 1978).

It has been argued that some of the professional terms and categories that were developed from a reductionist philosophy and the culture of technical rationality that it produced have now outlived their usefulness (Handy 1993). The constant reorganisation of social services, the challenge to community nursing roles, and the ever-expanding responsibilities of general practice and community care are symptoms of fundamental change. This change reflects a shift in the paradigms that underpin professional life away from reductionist philosophies and towards more holistic or integrative ways of thinking, in which clusters of ideas and practices can move in varying combinations through more transitional forms of organisation. In this new world flexible and often short-life structures are both necessary and desirable, in spite of the stress with which they are often associated, because they allow some order to be maintained in the midst of seeming chaos.

Singular professional roles and identities are also becoming less common since they too relate to specific tasks or fields of activity that were constructed at a time when services were broken down into smaller and smaller parts. Until quite recently the specialist expert headed the professional hierarchy and models of social authority and privilege were taken as given. Now it is becoming clearer that generalist professionals, such as fund-holding general practitioners and senior social services managers in voluntary and statutory sectors, have to contribute more to local inter-agency policy-making and they are being encouraged to do so because they have more chance of the integrative and collaborative thinking that is required to hold complex parallel policy changes in mind.

Workers in the field of health and social care are now therefore having to develop new languages and forms of organisation which are outside of traditional agency structures and professional categories. These new formations often take the form of trusts, partnerships and consortia. Traditionally the grassroots movements and to some extent the voluntary sector have been their originators. Now they are being generated by central government policy, for example through the promotion of joint commissioning agencies and community trust provider agencies. In this way the organisational potential for continuous change has been institutionalised and the leadership functions have been handed over to a new kind of troubleshooting manager, who may but probably does not have professional training and whose values are not necessarily aligned with the professional staff of the service concerned.

This shift in professional roles and identities, and the accompanying shift in values and organisational structures, has essentially been top-down and has been initiated by the political right (Statham 1987). It has been accompanied, however, and ultimately has joined forces, especially in social work itself, with grassroots movements with cultures that give high priority to equality and democratisation. These date back to Mayer and Timms' landmark publication *The Client Speaks* (1968) and are exemplified over the last decade by the work of Croft and Beresford (1989, 1992). These writers and workers have promoted collaborative practices and shared languages that are understandable not only to each other but to carers and users of services as well. The integrity of their commitment, however, once adopted at policy-making level, is at times parodied by a new kind of jargon that constructs a kind of politically correct 'newspeak', for example, 'user-centred seamless service' and 'needs-led assessment'. Such phrases are at one and the same time serious and ridiculous and within them lie the ethical labyrinths of current practice to which professional education and training must give focussed thought.

Woolgar (1983) argues that in such a world irony needs to become the project rather than a mere instrument of enquiry because it opens up co-existent, changing and contradictory meanings in a way that can allow creative thought to replace the more usual depression and disorientation. He attributes this liberation to the potential offered by moving from one level of interpretation to a newly created one and standing back to consider the relation between them. Whether this is the return of the dialectic or, as Ricoeur suggests (1970), a new discipline of reflection, remains to be seen. If there is validity in Woolgar's argument, as I believe there is, it is relevant to the focus of this chapter.

Social work education has to respond to the fundamental contradictions which exist in both the content and context of practice. This deep instability not only of the term and the idea, but also of the practices and values, of social work has to be faced. Indeed, the transitory nature of whole language sets is a more general feature of our age. It is therefore worth considering how that kind of instability itself has been theorised in order to understand at least momentarily the implications of it for professional education.

In this chapter I intend first to take a fairly old-fashioned overview of some aspects of social work in this turbulent environment and then to move on to look at three deliberately disparate theoretical perspectives that seem to me to have something to offer to understanding the unstable nature of professional education today: the work of Wilfrid Bion, of Donald Schon, and of the writers on post-modernism.

An Old-Fashioned Overview

The context in which social work is practised is usually bureaucratic: a social services department, a hospital or clinic, or a voluntary organisation. Where social work teams still exist in health care settings, they have often to accommodate a double dose of bureaucracy with the NHS as well as their local employing authority.

Social workers can therefore be seen as 'bureau-professionals', who are expected to exercise individual judgements of great complexity in conditions of extreme uncertainty within the constraints of a bureaucratic decision-making structure. There is and always has been an intrinsic contradiction between the complexity of individual judgements that have to be made in practice, and the often lumbering organisational procedures through which practice guidelines are issued. As bureau-professionals social services workers have to work within those frameworks and are accountable to them.

Any continuing education for social workers therefore needs to take into account this organisational context as well as the work itself. Furthermore, the newly defined basic training in social work set out in the Statement of Minimum Requirements (CCETSW 1989) is, at a length of two years, relatively short compared with that of other professions. Social work career paths, though now emerging, have previously not been mapped out very clearly, and until recently management or training were the only options at the higher levels, leaving practice standards to atrophy at just above a senior practitioner standard. Now that advanced practice specialisms are once more being established, notably in the field of child protection, mental health and learning difficulties, the idea of the individual expert is once more overcoming in-built prejudices and is achieving respectability. It will take some time, however, before a range of standards of excellence are articulated and have the chance to win general acceptance. The establishment of a General Social Services Council (at present mooted) would go some way to promoting improved standards, but attitudes within social work toward professional excellence seem likely to remain ambivalent making rapid change unlikely.

Some reasons for this slow pace of change are as follows:

- under-resourcing and slow implementation of CCETSW Paper 31 – the Framework for Post-Qualifying and Advanced Awards in Social Work (CCETSW 1990)

- lack of individualised budgets for continuing and advanced training to offset the bureaucratic impediments to individual professional development (Pietroni 1991)

- policy and organisational bifurcations between specialist fields such as child care and more generalist fields such as community care which inhibit cross-fertilisation of improving standards of knowledge and practice

- the nature of social defences in social work organisations that ensure (a) continuing inhibition of the more positive aspects of a professional elite and (b) a continuing primary identification with the deprived, damaged and distressed users of social services

- the swift pace of social policy change in the last five years which has infused the context of social work with basic anxieties about job security and organisational survival.

Before considering in more detail the nature and aims of professional education as it applies to social workers, however, it is necessary to consider this working context in more detail.

The Context of Social Work

Whatever precise local structures are in place (and they do vary considerably), certain features are fairly common, of which three have special relevance for this discussion. First, guidelines and policy on practice have frequently replaced or superseded individual professional judgement, for example,the use of eligibility criteria in selecting which clients receive a full needs assessment. Second, the locus of authority and decision-making is rarely individual and is often spread across a team or hierarchy and sometimes across several geographical sites (cf. Balint 1957, on general practice). Third, links between information on different systems of practice (for example, child care and mental health) are weak and sometimes non-existent.

Perhaps most fundamentally, social work practice is determined by the statutory framework which governs the care of children, of people with mental health problems, of elders, of disabled people and those who are ill. These national frameworks, filtered through local bureaucracies with their idiosyncratic patterns of authority and organisation, serve to ensure that the social worker is rarely, if ever, in the position of the autonomous professional fully responsible for his or her own decisions. These Spaghetti Junction-like laws, guidelines and structures are often confusing in and of themselves and undermine the capacity for individual thought and professional judgment. Furthermore, the adversarial, either-or nature of British judicial culture tends to produce somewhat crude and oversimplified responses to real practice dilemmas that ill-reflect the complexity of many clients' lives. Yet social work practice is often determined by the requirements of the rules of evidence and the guidance of statutory instruments.

Add to the conditions described above: a short social work basic training, no nationally recognised career path or consistent professional development structures, an inhibition of or antipathy towards individual authority and excellence, and a context is produced which is intrinsically antagonistic to thoughtful practice. What is perhaps surprising is that so much good social work practice does manage to take place, and that there are still so many good social workers prepared to battle against these odds, and doing excellent work. Recent recruitment figures are, however, falling which suggests that these extremely difficult conditions are now being recognised and expressed by a reluctance to enter the field (CCETSW 1993).

These complex and somewhat hostile conditions to some extent pit the individual social worker and their organisation against each other. The social work team then inevitably becomes a potential mediating structure that advances or inhibits high quality practice through powerful peer group norms. The quality of team leadership or middle management is then critical in determining whether the highest common factor or the lowest common denominator of practice is actually established; sometimes quality of thought and judgment survives, but commonly individual and team mentally join forces against the management of the organisation who, since quality and inspection units have been introduced, are often seen as part of a general 'more for less' climate rather than the protectors of good practice. Such shared antagonism towards higher organisational levels is a further disincentive to assuming conspicuous positions of managerial or professional authority, since inevitably to do so would mean being on the receiving end of that same antagonism.

These contextual features provide some of the reasons why, when developing continuing professional education for social workers, it is often useful to turn to the work of people who have theorised turbulence in the relations between individual thought and organisation culture in some depth. I refer here particularly to the work of Wilfrid Bion and Donald Schon, but I will also draw on the cultural perspective of post-modernism for the description it provides of the broader contemporary conditions which I have so far only signalled.

I will describe the work of Wilfrid Bion first. Later the work of Donald Schon in the USA will be approached through the concept of the reflective practitioner (1983). Finally, I will indicate some features of post-modernism which I have found helpful in keeping my own feet in these slippery conditions.

The Importance of Wilfrid Bion's Work on Group and Individual Behaviour

Bion's approach was always to think of the group as-a-whole with a particular group culture expressed unconsciously through the verbal content, non-verbal behaviour and 'the feeling tone' or atmosphere of the group (1968). Bion's theories of group behaviour have found their way on to most basic professional curricula which address that topic. His well-known theory of work group behaviour (which addresses an agreed common task) and unconscious basic assumption group behaviour (a potentially anti-task culture of pairing, fight-flight or dependency) seems to have stood the test of time. His influence, however, has gone far beyond this basic theory and

has led to innovations in group therapy, small group teaching and organisational development.

Over time Bion explored how unconscious meaning was revealed
through language, grammar and syntax. He first sensed and later, through
research into individual clinical work, showed how verbal and grammatical
structures and the emotional rhythms with which they are associated, reflect
intra-psychic problems and interpersonal power relationships. This sensitivity to the relationship between whole and part runs throughout his work
with groups and individuals. His unique contribution was that he could give
meaning to the relationship between whole and part in terms that freed up
blocks to thinking; thus a group could be helped to resume its focus on the
work task, or an individual who was previously in a state of mental
fragmentation could hope to recover coherent thought. He understood in a
deep way how the links between fragments of thought become dis-articu-
lated, when crude or primitive emotions disrupt cognition.

According to Bion, however, this delicate thinking process could not
develop in an infant or an adult unless the quality of attention provided by
the mother or other was good enough. Here again, Bion introduced new
terminology (1970). His term 'reverie' described the state of calm receptive-
ness that is required for it to be safe enough for the inchoate and undigested
pre-conceptions to be projected, received, reflected upon and given back in
an articulate form. As a result of experiencing this containing and reflective
process, the subject can introject a capacity for reflection and thoughtfulness
in their own right. To this overall two-term relationship Bion gave the more
descriptive name of container-contained.

The idea of containment seems to have been more accessible and has been
widely used and taken up. Bion postulated that there were three basic forms
of containment: parasitic, symbiotic and commensal (1970). Commensal
refers to a relationship in which two objects share a third to the advantage
of all three; symbiotic refers to a relationship in which one depends on
another to mutual advantage, and parasitic refers to an instance where one
depends on another to produce a third which is destructive of all three. These
forms of containment are highly relevant to the relationship between the
social worker and educator, for they provide a gauge of the quality and depth
of the containment process.

These descriptive categories are very useful when examining the nature
of the relationship between the social worker, the organisation and the
working task. At best and rather too rarely, the individual social worker is
sustained and enabled by their organisation to carry out a very challenging
and difficult task commensally. Individual thought then fosters growth in

the organisation and the working practice itself is in Bion's terms the articulation produced from that containment. At worst, and parasitically in Bion's terms, the working task is done badly and a spiral of mutual recrimination between social worker and organisation takes place to their mutual destruction. Somewhere in the middle, symbiotically in Bion's terms, is the familiar ground of the bureau-professional and the bureaucracy depending on each other to their mutual advantage in a silent collusion that neglects key aspects of the working task.

The three patterns of containment – commensal, symbiotic and parasitic – can also be applied to the relation between the social worker, the educator and the educational programme. A further crucial feature of continuing social work education has to be the promotion of individual thoughtfulness, a thoughtfulness that is strong enough to offset the pressures towards peer group conformity and the limitations it places on independent individual thought that are often a feature of working life in small teams and large organisations.

Although developed in the course of research work with very disturbed individuals, Bion believed the thought processes he described in his theory of thought were to be found in all individuals in certain conditions (1956, 1967). Certainly his theorisation of the mental process of fragmentation and accompanying loss of the capacity to think, resonate with the inner experience of social workers who are trying to work in complex organisations.

Members of bureaucracies often feel that the meetings they attend are off-task and preoccupied with rivalrous fight-flight behaviour, or are unduly dependent on a diffuse source of central authority, or that they are working alone in a hostile world peopled, in Bion's terms, by managerial or political 'bizarre objects' (1956, 1959, 1967). These collective structures of thought and feeling are defensive processes that undermine individual rigour. They have much in common with the group mentalities and states of depersonalisation and fragmentation described by Bion and his theorisation has much to offer in understanding them.

For example in social work organisations the experience of being asked to assess need but not given sufficient control over the means of meeting it is disturbing. It is also ethically compromising to be asked to rehabilitate ex-mental hospital patients in the community but at such a pace and with such insufficient information, planning or resources that disasters are inevitable. Social workers who are care managers or team managers continually work in the space between what Bion called pre-conception and absence; internally they pay a price. The burden of thoughtfully digesting that internally disruptive experience and continuing to practice as a bureau-professional, rather than cynically constructing in the mind an organisational world of bad objects at the level of management or policy making is immense. It places particular demands on PQ training to enable social workers to confront these tasks in an honest but realistic way.

In summary, the important features of Wilfrid Bion's theories for the purposes of the continuing professional education of social workers are as follows:

- he differentiates between work-oriented group behaviour and basic-assumption mentalities which are anti-task

- he describes the hazards to the individual, the organisation and the quality of work of failures of rigour and emotionally sensitive thought

- he describes the continuous creative feedback loop of the container-contained relationship, at first between two terms, and then as a continuous internal process within the individual

- he differentiates between three different qualities of the container-contained relationship (commensal, symbiotic, parasitic) and describes the implications of each for the quality of collaboration that ensues.

The Reflective Practitioner

I want to turn now to the work Donald Schon developed in the USA at the Massachusetts Institute of Technology. Although derived from a somewhat different cultural tradition, it shares some structural features and common themes with the work of Bion. Schon's work is better known in educational circles than Bion's and he is an expert on professional education.

Over a period of twenty years, separately and together, Argyris and Schon examined the relationship between individual professionals and their organisational tasks. Two key conferences were convened in the late 1960s and early 1970s, to which a wide range of professionals were invited to discuss the current state and needs of professional knowledge and professional education. A crisis in professional knowledge was felt to exist; professionals described a gap between the academic rigour of their training and the complex, indeterminate problems which faced them in day-to-day practice. Schon famously describes this as the gap between 'the high ground of academic rigour and the swampy lowlands of practice' (1988).

Schon and his colleagues then identified a situation-specific model of four distinct professional roles:

- the expert professional who claims expert knowledge which may result in being distanced from everyday problems

- the managerial professional who leaves behind his discipline of origin and assumes responsibility for planning, resource allocation and personnel

- the practical professional who takes a pragmatic problem-solving approach, arriving at solutions by trial and error, and who does not eschew everyday problems

- the reflective practitioner who recognises the limits of professional knowledge and action, builds in a cycle of critical reflection to maximise the capacity for critical thought, and produces a sense of professional freedom and a connection with rather than distance from clients.

Although, of course, not one of these categories occurs in pure form, it is with the last that Schon's main work has been concerned. He has been and still is preoccupied with creating educational conditions which are favourable to the development of reflective practice. He emphasises the need for educational experiences that challenge creativity and encourage intuitive problem-solving to make best use of previous practical experience. The role of the educator is therefore more like a musical conductor or drama coach than a professor.

Schon's work is one part in a long history of educational approaches designed to address the tensions between theory generated by practice and theory applied to practice, and it has close links with all problem-solving methods of education and practice, but there is something subtle and special about his concept of reflection, which describes a complex internal process in the individual (like Bion's theory of thinking) and an intricate series of exchanges with the outside world (like Bion's theory of containment).

Schon describes, in language which is drawn from systems theory (whereas Bion's is drawn from mathematics), a double feedback loop of action, reflection and learning. Practice is carried out in the first space, reflection in the second, and reflection and practice in the third. The examples he gives are described in meticulous detail and are drawn from a very wide range of professions from architecture, to music, to psychoanalysis.

In each example he describes a critical shift in thinking that takes place as a result of two factors: the reflective time, space and process and the dialogue with the educator. In his discussion of the educational environment required for this kind of shift to be possible, he emphasises how subtle and difficult it is to achieve, and how much time is required (1988).

His work on reflective practice can be summarised as follows:

- a crisis in professional knowledge exists – the high ground of academic rigour and the lowland of messy practice do not connect

- a form of professional artistry needs to be developed by stimulating living connections between theory, intuition and practice

- intuitive problem-solving needs to accompany hard knowledge and specific skills

- reflection-on-action and reflection-in-action ('a double feedback loop') are vital to advanced practice

- innovative educational approaches are needed.

Schon's two factors can be likened respectively to Bion's idea of containment and the attention and interpretation of the analytic process whether with an individual or a group.

The issues raised for contemporary professional education by Bion's work on groups and on the containment that enables thinking to take place, and by Schon's work on professional education are fundamental. From Bion's work on basic assumption behaviour in groups, it is clear how easy it is for groups to lose sight of their legitimate task and become engaged in anti-task behaviour. From his work on thinking, we learn that in certain conditions, thought can splinter and produce major perceptual distortions, not only in mentally ill people but also in normal adults. Combinations of basic assumption group life and disruptions to, or failures of, thought occur frequently in large organisations and particularly in bureaucracies, since they perpetuate in their own highly compartmentalised structures the fragment of disrupted individual thought. In this way, the opportunities for individuals to establish and sustain rigour and to find containment of primitive anxieties related to the primary task are minimal.

Professional Activities: A Post-Modernist Perspective

The dangers of a splintering of individual thought and its further fragmentation through bureaucratic compartmentalisation are considerable; poor quality practice, wastage of resources, duplication and lack of collaboration, inadequate information systems, high levels of stress and individual breakdown ensue. Because this splintered world is philosophically and structurally coherent with our age, however, it attracts little attention and raises too little concern.

Culturally, these features have been described by the term post-modernism; introduced in the 1930s, by 1960 one of the emerging keywords of academic life and reaching pre-eminence in the 1980s (Smart 1993). There is not space in this article to do justice to the many different strands of post-modernist thought so a synopsis is offered instead.

The term and ideas of post-modernism were founded on a disillusionment with radical politics and the socialist promise of the early twentieth century. They have been applied to the cultures and practices of all disciplines from architecture to electronics, and from art and literature to natural science. The loss of certainty, the acceptance of a relativist philosophy and the fragmentation of values, thought and beliefs described above in relation to social work have been identified as normal features of post-modernism. So the nearest that there are to facts in the post-modernist world are the constructivist nature of knowledge, the dizzy pace of change, the babel of professional languages, and the continuous erasure of categories of thought and formal structures of all kinds. The following synopsis of the distinctive features of post-modernist culture draws on a range of theoretical work:

- a cultural configuration constituted through complex relationships with a new generation of technologies, which are themselves linked to the emergence of a global economic formation

- the 'waning of affect' – people become 'commodities', 'bits', 'episodes', giving the impression of a new depthlessness

- a fragmentation of the privileged subject and a consequent breakdown of narrative order in favour of parallel or co-existing narratives that join in varying combinations as a result of articulation and commerce at the interface; no fixed positions and constant adaptation (Zohar 1993)

- the omnipresence of pastiche and prevalence of a 'nostalgia mode', particularly in the inner city which also has a near mediaeval quality of danger (Eco 1987)

- a crisis of representation resulting in empty language that lacks meaning and authenticity often producing 'language games' (Lyotard 1984)

- a culture increasingly dominated by space and spatial logic (Jameson 1991)

- knowledge and information becoming commodities in the market (Huyssen 1984).

It seems to me that those who have identified these key characteristics of our contemporary culture point to the following problematic features of the professional world of social work and of disciplines allied to it, highlighted by the introduction of market mechanisms:

- the commodification of care through needs assessment, care packaging and care management

- the emphasis on audit, information and databases especially to serve the welfare exchange market structured around the purchaser-provider split

- the near erasure of the term social work without official acknowledgement in the glossaries and directories accompanying the NHS and Community Care Act, 1990

- a world where the term quality can mean quantity, and care management is defined by resource-based eligibility criteria and therefore also means managing the lack of care

- the rhetoric of 'user-centred seamless service' and 'partnership' with a seductive undertow that evokes sentimentality in the place of a more rational appraisal of the viability of new policies given the existing resource framework

- the constant change of senior managers and organisational structures leading to an absence of authoritative leadership.

Implications: The Nature and Aims of Professional Education: Three Statements

Without containment and without a more benign and facilitating feedback system between the individual social work professional working in a bureaucracy, and their organisation, the dangers of making categorical errors in thought and in practice are bound to remain high. With Bion's concept of container-contained and Schon's concept of the double feedback learning loop which provides the foundation for reflective practice, however, it is possible to arrive at a series of statements of the aims of professional education which are capable of enduring the fragmentary post-modern world with its continual turbulent change.

The three statements that follow are derived from the three perspectives of Bion, Schon and the theorists of post-modernism as outlined above.

The contribution of Bion indicates that it is important:

- to give primary importance to the stimulus of individual thoughtfulness and integration (ethical, emotional and across the personal/professional divide)
- to create the conditions in which individual meaning, organisational purpose and the quality of work can be identified and examined
- to foster creative exchange between theorisations of the individual and of group and organisational dynamics and to consider their relevance to the nature of working tasks where possible
- to allow the painful truths of discrepant individual and organisational 'stories' (subjectivity and context) to emerge where necessary
- to provide containment, where needed, for the emotional and intellectual repercussions that can arise as a result of individual and organisational discrepancies
- to stimulate further professional development, by enhancing understanding of the nature of responsibility to the primary working tasks.

These aims beg many questions, first about how much time is needed but also, and perhaps more important, about the nature of the containment required. Educational and training courses at the Tavistock Clinic usually provide strong containment through a form of tutorial support that does not flinch from addressing personal development issues where they arise. In addition, course members often undertake a personal analysis, psychotherapy or counselling, either by choice or as a course requirement. The Tavistock is either reactionary or wise. Elsewhere the meaning that has been attributed to equality of opportunity in training has tended to preclude a focus on personal development.

The work of Donald Schon suggests the following aims for professional education:

- to educate for creative thinking in the course of practice in an uncertain and rapidly changing world
- to enable a close examination of specific problems and narrative discontinuities (breaks in the story) in an individual's professional practice to take place

- to create the conditions of both safety and challenge in which unconscious creativity can be brought to bear on problem-solving, exploring those discontinuities

- to encourage a cycle of continuous learning eg. rehearsal in the classroom, followed by 'new' practice in the workplace, followed by review and revision and further practice

- to develop new educational roles based on partnership rather than on the old style expert/student relationship.

These aims overlap with the first statement but they are not co-terminous with it. Perhaps because of Schon's background as a philosopher, they point to the potential for what could be called 'operational category error' in the processes of professional thinking and practice (1992). Schon's work is intellectually located in a world in which critical change is not only recognised but was responsible for the generation of his theory. Schon started from the premise that categories of language, thought and practice are unstable, and have a very limited shelf-life. Indeed his first book was originally entitled *The Displacement of Concepts* (1963) and later became known as *Beyond the Stable State*.

The third statement that now follows is a synthesis of the other two that takes into account the post-modern perspective and the issue of task competency which has not been addressed in this chapter as it is addressed elsewhere in this book:

- to provide a containing environment in which individual practitioners are given the opportunity of recovering or establishing creative individual thought

- to offer a partnership in learning between educators and learners

- to provide a learning environment in which the log-jams and messiness of day-to-day practice can be faced and scrutinised in detail

- to provide continuous workshop environments (Schon's 'practicum') in which new ideas and approaches can be explored before and after their use (the double-feedback loop)

- to enable the nature of the organisational structures and defences that frame the work to be examined in relation to identified tasks

- to educate for a context of continuous change in which professional categories and languages, and organisational structure, are constantly by definition under erasure.

Conclusion

It has been argued that some of the professional categories that developed from specialisation, including the category of social work itself have to some extent outlived their usefulness. The constant flux and reorganisation of social services require of professionals that they are able to reframe their knowledge, skills and practices into new combinations and categories to suit a world where skill-mixes of a radically new kind are required and ethical dilemmas are often profound. How else can they meet the individual and organisational confusion produced by critical change and the ensuing indeterminacy of professional knowledge? Social work education has to be allowed to address the fundamental contradictions which exist in the context and content of social work practice including the likelihood that the very professional category of social work like others in health and social care is under erasure.

References

Balint, M. (1957) *The Doctor, His Patient and the Illness.* London: Churchill Livingstone.

Bion, W. R. (1957) The Differentiation of the Psychotic from the Non-psychotic personalities. *International Journal of Psycho-analysis* Vol.38, 266–275.

Bion, W.R. (1956) The Development of Schizophrenic Thought. *International Journal of Psycho-analysis* Vol.37, 344–6.

Bion, W.R. (1959) Attacks on Linking. *International Journal of Psycho-analysis* Vol.30, 308–15. Republished (1967) in W.R. Bion *Second Thoughts.* London: Heinemann pp.93–109.

Bion, W.R. (1968) *Experiences in Groups.* London: Tavistock Publications.

Bion, W.R. (1970) *Attention and Interpretation.* London: Tavistock Publications.

CCETSW (1989) *Rules and Requirements for the Diploma in Social Work.* London: CCETSW Paper 30.

CCETSW (1990) *The Requirements for Post-qualifying Education and Training in the Personal Social Services: a Framework for Continuing Professional Development.* London: CCETSW Paper 31.

CCETSW (1993) *Annual Report.* London: CCETSW.

Croft, S. and Beresford, P. (1989) User-Involvement, Citizenship and Social Policy. *Critical Social Policy,* Vol. 9 No.2 Autumn.

Croft, S. and Beresford, P. (1992) The Politics of Participation. *Critical Social Policy,* Vol.12 No.2 Autumn.

Derrida, J. (1976) *Of Grammatology.* Baltimore and London: Johns Hopkins University Press.

Derrida, J. (1978) *Writing and Difference.* London: Routledge and Kegan Paul.

Eco, U. (1987) *Travels in Hyper-reality.* London: Picador.

Handy, C. (1993) *The Empty Raincoat.* London: Hutchinson.

Huyssen, A. (1984) Mapping the Postmodern. *New German Critique* 33.

Jameson, F. (1991) *Postmodernism or the Cultural Logic of Late Capitalism.* London and New York: Verso.

Lyotard J-F. (1984) *The Postmodern Condition: A Report on Knowledge.* Manchester: Manchester University Press.

Mayer, J.E. and Timms, N. (1968) *The Client Speaks.* London: Routledge and Kegan Paul.

Pietroni, M. (1991) *Right or Privilege?* London: CCETSW Study 10.

Ricoeur, P. (1970) *Freud and Philosophy.* Newhaven, Connecticut: Yale University Press.

Schon, D. (1963) *The Displacement of Concepts: public and private learning in a changing society.* London: Tavistock Publications.

Schon, D. (1983) *The Reflective Practitioner.* London: Temple Smith.

Schon, D. (1988) *Educating the Reflective Practitioner.* London and San Francisco: Jossey Bass.

Schon, D. (1992) The Crisis of Professional Knowledge and the Pursuit of an Epistemology of Practice. *Journal of Interprofessional Care* Vol 6, No 1.

Smart, B. (1993) *Postmodernity.* London and New York: Routledge.

Statham, D. (1987) Women, the New Right and Social Work. *Journal of Social Work Practice.* Vol.2, No. 4, pp.129–149.

Woolgar, S. (1983) Irony in the social study of science. In K. Knorr-Cetina and M. Mulkay (eds) *Science Observed: Perspectives on the Social Study of Science.* London: Sage. pp.239–149.

Zohar, D. (1993) *The Quantum Society.* London: Bloomsbury.

Chapter 3

Professional Competence and Higher Education

Margaret Yelloly

All professional trainings in social work have been influenced by the growing emphasis on competence and clear outcomes described by Jones and Joss, though for social work educators there remains a tension between this and the historic emphasis on process, and on personal and professional growth. Major shifts in vocational education and training have been prompted by the advent of the National Council for Vocational Qualifications (NCVQ) and the Scottish Council for Vocational Education and Training (SCOTVEC), and the massive developments in competency-based education and training which have come about under their aegis and that of the Training Agency have been termed a silent revolution. To date the effects have been most powerfully felt in Further Education, since National Vocational Qualifications (NVQs) at levels 1 – 4 have affected courses mainly located in that sector. But the idea of competence has also profoundly influenced professional training and can be seen in CCETSW's Paper 30, the *Regulations and Guidance for the Diploma in Social Work*, and (even more self-evidently) Paper 31, *The Requirements for Postqualifying Education and Training in the Personal Social Services*. We would expect, therefore, that a focus on outcomes and competences, rather than on structure, inputs, or process, would strongly characterise recent developments in social work education.

The tides of competence are running and as Burke (1989) notes, the changes have already touched the lives of millions, and are set to expand yet further and more rapidly. The impact of competence is likely to be even more massive as NCVQ now moves into the professional areas at Level 5 and above, to enable it to achieve the original objective of 'providing opportu-

nities for progression, including progression to higher education and professional qualifications...' (DOE and DES 1986). The relationship between
NCVQ, the professional accrediting bodies, and higher education institutions are likely to be a key and contested area within the next few years. It
may well be that social work education and training will be brought firmly
within NCVQ's orbit, and be organised around its key educational philosophies and features, even though (as this chapter will argue) these central ideas
may change out of all recognition in the process of transmission into higher
education.

The Origins of Competency-Based Education and Training

Initially competency-based training developed from pilot projects in teacher
education in the USA. In this country its introduction was into further rather
than higher education and stemmed from the new approaches to training
policy contained in a series of White Papers in the 1980s (DOE 1981, 1984;
DOE and DES 1985, 1986) which set out the Government's aim of creating
a unified and coherent national framework for vocational certification across
the whole range of occupations, with a view to specifying clearly the
competences which employers might expect from those holding particular
qualifications. To achieve this a new body was set up, the National Council
for Vocational Qualifications, and a system of S/NVQs was introduced. The
developments for various occupational groupings are guided by Industry
Lead Bodies (ILBs), of which the Care Sector Consortium is the relevant one
for social work, and these formulate 'clear and precise statements' or
Occupational Standards. The Care Sector Consortium has now been incorporated in the Occupational Standards Council for Health and Social Care.
A number of distinctive concepts and features derive from the competence
focus and philosophy of NCVQ: the concept of competence; the methods
of deriving competence statements; standards, and the means of assessing
them. This chapter considers only the concept of competence itself, recognising but not addressing the very considerable difficulties involved in
assessment. Competence is in fact all about assessment; it is only indirectly
about training, though paradoxically, training in the vocational and professional arenas must increasingly be about competence.

What is Competence and How is it Identified?

The Training Agency has this to say:

> ...occupational competence is defined as 'the ability to perform the
> activities within an occupation or function to the standards expected

in employment'. This is a wide concept which embodies the ability to transfer skills and knowledge to new situations within the occupational area. It encompasses organisation and planning of work, innovation and coping with non-routine activities and includes those qualities of personal effectiveness required in the workplace to deal with co-workers, ·managers and customers. It stems from an understanding that to perform effectively in a work role an individual has to be able to combine

- performance of various technical and task components

- overarching management of the various technical and task components to achieve the overall work function

- management of the variance and unpredictability in the work role and wider environment

- integration of the work role within the context of the wider organisational, economic, market and social environment.
  (Training Agency, 1988)

This is a broad conception of competence which includes the need for flexibility and coping with the unique and unpredictable, as well as the network of systemic relationships necessary in any occupational role, from paediatrics to hairdressing. It also implies a knowledge and understanding of principles which enable competence to be transferable. This breadth of conception is especially noteworthy in the face of the criticisms of competency-based training as leading to a narrow, mechanistic, and rote-learning approach to education and training.

Statements of competence are arrived at by undertaking functional analysis of specific occupational tasks, breaking these down into units, and deriving from them a set of task-specific competence statements (what someone must be able to do). Increasingly these are expressed in the NVQ model as 'range statements', that is, statements which define the boundaries within which a particular element operates and provide a more detailed specification of what the element covers. Range statements have been developed to try to deal with ambiguities which may lead to varying interpretations (and thus assessments) of the same performance. In NVQ methodology, elements are grouped into clusters or units, for which credit is given, and which can build up into a full NVQ. Inevitably the attempt to specify behaviour more and more minutely, as range statements do, makes the process much more complicated and increases the difficulty of an holistic approach to assessment.

The Shift to Competence in Social Work Education

These developments in further education have been paralleled in higher education by a move towards competency-based practice and training for the professions (Clark 1990) though here it has not developed in the same way as a single unified model. The Guidelines for the Certificate of Qualification in Social Work left the specification of outcomes largely to individual programmes; these were indicated only in a broad general way and their interpretation, balance, and curriculum implications were very much a matter for programmes and educational institutions to work out. Often course content reflected the predilections of the teachers as much as the needs of employment, and frequently embodied an idiosyncratic view of the nature of social work and the right preparation for it. The advent in 1989 of the Diploma in Social Work, the new professional qualification for social workers in all fields and settings, heralded a very significant change of emphasis. Embodied in the·new Regulations are explicit shifts, first towards *the specification of the knowledge, skills and values needed to achieve competent social work practice of a national minimum standard*; and second, towards the assessment of competence on the basis of *specified practice outcomes* at the point of qualification. It was CCETSW's hope that an outcome focus would allow for and encourage innovative and flexible models of training (CCETSW 1989 p.6). Although the Statement of Requirements for Qualification in Social Work identifies knowledge, values and skills necessary to competent practice, and not competence itself, competence is assumed to involve all three. However the Statement does also contain some explicit statements of competence which can potentially be assessed on the basis of specified performance criteria, though these criteria are not part of the Paper. The specification of areas of competence was not new: for very many years courses produced guidelines for practice assessment which provided a detailed statement of the main areas to be assessed, and some provided checklists of criteria. What *was* new was a common national statement of competences, and the importance attached to them, not only for assessment, but for curriculum building.

The Statement of Requirements was reached by a process of consultation with experts in all fields of social work, and was intended to reflect the cumulative wisdom and experience of practitioners, educators and managers. Unlike later competence statements, however, such as those developed for the Residential and Day Care Project, by the ASSET Programme, and for the Registration and Inspection of Homes, the CCETSW Statement was not derived from functional analysis. It covers a wide range of social work practice and is necessarily broadly conceived and unspecific in respect of occupational role. Furthermore, it was profoundly affected by political considerations; the Statement was originally part of a bid to attract government funding to introduce a three-year qualification in social work. It has been generally welcomed by practitioners and educators as providing a clear statement of what social work is about, and one which manages to incorporate most of the key elements without unmanageable detail. But in trying to achieve at one and the same time a statement which was broadly acceptable, on the one hand to practitioners and employers, and on the other to the government, the product is open to the charge of romanticism: are these competencies what is actually required of all social workers in real-life jobs? Or do they reflect an idealist position, an expression of professional aspirations rather than a realistic expectation of what social workers with a two-year training at non-graduate Diploma level can actually be expected to do? Few would claim to meet all of the requirements listed so comprehensively in Paper 30, and almost certainly not on the basis of a two-year training. At the time of writing CCETSW has announced its intention to embark on a new study of social work competences, using functional analysis, in collaboration with the Occupational Standards Council.

In developing the Postqualifying Framework, CCETSW was much more explicitly guided by ideas of competence, in part because they are more compatible with part-time and Credit Accumulation and Transfer modes of training delivery which were principles of Paper 31 (CCETSW 1990). Part II of the Paper contains competence requirements for each of the four routes (practice, education and training, management, and research) and these have been further refined by a number of more detailed statements (or 'illustrative exemplars') covering such areas as child care, mental health, firstline management and supervision in group care, learning difficulties, work with older people, supervision, management and research, derived by a process of functional analysis – identification of role requirements in consultation with managers and expert practitioners.

These developments in education and training for social work have clearly been powerfully influenced by NCVQ thinking. But there are also factors specific to it as an occupation which have fuelled the shift towards competency-based education, and are summarized in *Care for Tomorrow* (CCETSW 1987). Social work has been rocked by a number of scandals which have called into question the professional competence and the quality of training of its members. Public criticism has been underlined by challenges from employers to the educational objectives espoused by social work training in institutions of higher education. The greater employer influence on the Certificate of Social Service programmes sharply pointed up the difference between the explicit employer-led objectives of CSS, and the more theoretical, critical and intellectual objectives traditional HE-based courses held sacred. These differences were often exaggerated and stereotyped; CSS courses were taught more often than not by CQSW-trained staff, and were by no means uncritical; nor were university and polytechnic courses uninterested in practice outcomes. However, they came to stand for identifiably different approaches to professional education and training. This tension between the intellectual endeavours valued in higher education and the practical abilities needed in the job affects all the professions, from lawyers, doctors and accountants to engineers and nurses. It is by no means unique to social work and indeed is an issue at the heart of all professional education. What we now see universally is a move towards greater employer participation in the defining of training objectives and their implementation, through partnerships of varying degrees of intimacy. *Enterprise in Higher Education*, for instance, is based on partnership with employers and expects nothing less than 'the involvement of employers in curriculum review, development and change, in the assessment of outcomes and in the learning process' – traditionally the professional sphere of the educator (DOE 1988). In the case of social work, whose claims to professional status have always been fragile and marked by theoretical insecurity, uncertainty, and an 'indeterminate zone of practice' (Schon 1987) the influence of employers and of the State (via the Department of Health) has been wielded more strongly and to more obvious effect than in the major professions such as the law and accountancy. No programme of professional training for social work can now be approved unless it is submitted jointly by such a formally constituted partnership.

The Department of Health's *Personal Social Services: Resourcing Strategy for 1991/2 to 1993/4* (SSI 1991) summarised the problems facing social work training as follows:

- concern about the general competence of newly qualified social workers to work effectively in the field

- the failure of qualification training to provide adequately for meeting the special needs of particular client groups (such as abused children) or to provide sufficient training in important areas including legal powers and responsibilities

- lack of consistency in what people completing social work courses are trained and equipped to do, resulting from too much variation in the process and contents of theory and practice teaching, and under-resourcing of both the academic and practice elements

- problems of credibility and quality control in a two-tier structure of social work qualification training, exacerbated by a progressive decline in people qualifying from the higher status CQSW courses (11% over a decade).

The government priorities for CCETSW set out in the recent policy review indicate a strong emphasis on the need to demonstrate the quality of the output from social work courses (SSI 1993, para. 4.7).

The Advantages and Limitations of the NVQ Model

The advantages of a competency-based model are well-rehearsed. Perhaps most significantly, it provides a means of comparing levels across a range of occupations in order to develop a comprehensive framework for a progressive system of education. Thus it offers a welcome opening of access to professions and occupations which have traditionally controlled entry by way of discrete and occupation-specific educational ladders, of which even the lower rungs were never open to all. Further, the emphasis on outcome introduces clarity and focus into vocational education, ensures it is relevant and meets the needs of the workplace, and has ethical advantages in making the criteria for assessment more transparent and open than has traditionally been the case. It also provides a rationale for curriculum building. These advantages are very considerable.

But there are also criticisms. The first is of *atomisation*. The attempt to analyse competence into discrete elements of behaviour (even if these are subsequently re-grouped as 'units') results in a fragmentation of complex interrelated activities, which does violence to the way that people actually behave in real-life situations. Ashworth (1992) is critical of the inadequate specification of competence in the NCVQ model and believes that the notion of competence involves an over-mechanistic way of thinking. He suggests that this model provides 'solutions' to the specification of learning outcomes which are normally inappropriate to the description of human action, or to the facilitation of the training of human beings. The more human the action, the more likely it is to involve creative thought and understanding, and to involve a team rather than the activity of an individual.

A second concern is the *lack of dynamism* said to be inherent in functional analysis. NVQ clearly aspires to a dynamic view of competence. Jessup writes:

> Closely related to the issue of developing broadly competent people for current roles, is the need to prepare people for changes in the future. How can we not only train people for the jobs they have to do now, but also give them a basis of competence to cope with, or acquire

quickly, the skills they will need for work they might be performing in two years or five years from now?... The emphasis placed upon task management, contingency management and role/environment skills, encourages the development of the 'process' or core skills associated with employment, which are likely to endure and remain relevant as technology and work practices change. (Jessup 1991 p.28)

Nevertheless, the encapsulation of detailed competences, in the NVQ handbooks, if not in tablets of stone, is not easily compatible with a dynamic view of competence, and makes them difficult to adapt or modify in the light of changing circumstances. It is often remarked how easily competence statements can become dated.

A third criticism relates to the difficulty in dealing with *knowledge and values* in any very satisfactory way. Professionals typically emphasize the cognitive and value components of their work which (though they can also be incorporated in competence statements) are more typically seen in NVQ terms as the knowledge and understanding underpinning competence. The metaphor of 'underpinning' raises more questions than it answers in respect of the complex interaction of knowledge, cognitive activity, and competence in work performance; at best it reduces knowledge and understanding to a subservient status. Yet for work-roles involving problem-solving (as virtually all jobs do since they are rarely totally repetitive) cognitive abilities which cannot be directly observed or assessed may be the key feature. The interrelationship between this and action is complex.

Joss emphasizes the potential disadvantages of the model for professional work:

'it denies the holistic nature of such work; shows what people must do but not how or why; completely fails to provide an explanation of the importance of the exercise of discretion in work and thus devalues the fact that equally competent performances can arise from quite different actions; it may thus discourage creativity and risk-taking, (indeed, lead to inappropriate application of policy or procedures on occasions); it is over-reliant on quantitative measures to the exclusion of qualitative ones; being output oriented, it denies the importance of process; cannot handle abstract concepts, such as reflective insight, which are not easily amenable to observation; and similarly, is a very poor training tool since it cannot shed light on the learning process, only on the acquisition of (or lack of) competences'. (Joss quoted Hey 1991)

Despite these strictures (which seem to relate to the more mechanistic model) Joss and Hey were nonetheless able to produce a detailed social work practice exemplar involving competence specification at the advanced level which demonstrates that statements of competence *can* be made with some conviction in the professional arena, in a way which clarifies the bases of assessment, enables differentiation to be made between levels of competence in different occupational roles, and acts as a guide for educators. Moreover, this can be done without the wearisome lists and over-specification of detail which renders some competence (and their accompanying range) statements so user-unfriendly.

Knowledge and Competence

Warren Piper (1992) calls attention to the growing preference within higher education for cognitive and epistemological approaches to the study of student learning, as opposed to behavioural objectives. That there has been a discernible shift towards a wider notion of competence capable of encompassing higher order cognitive abilities is undeniable. Wolf (1989) usefully points out that competence, like knowledge, is a construct; it cannot be directly observed or measured, only inferred from behavioural indicators. There is thus no qualitative difference between the two, and both knowledge and cognitive ability are capable of being behaviourally referenced, for example, through reflective case studies or clinical papers.

Eraut (1991) includes in his account of 'underpinning knowledge' activities not normally designated in this way – self-awareness, self-management, self-development; and also abilities or skills such as planning, problem-solving, analysis, modification and evaluation. These are a very long way from a narrowly behavioural conception of competence. There appears to be no dispute that knowledge and understanding are present in most work-roles to varying degrees. What is at issue is whether the NVQ model is capable of incorporating these areas of human cognition both conceptually (without extraordinary intellectual contortions) and practically in the actual processes of assessment. There appears to be a very considerable gap between aspirations for a broad view of competence, and existing competence statements. While the broad definition of competence increases the ability to use relevant knowledge, curriculum is not generally spelled out, except in very general terms. It is the task of the educator to identify and introduce the learner to 'relevant knowledge'. While this might at first sight allow of a flexible approach to curriculum content, in practice defined outcomes contain an implicit specification of the nature and types of knowledge necessary to the performance of the role; other areas may be pushed to the periphery. For example, sociology as a discipline now has an increasingly marginal place in the epistemology of social work, by comparison for instance with law. While in approving DipSW courses, CCETSW's emphasis was originally to be firmly on outcome, experience suggests that in fact curriculum areas are increasingly being prescribed; for example, in relation to law, child protection, and teaching which supports antidiscriminatory practice.

Webb (1992) provides an interesting and sceptical analysis of these developments in vocational education. He takes issue with the whole idea of competence and sees the 'vocationalist discourse' as leading to a national curriculum and massive circumscription of education and training in response to demands set by employers. In his view semi-professions such as nursing and social work are subject to advancing degrees of control by the state as part of an increasingly explicit subordination to policy agendas; '...any discretion or latitude that ever applied to these bureau-professionals (as 'caseworkers' for example) has been channelled elsewhere.' All this, in his view, reflects increasing control by the centre and an accompanying curtailment of autonomy and discretion. Indeed, such an agenda is explicit in the role of the Training Agency and the literature of NVQ. It is instructive to recall that the CCETSW Statement of Requirements was widely seen in universities as presaging the loss of the independently-minded practitioner, able to challenge inequitable or oppressive environments, and her replacement by the biddable employee trained not to reason why. The increasing marginalisation of sociology as a subject of study for social workers attests to the increasing restriction and technicisation of the curriculum. This trend is in sharp contradiction to the tradition of social inquiry and analysis within which social work in the UK has traditionally been rooted; no longer is an understanding of the social and economic context which shapes the lives of citizens and the professional activities of social workers regarded as necessary to informed practice.

What a competence approach does usefully value is that kind of implicit practical knowledge or practice wisdom, 'the experience-derived know-how which professionals intuitively use' (Eraut 1985), which is acquired through practising an art or craft, and learning through doing it. Much of this knowledge cannot be described or taught by verbal means. When I learned to tune a keyboard instrument, my instructor described the sound of the perfect fifth as 'like strawberry jam.' This was a pretty good shot at describing an aural sensation, but no one could learn to recognise the unique sound of the perfect interval through description alone, only through repeated familiarity with the actual experience. (There are technical ways of tuning intervals with scientific accuracy, for example, electronically, but the human ear is generally regarded as superior for practical purposes). There is nothing mystical about tuning skill; the facility to tune an interval quickly and 'intuitively' has been acquired through a process of reflection, analysis, and repeated trial. An interval sounds 'sour'; is it correct for that musical temperament? Is it too wide or too narrow? Is a note sharp or flat? Such reflections lead to minute adjustments which are found to improve the quality of the sound, to which the ear itself, through constant application and attention, becomes more sensitive over time. So too with interpersonal skills, though the right balance between 'know-how' and more formally-acquired theoretical or 'book' knowledge remains an issue in social work education.

Reflective Practice and the Learning Process

Underlying many of these criticisms seems to be a feeling that the outcomes of professional education are not reducible to a set of competence elements, and that the attempt to do so damages the 'artistry' and creativity the professional needs to bring to the job. An influential notion, which has made sense to professions as different as social work, accountancy, and engineering, is that of the reflective practitioner. Schon (1987) has pointed to the crisis of confidence which can be observed in many professional schools. Professionals are under ever more powerful public and political scrutiny, and pressure from increased expectations of their performance in an environment which 'combines increasing turbulence with increasing legislation of professional activity.' They work in larger systems over which they have little control, and (in the caring professions especially) their work lacks technical precision and certainty. Uncertainty, uniqueness, value-conflict are the characteristics of the 'swampy lowlands' inhabited by messy human problems where these staff work. Training for artistry or reflective practice Schon sees as more akin to the training of a musician or a painter than that of a technician. The musician requires technique, a knowledge of musical form and the laws of harmony; but interpretation in performance is essentially personal. Performances of the same work may vary hugely in terms of tempo, style, phrasing and so on, and all may be acceptable. Hence the importance of the 'practicum', providing conditions like those created in the studios and conservatories, where there is freedom to learn by doing in a setting relatively low in risk, with access to coaches who initiate students into the 'traditions of the calling'. The work of Winter and Maisch (Maisch and Winter 1991, Winter and Maisch 1992) is of special importance in this context, since their ASSET model attempts to bridge the notions of competence, on the one hand, and artistry on the other. It is one of the few attempts to frame professional work at Honours degree level in terms of a fully-fledged NVQ model, and the project followed the whole process through from planning to implementation and evaluation. The papers produced by the Project are the result of identifying, thinking through, and resolving a host of problems, both practical and intellectual, encountered on the way. This is a very different matter from a conceptual paper produced for a conference, which may never be tested out in the refining fire of educational practice.

It is worth noting that a competence emphasis does not of itself imply any necessary relationship with a particular kind of educational process or method. Winter (1991) sees the attainment of competence as involving experiential learning through a constant cycle of concrete experience, reflective observation, conceptualisation, active experimentation and concrete experience. It is thus possible to see the model of learning set out by Schon, involving a process of reflection-in-action, problem-solving, and experimentation as compatible with the acquisition of professional competence which includes the capacity to address non-routinised work and unique situations. Indeed the capacity to reflect is itself amenable to specification as a statement of competence, and to behavioural indicators. For example, a case study may include an account of the thinking process which led to a course of action, and the learning which accrued from it.

Winter maintains that the idea of experiential learning underlies and informs reflective learning: 'Good practice...for professional workers, is practice whereby knowledge is developed through forms of reflection which practice itself requires' (1991 p18). A theory of professional competence must in his view incorporate principles about the nature of professional work and the educational models best suited to promote it. Self-evaluation and self-knowledge are part and parcel of the professional task, and must feature both in outcomes and as process. It must be said, however, that this is a somewhat idiosyncratic view of competence, and one which represents a significant departure from the older NCVQ model.

There are many unresolved questions as to the educational models which best promote reflective practice of the kind noted by Schon, due at least in part to the paucity of educational evaluation on which teachers can draw. The traditional approach is top-down; the learner reads books or papers, attends lectures or seminars, and is introduced to ideas and theories which are then applied. By application is meant more than a self-conscious reference to organising ideas or frameworks for action; educators look for an integration of knowledge which becomes part of the learner's own frame of reference, and informs practical action in a way which appears natural and unforced. The bottom-up approach, by contrast, starts with the problem to be solved or the situation to be attended to, and seeks out the knowledge, factual or theoretical, which is needed to deal with it effectively. This more nearly reflects the way that knowledge is used in practice, and is typified by the Enquiry and Action Learning approach pioneered in this country by the University of Bristol (Burgess and Jackson 1990). Such differing models reflect both theories of learning and educational ideologies; research can throw light on their relative effectiveness in achieving educational objectives, but the research evidence suggests that there are different learning styles (Gardiner (1989) for instance, distinguishes serialist and holistic learners) and that no one approach is likely to be universally applicable. Studies of student satisfaction suggest that a variety of teaching and learning modes are valued. Many educators would take the idea of experiential learning even further; they would say that for knowledge to be utilisable in social work practice, cognitive learning has to be accompanied by affective change, and that much of the really significant lifelong learning is of this kind. Maier's concept of 'transformational learning' (Maier 1984) involving the relinquishment of old conceptions, accompanied by the pain and discomfort of uncertainty, which leads to a fundamental paradigmatic shift illuminates particularly well the kind of powerful experiences which learning for the caring professions may involve (Stanford and Yelloly 1994).

While Winter and Maisch describe the ASSET model as a refinement of NVQ, we should not underestimate the enormous differences in emphasis. ASSET places far more weight than does the older NVQ model on the kinds of cognitive, reflective and affective processes that are discussed here. It feels a much more acceptable and compatible approach to professional education in universities, but it is in essence a different conception of competency-based education, with different intellectual antecedents, rather than a modification of NVCQ thinking. As these two systems (the Higher Education and the employment-based) begin to interrelate, we can already see profound shifts in the delivery and assessment of professional education. ASSET has shown that these need not be at the expense of concern with educational process and intellectual inquiry, and social work would be deeply impoverished if the research outlook and intellectual traditions of the universities were to be lost through through uncritical acceptance and imposition of narrowly-conceived and inappropriate industrial models.

Conclusion

The development of competence as a unifying concept across the whole spectrum of vocational and professional qualifications is intended to promote consistency, differentiate between levels, and promote access throughout the

whole continuum. To the extent that this has been achieved it has considerable pragmatic value. In the course of its application to professional education, the concept has been revised and considerably extended, as we have
seen, to take account of the less technical aspects of professional activity. In
the process it has been broadened, sometimes out of all recognition, to
include a number of cognitive and affective aspects related to, but not
normally subsumed within, the notion of competence. The new focus on
outcomes sharpens up the aims and objectives of education in the vocational
and professional spheres. This is welcomed not only by employers but by
students who often have definite vocational aims and value training which
is directly related to the job. However there remain powerful tensions
between traditional conceptions of the educative role of higher education
institutions and those which are competency-driven. While clear objectives
must guide formal structures for learning, educators are inescapably involved
as participants in the processes of teaching and learning. A primary objective
of maximising individual potential and excellence is difficult to marry with
that of minimal universal standards, and the tension between them is reflected
in the transactions between outside regulatory and teaching institutions
(Pinker 1993, Trow 1993). Of course social work must be relevant and equip
its students for the real world of practice. But education driven only by a
search for competence is likely to promote a narrow, technicist, minimalist
and dogmatic approach at the expense of concern with intellectual inquiry
and social analysis, with processes of learning, with the cognitive and ethical
foundations of professional practice, and with the idiosyncratic and creative
aspects of practice (the artistry) which lie at its heart.

References

Ashworth, P. (1992) Being competent and having 'competence'. *Journal of Further and
Higher Education* Vol.16, 3, –17.

Burgess, H. and Jackson, S. (1990) Enquiry and Action Learning: a New Approach to
Social Work Education. *Social Work Education* Vol.9, 3, 3–19.

Burke, J.W. (ed) (1989) *Competency-Based Education and Training*. Lewes: Falmer Press.

CCETSW (1987) *Care for Tomorrow*. London: CCETSW.

CCETSW (1989) *Regulations and Guidance for the Diploma in Social Work (Paper 30)*.
London: CCETSW.

CCETSW (1990) *The Requirements for Postqualifying Education and Training in the Personal
Social Services (Paper 31)*. London: CCETSW.

Clark, C. (1990) Key Issues for Research on Competence. In P. Marsh and C. Clark (eds), *Research Issues in Social Work Education and Training*, University of Sheffield.

DOE (1981) *A New Training Initiative; A Programme for Action*. Cmnd. 8455, London: HMSO.

DOE (1984) *Training for Jobs*. Cmnd. 9135, London: HMSO.

DOE (1988) *Enterprise in Higher Education*: Supplementary Notes of Guidance, unpublished.

DOE and DES (1985) *Education and Training for Young People*. London: HMSO.

DOE and DES (1986) *Review of Vocational Qualifications in England and Wales*. London: HMSO.

DOE and DES (1986) *Working Together: Education and Training. Cmnd. 9823*. London: HMSO.

Eraut, M. (1985) Knowledge Creation and Knowledge Use in Professional Contexts. *Studies in Higher Education* 10, 2, 117–133.

Eraut, M. (1991) In N. Jessup (ed) *Outcomes: NVQ's and the Emerging Model of Training*. Lewes: Falmer Press.

Gardiner, D. (1989) *The Anatomy of Supervision. Developing learning and professional competence for social work students*. Milton Keynes: Society for Research into Higher Education and Open University Press.

Hey, A. (1991) *CCETSW's Advanced Award: project report*. Unpublished study for CCETSW.

Jessup, N. (ed) (1991) *Outcomes: NVQ's and the Emerging Model of Training*. Lewes: Falmer Press.

Maier, H.W. (1984) A simple but powerful concept poses a challenge for the teaching and learning of social work practice. *Social Work Education*, 4:1.

Pinker, R.A. (1993) A lethal kind of looniness? *The Times Higher*, September 10, 19.

Schon, D. (1987) *Educating the Reflective Practitioner*. MA: Jossey Bass.

Stanford, R. and Yelloly, M. (1994) *Shared Learning in Child Protection*. London: English National Board for Nursing, Midwifery and Health Visiting, and the CCETSW.

SSI (1991) *Personal Social Services: Resourcing Strategy for 1991/2 to 1993/4*, Department of Health, 1991.

SSI (1993) *Policy and Financial Management Review of the Central Council for Education and Training in Social Work*. Department of Health.

Training Agency (1988). Quoted in J.W.Burke (ed) (1989) *Competency-Based Education and Training*. Lewes: Falmer Press.

Trow, M. (1993) The business of learning. *The Times Higher*, October 8, 20 –21.

Warren Piper, D. (1992) Are Professors Professional? *Higher Education Quarterly* 46, 2, 145–156.

Webb, D. (1992) Competencies, contracts and cadres: common themes in the social control of nurse and social work education. *Journal of Interprofessional Care* 6, 3, 223–230.

Winter, R. (1991) Outline of a General Theory of Professional Competences. In M. *Maisch and R.Winter (eds), Asset Programme: Vol 2. Development and Assessment of Professional Competences.* Chelmsford: Anglia University and Essex County Council.

Winter, R. and Maisch, M. (1992) *Assessing professional Competences: Final Report of the ASSET Programme.* Chelmsford: Anglia University and Essex County Council.

Wolf, A. (1989) Can Knowledge and Competence Mix? In J.W. Burke (ed) (1989) *Competency-Based Education and Training.* Lewes: Falmer Press.

Chapter 4

Conceptions of Knowledge and Social Work Education

Mary Henkel

Introduction

Like most other groups in the public sector of the UK those involved in the education of human services professions are being required to adapt to a public policy environment which is being fundamentally reshaped within the framework of a strongly regulated market. These changes are being made in the name of radical reduction of the public sector and of freeing individual enterprise as far as possible from the restrictions of state intervention. The disciplines imposed are to be those of competition, contracts, limited state funding and evaluation against centrally imposed norms, in which individualism, economic instrumentalism and authoritarianism are prominent. They are informed by a model of rationality predicated on the need to use scarce resources with maximum efficiency and to match means to ends that are determined ultimately by individual self-interest.

If resources are still seen primarily in financial terms, the definition has widened, most notably to include knowledge. For in the contemporary world, knowledge is increasingly regarded as a, if not the, critical commodity for economic welfare. It is overwhelmingly for use. Hence the insistent emphasis on the need to manage the production of knowledge and on skills and competences and performance. Knowledge and understanding are to be harnessed to the achievement of measurable goals.

Within this environment, professionals are under pressure: no longer can they hide within the protective limits of peer review. Evaluation is against visible output or publicised targets rather than less tangible process criteria; quantitative measures are sought to provide performance indicators. Prominent amongst such measures, particularly in contexts where they are difficult to devise, are those of customer or consumer satisfaction. Professionals are encouraged to revise concepts of professional excellence, to take more account of, or in some cases yield place to, ordinary knowledge or common sense and to frame their practice from within customers' priorities and perspectives.

These developments seem in some ways to represent a welcome attack on entrenched privilege, arcane knowledge and arrogant assumptions that individuals cannot understand their own needs. At the same time, they represent another form of arrogance: a disregard for the complexities of human endeavours and problems, and therefore for the need for specialist or theoretical knowledge, critical reflection and openness to uncertainty; and a focussing on means to uncontested ends.

This chapter aims to examine some of the profound shifts in theories of knowledge that have been made in the course of the twentieth century with a view to showing how they both inform and challenge such developments. While they can be seen to be reflected in the changing world described, captured by those who hold power in that world, they also point to quite different possibilities, not least for the practice and education of social workers and other human service professions.

Two main theories of knowledge are explored, pragmatism and herme-neutics. They derive from the different traditions of North American and Continental European philosophies respectively but have much in common. Both challenge the Cartesian paradigm, at the centre of which are dualistic forms of thought (mind and body; subject and object; theory and practice; knowledge and action) and the ideal of the individual knowing subject contemplating an external object. Instead they assert the active and collective nature of knowledge acquisition and development, together with the role of language and disciplinary tradition in shaping knowledge and confounding the clear cut division between subject and object. At the same time, they facilitate a review of the relationship between conceptions of knowledge as a means of control or practical intervention and knowledge as understanding and dialogue.

In contrast to what is emerging as the dominant framework for contem-porary British society – individualism, atomism and an instrumental concep-tion of rationality – quite other ideas and values are found to underpin these conceptions of knowledge: communitarianism, interaction and a conception of rationality that is both communicative and practical.

They provide an epistemological framework for the idea of reflective professional practice and education and an alternative rationale to that of consumerism for involving service users and students in these processes. But there must be doubts about how adequately they can deal with the politics of knowledge and of welfare. This question is explored in the last section of the chapter.

Away with Polarities: Knowledge and Action

Bernstein characterised one of the key changes in philosophy during the twentieth century as a move from 'the spectator theory of philosophy': 'from (quoting Anscombe) "an incorrigibly contemplative conception of knowledge" to recognition of the need to understand man as an agent, as an active being engaged in various forms of practice', including the development of knowledge (Bernstein 1972). Within the Cartesian paradigm that had dominated the philosophy of knowledge since the seventeenth century, the concern was to establish how the individual knowing subject could apprehend an external reality. The task was to discover the laws governing the natural world, within a correspondence theory of truth (the idea that knowledge reflects or 'corresponds' to the reality it has grasped). For the empiricist successors of Descartes, the key to that discovery was observation. But gradually the idea that it was possible to apprehend or represent reality directly was undermined and correspondence theories of truth gave way to coherence theories of truth (to meet the criterion of truth propositions must be consistent with each other and the theoretical framework in which they are made). Attention was in some cases directed towards knowledge as practice which is regulated within communities: scientific communities or disciplines, which developed and controlled epistemic rules and criteria of evaluation, a subject of growing interest to sociologists as well as philosophers of science in the twentieth century (Mulkay 1979).

One source of these changes was the pragmatist tradition of philosophy developed from the nineteenth century in the USA, particularly in the work of Peirce and, later, Dewey. Another was the critical rationalism of Popper, prefigured in some respects by Peirce. All three brought together the idea of man (sic) as agent and man as inquirer (see also Henkel 1993). For Peirce, 'the concept of self-controlled conduct provides the mediating link between the traditional dichotomies of theory and practice, thought and action. Man as knower or inquirer is viewed as an agent...not a passive spectator of reality.' (Bernstein 1972). The goal was the 'development of concrete reasonableness'.

Peirce and Popper were, of course, scientists and their conceptions of human action were that it is fundamentally scientific. Scientific inquiry is a refined form of normal human action. For Popper, whose theories of knowledge were embedded in theories of evolution, the primal human activity was problem solving, his paradigm of scientific inquiry. But at the same time, he, like Peirce, regarded knowledge, theories and solutions as inevitably incomplete and provisional. New theories and solutions opened up, indeed often created, new problems, requiring the generation and testing of new solutions.

For Peirce a key theme was the social structure in which rational activity could be realised. This would happen in the context of a free, open, self-critical community of inquirers which constructs and keeps under critical review the epistemic rules and evaluative criteria.

Both Peirce and Popper had highly normative theories of scientific behaviour, in which personal values and scientific excellence were integrally linked. Their conception of the practice of science and the pursuit of rationality entailed values of openness, self-criticism, integrity and courage.

However, Dewey, in developing Peirce's ideas, went further towards relating disciplined inquiry to moral and social issues. His primary project, according to Bernstein, was to 'bring the problems and procedures of moral and social life into closer harmony with advances in experimental, scientific inquiry' (Bernstein 1972). Dewey's conceptual framework was strongly biological. Human experience held a central place in his philosophy but, again, as an active and future-oriented rather than a passive and past-oriented concept. Experience meant, for him, an 'active transaction between a living organism and its environment'. He saw human beings as active agents seeking to transform the situations in which they find themselves. He rejected any antithesis between thought and experience: for him the contrast was between experience that 'is funded by the procedures and results of intelligent activity and experience which is not'. He assumed that intelligence should be exercised in all aspects of living, including moral choices, and thus rejected sharp distinctions between theoretical and practical judgements.

Thus the Cartesian ideal of the individual subject or the individual self as the source of reason and knowledge, contemplating the representations of an objective reality, can be contrasted with the pragmatist ideal of a community of inquirers working within conceptual frameworks formulated, criticised and adapted over time to construct new theories and solutions: knowledge as individual contemplation of an objective reality as against knowledge as continuous, self corrective activity or practice generated in and shaped by a community (see also Toulmin 1972).

This set of ideas is grounded primarily in theories of science, but although Popper, in particular, was adamant that clear distinctions could and should be maintained between science and non-science, key features of the scientific mode are seen as fundamental for the development of a good society. These include scepticism, regulated conflict and readiness to abandon cherished ideas in the face of reasoned argument; at the same time a high value is placed upon boldness and an experimental approach to problem solving of all kinds (Popper 1966).

Knowledge as Dialogue: The Hermeneutic Paradigm

The hermeneutic paradigm of knowledge development also rejects the Cartesian emphasis on the individual knowing subject. Unlike pragmatism, its origins lie primarily in the humanist rather than in the scientific tradition. Key figures in the development of this set of ideas were Heidegger, Wittgenstein and Gadamer. Wittgenstein's contention that it is language that constitutes the limits of our understanding and thus the limits of our world has been profoundly influential. Our conceptions of the world are unavoidably informed by presuppositions which we absorb with our language and which we cannot wholly discard. There is no way in which human beings can apprehend the 'true nature' of reality; all learning is mediated through language and the theories embedded in that language.

Hermeneutics, in which language and its interpretation are central, was embraced in the context of humanistic studies on the continent in the nineteenth century and 'developed into a system which made it the basis of all the human sciences' (Gadamer 1975). But in Gadamer's eyes it had a greater significance still: interpretation for him, is at the heart of what it means to be a human being. We become who we are in the process of understanding, which is inextricable from interpretation and application and is something in which we are engaged all the time. It is achieved through dialogue or encounters with other people, beliefs, traditions and cultures, sometimes contemporary but often past, and thus represented by texts and other cultural artefacts.

He maintained that nothing was in principle incomprehensible, but understanding had to be gained not only through honest and open engagement with the other but also through acknowledging and more fully understanding the presuppositions or prejudices that we bring to such engagement. Learning about something new required understanding one's own context and tradition more deeply. Under these conditions, prejudices are to be seen not as barriers but as gateways to understanding. But within such a theory, knowledge again is always provisional: adapting and changing as people from different traditions confront, interpret and appropriate different ideas.

Thus the hermeneutic paradigm is one in which all understanding is moulded within communal traditions, themselves shaped and transmitted through language. Through self-critical awareness of those traditions and belief in the values of openness, understanding and freedom it is possible for people to achieve consensus, which will often mean a reformulation of ideas or new learning on the part of all participants.

Moreover, the perception of application or, as Bernstein suggests, 'appropriation', as inextricable from understanding and interpretation meant that the knowledge gained was not only theoretical but also moral and practical. Appropriation of ideas meant that those ideas would influence a person in the conduct of their lives or their praxis. According to Bernstein, Gadamer's encounter with Aristotle was decisive in his formulation of this theory, and in particular his encounter with the concept of phronesis, 'a form of reasoning and knowledge that involves a distinctive mediation between the universal and the particular' (Bernstein 1983). Appropriation entails just such a linkage or mediation. For Gadamer, then, embedded as he was in humanistic studies, the intellectual, the moral and the personal were not separable dimensions of the development of knowledge. Indeed, the greatest danger of the modern world, was that it was dominated by technical knowledge that had become separated from human understanding and being. For him the main task of philosophical hermeneutics was 'to defend practical and political reason against the domination of technology based on science.' (Bernstein 1983)

Gadamer has been criticised on a number of counts: in particular for his failure to articulate why understanding, even between the most distantly separated of traditions, is fundamentally unproblematic; for his belief in the authority of tradition and thus the tendency to conservatism in his theory; for his failure to take account of the social and political forces that impede understanding; and for his dismissal of the role and value of technical knowledge.

Habermas was well aware of these and other weaknesses in his thought. He sought to ground his ideas in an analysis of communication that demonstrates its potential to bring people together by genuine consensus rather than coercion. He is profoundly critical of the structures and processes through which power is, he thinks, increasingly unequally distributed. And while he sees science and technical knowledge as deeply implicated in them, he nevertheless recognises the essential role they have to play in advanced societies. But he entertains a similar set of ideals to those of Gadamer and the concept of rationality in which he places his hopes was shaped by the hermeneutic tradition.

Habermas' project was concerned with rationality as the core of enlightenment philosophy and the central feature of modern society. Despite his radical criticism of the nature and function of rationality in the Western world, he aimed to explore how it could be held onto as a positive force in the modern state. This entailed recognising that historically rationality had had two modes.

The first and dominant mode is cognitive-instrumental and directed towards the achievement of goals; individual success – within the concept of rationality as the pursuit of self interest – is embedded in and a necessary component of the individualism underpinning capitalism. This concept of rationality is, in Habermas' view, grounded in the paradigm of individual subjectivism, in which the subject stands out against a world of objects to which it has two basic relations: representation and action. Within this paradigm rationality consists in the individual subject gaining knowledge about a contingent environment so that he or she can adapt to or manipulate that environment (McCarthy 1984). Criticisable validity claims concern propositions about observable external reality. Discourse on values and feelings is not concerned with propositional truth and therefore cannot be validated. Facts are clearly distinguished from values.

Second, there is communicative rationality directed towards the achievement of understanding: the idea of the 'unifying, consensus-bringing force of argumentative speech'. It is embedded in the notion of community and intersubjectivism.

Habermas is reaching for a theory of rationality as communicative action, which emphasises the role of coordinated action in modern societies (1984 and 1987). It is predicated on the argument that it is possible to reason about moral values and feelings as well as about predictive and explanatory theories and facts and that reasons in all these areas can be validated and refuted. Thus it is possible for people living and working within different worlds, different disciplines and different occupational groups to reach consensus on the basis of reason rather than coercion. But to achieve such understanding it is necessary to grasp the the structures of social interaction in which teleological actions are located: linguistic, institutional and cultural.

If a shift from the purposive to the communicative dimension is to be made, social theory must be founded on an analysis of language. He argues that when we speak to each other we are making broader validity claims than are thought to be possible in the positivist or subjectivist paradigm – about the rightness of actions and the authenticity of our feelings, as well as about the truth of theories or empirical facts or about the logical relationship between means and identified ends. Further that we can recognise these claims as they are made by other people and can assess their validity.

But that entails not only the analysis of language. It also means grasping the contexts in which meanings are developed, problems defined and solutions devised. This means mutual understanding of social institutions, traditions, texts, cultural artefacts.

Within his system, all social actors have intepretive capacities. Social scientists are reflective participants, part of the phenomenon they are trying to understand, rather than privileged observers or analysts occupying an external and unimpeded vantage point. They must derive much of their understanding from social actors but may in turn persuade those actors of the value of a reflexive treatment of ideas. In that way they themselves not only participate in but also accelerate the process of change. It will be argued later in the chapter that these arguments are transferable both to the interchange between social scientists and the professionals who derive the concepts that inform their practice from the social sciences and to the relationships between those professionals and their clients. (At the same time Habermas' own concern that the power implicit in his model also has to be understood and preempted will be addressed. For social scientists and the professionals whose practice is defined by their work have immense poten-tial, if not actual, power. Through the metalanguage that is at the heart of their disciplines, social scientists can determine the categories in which social understanding, and therefore social direction, is developed, even if these categories sometimes originate in other communities of actors. Habermas, whose recognition of this is only too clear, argues that they need to embrace a critical theory of society that confronts the implicit, as well as the explicit, processes by which power is achieved and sustained, if they are to make the case that the idea of communicative rationality liberates rather than op-presses.)

Within the hermeneutic paradigm the development of knowledge is a matter of continuing dialogue between and within communities. But more than that, the concept of knowledge as action is embedded in it. The idea of communicative action means that it is not necessary to set action and communication against one another. Rationality is communal, dialogical and also bound to the moral and practical concerns of human beings. 'Underlying the recovery of the hermeneutical dimension of the sciences is a practical-moral concern which seeks to root out the various forms of positivism and scientism still so prevalent and to open a space for concepts of learning from what is different and alien and for reclaiming the integrity of the concept of practical wisdom' (Bernstein 1983).

So it seems that two quite distinct philosophical traditions, American pragmatism and continental hermeneutics, have converged on a number of key ideas.

They have strong echoes in the work of Alasdair MacIntyre, which has recently been shown by Stanford (1992 and see also Chapter 8) to provide a productive framework for understanding the nature of professional practice. The concept of practice is central to MacIntyre's project to reclaim the idea of virtue in a modern pluralist world (MacIntyre 1981). He argues that much of human life is organised round practices and that these provide the arena in which virtues are demonstrated. Practices are coherent and complex forms of socially established cooperative activity (such as professions) with their own intrinsic goods and standards of excellence, through which human ideas of goods and excellence are systematically extended (p.175). They depend on the exercise of virtues or values: integrity, justice, courage, practical wisdom. They are developed by and within the traditions of a community. Moreover, practices are a core part of the narrative of each individual human life, which also has its roots in tradition and community.

Stanford has shown how the concept of a profession can be enriched by incorporating it within Macintyre's conceptual framework. The intricate relationships between the intellectual, the moral and the personal in the practice of a profession and the grounding of these in the living history of a community and its individual members come alive in her analysis. It might be seen as a bridge to the next part of this chapter in which the applicability of all these ideas to the education of social workers will be explored.

Pragmatism, Hermeneutics and Professions

Knowledge as action and action as knowledge/understanding

The idea of reflective practice is a central theme of this book (Schon 1983 and 1987). Pragmatism and hermeneutics can be seen as additional sources of illuminating reflective practice. These traditions emphasise the role of rationality in constructive dialogue. But it is an understanding of rationality, in which the emancipatory rather than the controlling potential is emphasised; in which reasoning is the foundation of moral decision but at the same time depends for its efficacy on the values of its exponents; in which feelings can be exposed and explained; and in which the presuppositions and values of participants are brought into the dialogue and seen as promoters of mutual understanding because they are open to continuing reflective criticism. The point can, perhaps be illustrated in the context of social work in community care.

Central here are the needs of dependent people and the formulation of responses and solutions to them. But social workers, like other professionals, currently stand accused of disregarding or distorting the needs of those seeking their help. They are said to be only too ready to interpret them in terms of the services they have available. A reflective form of practice should avoid that problem. A white practitioner meeting, for example, a Muslim woman recently arrived from Turkey who has now had a stroke and is paralysed on one side will need to understand what has been the pattern of her life, what that has meant to her and how far it has been lost. The worker will test her own assumptions and be ready to change them in searching with her client for a way of sustaining the meaning of her life. The worker may have to work out with the woman who else in her network needs to be involved. They may all need to face the question how far her existing conceptions of meaning can be sustained in the face of her losses. At the same time the worker may realise that her own frames of reference and practices are too limited for her to achieve an adequate plan. She might need to bring together a new or enlarged practitioner network.

The dialogues would therefore be between individuals but individuals who are members of communities or networks. They would also entail cognitive action: the involvement of the participants in imagination, inter-pretation, the testing of the validity claims of their own and others' statements, analysis, the testing of hypotheses, judgements. But woven into these would also be the exercise of feeling and of, for example, integrity, courage, respect for persons and for the culture of which they are a part. All of these might be construed as collaborative or communicative action.

But such concepts can illuminate the process of education for practitioners too. It is clear that practitioners as they operate in an environment where demands, assumptions and structures are changing at an ever-increasing rate are all the time having to adapt their practice to cope. Many of them are required to move into different levels of responsibility and kinds of role (supervisory, training, managerial, evaluative, policy making) with little by way of formal preparation. This may bring them into collaboration, nego-tiation or conflict with new groups embedded in different cultures and in pursuit of different goals. Alternatively, familiar tasks and priorities may have undergone radical change.

These are the people who come for post-qualifying education and training. In these circumstances, the notion of education as dialogue has much to offer. The thrust of a number of chapters in this book is that a key function of the educational experience is to enable participants to reflect on their current roles and demands and perhaps to reframe them. Without the opportunity of such a review, it may be hard to learn how to cope with them more effectively. Revisiting their experience through an examination of the prejudices and traditions which they brought with them to these new roles as well as of the presumptions and culture they found there is a way of opening up such understanding. At the same time, they might need to embark on a similar process of understanding the culture and assumptions of those from whom they are seeking further training: to engage critically but openly with the language, conceptual structures and practice traditions being presented to them.

But these processes are needed not only by them but also by their teachers, to enable them to review how far their assumptive worlds and working practices are adequate for the task of enabling participants to understand and manage their practice environments. They have to question the extent to which their paradigms can continue to accommodate, illuminate and help to translate or convert the constantly moving experiences of those operating along a different track in the larger policy environment from their own. If they cannot, how can can they refresh or adapt their frames of reference? This needs attention to change in the policy environment but also to changes in theory and in the constellations of theory. Is the solution to dig more deeply into their own roots or will they at the same time need to be open to how the theoretical horizon is changing or how they might need to make a move so as to shift it themselves?

A key issue raised here is that of the balance to be struck between certainty and uncertainty, openness and closure, continuity and disjunction. It is particularly relevant to the social work profession, because of its location at a number of margins in modern society. The aim is to explore how far conceptions of professional education and practice grounded in a theory of communicative action can help social workers to a stronger and more justifiable resolution of the problems of openness and closure. The context of institutional and policy change is crucial to this discussion. Strong pressures exist towards the fragmentation of existing institutions, such as local authorities; the need for inter-institutional and interprofessional collaboration is being increasingly emphasised; quality movements are requiring all kinds of professionals to reappraise internalist concepts of excellence and to reframe them in the light of the needs of those who use their services (Joss and Kogan 1994, Pollitt 1992).

Dialogue, Openness and Closure and the New Educational Frameworks

Control of professional education is being pulled out of the hands of the academics in the name of collaboration with employers. In this context, the question whether the polarities between theory and practice, knowledge and action and technical and moral reasoning have been destroyed or transcended is of central importance.

It has been argued here that there is an epistemological base for transcendence. Professional education has been presented within the pragmatist and hermeneutic frames as a process of moving between grounded understanding of one's own practices, strengthening those practices and confronting theories, paradigms and practices which challenge them. It rests on an assumption that new learning can be better appropriated by those whose existing ideas are well founded but developed in a tradition of openness. It is a parallel position to that of Bowlby about the relationship between dependence and independence (Bowlby 1971) and closely linked to that of Marris about the relationship between loss and change (Marris 1974). People are more likely to be in a position to face new things if they have a basic sense of security or trust (in this case in the strength of rationality) and are trained to reappraise the foundations of that security as their environment changes. But how do these ideas fare in the new principles and patterns proposed for post-qualifying education and training for social workers?

First, there is the movement towards modular rather than integrated curricula. Modular systems place a premium on adaptability to individual needs and career patterns, responsiveness to demands for new knowledge and skills, and ease of combining new learning with continuation in the work environment. They provide individuals with opportunities to select and construct their own learning programmes. They enable people to pinpoint and meet their learning needs precisely but within a predominantly aggregative model of learning. They also assume that individuals' existing conceptual structures are both strong enough and flexible enough to incorporate the new learning. Otherwise, learning might be fragmented. It also might be deeply conservative and severely limited, leaving basic assumptions untouched.[1]

Integrated programmes place a premium on deep learning, immersion in a particular tradition or paradigm and a critical reflective search for what can

---

1   For a discussion of some of these issues in the more general context of higher education, see Boys *et al.* (1988).

continue to feed that. They can thus reinforce existing belief structures and modes of operation. But they can, equally, provide new ones and require participants to engage in quite fundamental reframing of their practice. They are long term strategies. No individual can have the opportunity to experience many of them. However, the thrust of this chapter is that a place needs to be kept for them within the new educational environment because they can enable people to strengthen their capacity to understand and manage change.

But for that to happen, it is necessary to focus on where students come from as well as where they are going. The argument is that critical reflection by individuals on their own careers and their own practices needs to be part of the preparation for and the process of education. Those who are clear about their particular models of practice and what informs them are in the end likely to find that their encounter with new perspectives on that practice or with alternative frames of reference or alternative models is more substantial, challenging but ultimately more productive than a briefer and more superficial encounter. Some continuity is built into the process of new learning which can make it more secure. New approaches will not just be blown away by the next set of exciting or overpowering set of ideas put in the individual's way.

But the decisions reached about curricula will depend ultimately on the outcome of the more fundamental change in the social work education system: to joint responsibility and collaborative planning by employers and educationists. How far can those too be developed within a model of communicative rationality – of critical self reflection and open exchange, in the name of consensus? The issue is partly structural; for it concerns the location of both social work and social work education in society and how that affects their power. But it is also a matter of how prepared social work educationists and social workers are to reflect on the multi-faceted nature of their own and of employers' assumptions, self-perceptions and aspirations and grasp hold of the possibilities of dialogue. They may have to face how others see them as well as vice versa.

Openness, Closure and Marginality

A key strand in Habermas' theories of rationality and modern societies is that of the differentiation of the public domain with its systems and structures for the management of governments and economies from the 'lifeworld' or the domain of family, community and culture. His claim is that the instrumental rationality of the 'systems' world has increasingly silenced the communicative rationality of the 'lifeworld' which has been steadily invaded and colonised as 'subsystems of the economy and the state intervene with money and bureaucratic means in the symbolic reproduction of the lifeworld' (Crook *et al.* 1992, Habermas 1987). The thesis has echoes in feminist analyses of the division between public and private worlds, the dominance of the public and its capacity to encroach upon and enfeeble the private domain.

It has particular resonance for social work, particularly when a conception of social work practice centred on dialogue is accepted. For one way of characterising the place of social work in society is to say that it stands at a number of margins. First, along with other human service professions, it can be said to be located at the interface between the lifeworld and that of social systems (Habermas), the public and the private domains (Pascall 1986, Stacey 1981). This location can be understood in a number of ways. It can mean that the role of social workers is to interpret the needs of certain groups to other professions, officials and institutions or to ensure that those formal systems support the informal relationships of family, neighbourhood or community. Within this construction, social workers may confront official-dom with the experience of poverty, exclusion and disablement; articulate the perspectives of people in their domestic or informal settings, the language and structures of which have become etiolated in the world of formal systems and find a way to give them back some voice.

But their role may be perceived in quite a different light: as gatekeepers of scarce resources, mediators of government priorities and the means by which the holders of political power and wealth sustain and reinforce their dominance. They may be seen as prey to the power of the systems world so that they embed language, norms and cultures in their practice that have little to do with the 'lifeworld': managerial imperatives of economy, efficiency, measurement, outcome, performance; legal mechanisms of control and exclusion.

In fact, social workers would have to admit to wielding great power over the lives of disadvantaged people. But that power is now increasingly regulated. This leads into the second way in which social work is marginal. It is at the margins of the professional world (Henkel 1993). As such it is vulnerable to engulfment or to over-determination by the organisations in which its practitioners are located. The establishment of social services departments in 1971 to be led by the emerging profession of social work was a Pyrrhic victory for social workers. Although the departments were set up on an assumption that they would be defined by professional values, and although social workers continue to hold many of the key roles in them, that assumption has now been effectively reversed: social work practice is largely defined by legal and managerial values. It has become caught up in an instrumental concept of rationality quite alien to its claims for recognition as having a contribution to make to society.

But social workers and social work educators cannot walk away from the world of management and if they claim that dialogue across traditions and institutional boundaries is at the heart of their practice, they need to reach out to it, to seek for common ground. Some would contend that all, or almost all, systems are underpinned by primary human values, as well as by instrumental concepts or mechanisms. Kogan (1974) has shown how the apparently second order values of bureaucrats, such as due process, are expressions of primary values such as equity.

The hermeneutic paradigm provides one way of working towards change based on the power of communicative rationality, seeking out the other and finding a basis for dialogue that is both practical and analytic. It requires the energy and vision to work on a number of fronts and across rather than within boundaries. The aspiration to consensus is, however, misleading and dangerous: the potential in Habermas' vision for a new totalitarianism is evident. A less risky approach is to work towards identifying points of alignment and of difference between groups; to hold space for uncertainties and to provide opportunities for the tackling of problems by different groups with different perspectives on them. For social workers it means internal preoccupation to found their own practices on practical and moral reasoning as against expediency or immediate attraction. But at the same time it requires external engagement with a clear-eyed awareness of the workings of power as well as a capacity to tune into others' idealisms. Social workers and social work educators must exploit their multiple marginalities and their ambivalences as they negotiate with employers, managers and politicians.

References

Bernstein, R. (1972) *Praxis and Action*. London: Duckworth.

Bernstein, R. (1983) *Beyond Objectivism and Relativism*. Oxford: Blackwell.

Bowlby, J. (1971) *Attachment*. London: Penguin Books.

Boys, C., Kirkland, J. (1988) *Career Aspirations and Destinations of College, University and Polytechnic Graduates*. London: Jessica Kingsley Publishers.

Crook, S., Pakulski, J. and Waters, M. (1992) *Postmodernization: Change in Advanced Society*. London: Sage.

Gadamer, H. (1975) *Truth and Method*. Translated and edited by G. Barden and J. Cumming. London: Sheed and Ward.

Habermas, J. (1984 and 1987) *The Theory of Communicative Action*. Cambridge: Polity Press, Vols I and II.

Henkel, M. (1993) 'Social Work: an Incorrigibly Marginal Profession?' In T. Becher. (ed) *Governments and Professional Education*. Buckingham: SRHE and Open University Press.

Joss, R. and Kogan, M. (1994 forthcoming) *Total Quality Management in the National Health Service: Final Report of an Evaluation*. London: Centre for the Evaluation of Public Policy and Practice, Brunel University.

Kogan, M. (1974) 'Social Policy and Organizational Values' in *Journal of Social Policy*, Vol.3 pt.2.

McCarthy, T. (1984) Translator's Introduction to Habermas J *The Theory of Communicative Action*. Cambridge: Polity Press.

MacIntyre, A. (1981) *After Virtue: A Study in Moral Theory*. London: Duckworth.

Marris, P. (1974) *Loss and Change*. London: Routledge and Kegan Paul.

Mulkay, M. (1979) *Science and the Sociology of Knowledge*. London: Allen and Unwin.

Pascall, G. (1986) *Social Policy: A Feminist Analysis*. London: Tavistock Publications.

Pollitt, C. (ed) (1992) *Considering Quality: an Analytical Guide to the Literature on Quality and Standards in the Public Services*. London: Centre for the Evaluation of Public Policy and Practice, Brunel University.

Popper, K. (1966) *The Open Society and its Enemies*. London: Routledge and Kegan Paul, 5th edition.

Schon, D. (1983) *The Reflective Practitioner*. London: Temple Smith.

Schon, D. (1987) *Educating the Reflective Practitioner*. San Fransisco: Jossey-Bass.

Stacey, M. (1981) 'The Division of Labour Revisited or Overcoming the Two Adams' In P. Abrams, R. Deem, J. Finch and P. Rock. *Practice and Progress: British Sociology 1950–1980*, Allen and Unwin.

Stanford, R. (1992) *A Study of Police and Social Work Joint Investigations of Cases of Suspected Child Abuse*, M Phil Thesis, Brunel University.

Toulmin, S. (1972) *Human Understanding*. Oxford: Clarendon Press.

Part Two

Emerging Theory for Practice

Chapter 5

The Intersubjective Mind
Family Pattern, Family Therapy and Individual Meaning

Gill Gorell Barnes

In this chapter I shall attempt to put together some of the theory and research which links a systemic approach to working with families to the idea of intersubjectivity. In the meaning individuals make of family pattern in intimate relationships the mutual influence of the family in meaning making is one of the constructs that influence both systemic family therapy and a systemic approach to individual therapy.

What leads someone who works with individuals to consider working with families? It has always seemed to me that there are infinite aspects of working with individuals and families that lend themselves to ongoing curiosity about human behaviour and the relevance to professionals of both ways of seeing; a systemic approach and a psychodynamic approach. These include the development of individual beliefs and ways of construing the world; the way individual beliefs are constrained by family beliefs and family patterns; the way families communicate with one another and how that affects the individuals within them and their freedom to think, act and speak; the nuances of family languages and their specific context-determined meanings, and the way these relate to the development of individual meanings and individual narrative. In sum, the processes by which the family and the individual interact over time and how these processes contribute to the development of the individual and his or her identity and functioning become complementary within the double description of an individual and a systemic perspective. At a higher level of social patterning the way the family itself is constrained by culture, by race, by class, by poverty or social conditions and the way in which men and women are affected by beliefs about gender and gendered behaviour, are all scripted into family life.

What are the aspects of family systems therapy which practitioners believe are different from a psychodynamic approach? First the perspective on the patient. Individual psychotherapists view the patient from the standpoint that he or she is an integrated discrete organism. Family and other systems therapies view the patient as one component in a human social system, the family, which can show malfunction through the behaviour of one component, the patient. Two important aspects of this thinking are that people are not islands; and their behaviour can best be understood in the context in which it occurs. This is an interpersonal perspective which sees behaviour as principally responsive to the context of a person's relationships. It is the communicative behaviours, not the intra-psychic attributes, that are the focus of interest, the relations between rather than the relations within. This differs from most psychodynamic views in which the individual's internal world is seen as the principal organiser of behaviour. The term 'internal' is frequently used as a synonym for psychic or mental, on the assumption that psychic processes are located in an inner space. Thus internal reality and internal conflict are defined in contrast to the external equivalents or actual external relationships in which people are currently engaged.

Viewed this way the internal world may be seen as relatively impermeable and intact, accessed principally through dreams, associations and play, or manifested in aspects of the exchange between therapist and patient where inappropriate structural patterns may repeat. In family systems therapy the individual's internal world is also seen as responsive and accessible through the day-to-day interactions with intimate others. These interactions and the meanings individuals attribute to them are dependant on the context in which they occur. Meanings may be developed with the belief system of one generation of a family or may be handed down over many generations (Byng-Hall 1982, Selvini Palazzoli *et al.* 1978). A second major component of family systems thinking is that people in close emotional proximity readily set up stable patterns of interaction. These patterns are made up from a whole series of sequences, repetitive short events involving two or more people. The sum of all these sequences and the idiosyncratic way in which each family arranges them is referred to as family pattern (Cooklin and Gorell Barnes 1993).

Family systems thinking assumes that the actions of all participants in a sequence affect one another and in as much as each is reacting to the behaviour of others, the sequences over time become self regulatory with the regular boundaries of place, routine and role that family life entails. As with other open systems, characteristics include wholeness; the interrelation and interdependence in 'family' behaviours; non summativity, the idea that the whole is greater than the sum of its parts, which is particularly important in considering the impact of 'pattern' on the individual especially in intergenerational work; and feedback, the response to input from within or without the family in which characteristics of the family are either amplified or diminished in the way that most fits the continuation of sustainable family life.

In intimate human systems, connected and developed over time, systemic therapists have taken the view that there are no protagonists or victims but that each enters into the interactions and complements each other's behaviour within the overall balance of the family as a whole. For this to happen each participant would notionally be equally bound by the ground rules of the group and would share similar sets of beliefs and values. As systemic theory was in its early years largely constructed by white middle class men, these views have been widely critiqued in the last decade. Researchers and women therapists have drawn attention to the imbalance of power in families (Boh et al. 1989, Boss and Weiner 1988, Goldner 1985, 1988, Goldner et al. 1990, Hare-Mustin 1987, Henwood et al. 1987, McGoldrick et al. 1989). A debate has been created in which a wider discussion of power and coercion in social systems has enforced the need for more distinctions in systemic thinking as it relates to therapy with families and intimate human relationship groups. The way in which people become drawn into habitual patterns which may not be to their individual liking, for reasons of economic survival or protection of their young requires a different lens for examining theory, as do the creation of abusive patterns through structures of race, class and caste (Fernando 1991). In any interactions people may not be equal in the degree to which they choose to be bound by a particular set of beliefs. Choice may also be dependent on relative power related to age. While each adult participant to some extent chooses to continue to participate in the life of the family, the cost of trying to give up that participation may be dramatically different for different family members. The child cannot leave home and this is frequently true of the abused wife.

Systemic therapy has therefore adopted a number of different lenses with which to consider the respective relevance of interconnection through choice and interconnection through circumstance as these affect people's freedoms within families and households. Those relating to race and ethnicity (Boyd Franklyn 1989, Cook and Watt 1987, Ho 1987, Lau 1988, Messent 1992, O'Brien 1990, Weiselberg 1992) indicate the variety of applications of systemic thinking within therapists of different cultures. Those which stem from work with coercive power, and the abuse of women and children from a feminist perspective, reflect the tension between attempting to hold a 'non blaming' systemic position at the level of 'family', and the anger deriving from the recognition of how such imbalances are built in and reinforced at wider and more powerfully institutionalised levels of society (Burck and Speed 1994, Gorell Barnes and Henessy 1994, Jones 1991, Perelberg and Miller 1990, Smith 1994).

Family Pattern and Individual Habit

Bateson (1973), arguably the early theorist whose influence on the practice of systemic family therapy has been greatest, described 'habit' as a 'major economy of conscious thought' (p.115), the sinking of knowledge down to less conscious levels. 'The unconscious contains not only the painful matters which consciousness prefers not to inspect, but also many matters which are so familiar that we do not need to inspect them' (p.114). Much of what systemic family therapists do, therefore, using a number of different techniques stemming from their own different belief systems, is to restore the capacity to think and reflect in situations where this capacity is lost. Family therapists look for 'habit' or ways in which families behave which are not necessarily responses only to the current situation but are ways of behaving laid down at levels not immediately accessible to awareness. Some of these behaviours may be redundant, that is no longer have relevant meaning, and may actively impede the development of behaviours which would be more functional for the family in their current context.

To summarise, the systemic family perspective assumes that:

- people are intimately connected and those connections can be as valid a way to both understand and promote change in individual behaviour as can any individual responses

- people living in close proximity set up patterns of interaction made up from relatively stable sequences of interaction

- the patterns that therapists engage with must, to some degree and at the same time, act as cause and effect of the problem they are presented with

- problems within patterns in families are related to inappropriate adaptation to some environmental influence or change.

Family therapy therefore addresses itself to changes in patterns of relationships, to those which are lived and witnessed on a daily basis and to those which are carried in people's minds (Reiss 1989). The fact that members of a family not only live the pattern but also witness it allows the development of different degrees of reflective capacity within the same family and between different members of the same family. Much of what may be shared as an area of interest between a psychodynamic approach and a systemic approach relates to this question of how the reflective capacity in different members develops, how it is protected or destroyed through individual developmental processes and how the capacity to reflect on experience affects children grown up when they themselves become parents. The way this can be monitored and supported within therapeutic intervention of any kind is of key concern to all professionals working with children, with adults as parents and their families.

Pattern and Meaning: Individual and Systemic Perspectives

The meaning systems that are developed between people who live in intimate relationships developed over time have been thought of as 'intersubjective realities.' Ideas and theory relating to this perspective come from the study of infant development, and in particular of children's language and under-standing of symbolic and abstract meaning; as well as from constructivist developments within family therapy theory. In the last twenty years transitions in family living have increased; within the family due to cohabitation and childbirth outside marriage (Kiernan and Wicks 1990) and also due to divorce, subsequent parenting apart and remarriage (Gorell Barnes 1991). Families are thus constituted and reconstituted many times and the intersubjective realities with which children begin their lives will not be those within which many of them grow up (Robinson 1991, Gorell Barnes *et al.*, in press). For some children, and for their parents, realities will have to be deconstructed and reconstructed as families change.

From a research perspective the idea of systemic properties in family pattern have been built up over the last fifteen years. The interactions between two people, the way aspects of this interaction continue to affect people when they are apart, and the way the qualities of that interaction are affected by the introduction of a third person have been studied in a variety of family situations. Models of the systemic properties of pattern in families have been built up theoretically from the properties of a two person relationship. From the interactions between any two people some characteristics will emerge as belonging to that particular interaction whereas others will be seen as specific to the relationship over time. Some studies have looked at and measured the behaviour of families, whereas other have assessed the less tangible aspects of mutual influence such as changes in perception, emotion, affect and expressed opinion. (Further details of relevant research and its implications for the study of family pattern can be found in Gorell Barnes 1981, 1985, 1992 and 1994). While the effect of systemic family pattern on the freedom of any individual is part of the assessment in relation to each presenting child and family it may be presumed that because of the repetition of daily sequences in family life and through the attitudes, beliefs and principles expressed in these, family pattern carries a powerful influence on aspects of individual development.

How does the idea of patterning in families relate to a systemic approach and to the question of an individual perspective? Systems thinking in family therapy with children and adults derives principally from the concept of mutual causality or mutual influence, the interrelationship of events within a given framework. The familiar notion that the whole is greater than the sum of its parts is given weight from a developing 'mass' in the literature from child development research. A system can be defined as an organisational arrangement of elements consisting of a network of interdependent and co-ordinated parts that functions as a unit. This arrangement is often referred to as the coherence of the family (Reiss 1981). Family coherence contains the idea of core family characteristics (Dunn 1988) that are held in balance in relation to one another over time in a family, that may be taken in by children as whole patterns – mental representations of sets of relationships that may be carried forward in life in subsequent social contexts.

Mutual influence and systemic patterning are now well established concepts in child development research (Emde 1991, Fivaz-Depeursinge et al. 1994, Hinde and Stevenson Hinde 1988, Stern 1977, 1985). In the study of self-regulating mechanisms in families, researchers underpin the elusive notion of the coherence of a family which family therapy tries to address. An additional concept borrowed from Trevarthen (1979) is the concept of intersubjectivity. He studied the way in which infant and mother patterns of communication, both verbal and nonverbal, rely on a fine-tuning based on former experience of one another from the moment of birth and possibly before. The pattern of finely tuned anticipation and responses known within a family to the members of that family is the core construction of family living that is currently being unpacked by researchers working from widely differing perspectives (Dunn 1990, 1991, 1993, Murray 1991, Murray and Trevarthen 1985, Stern 1985, Trevarthen 1979, Trevarthen and Hubley 1978, Trevarthen and Marwick 1986). Within the field of research many of the questions relevant to therapy are also being debated, principally the question of how many relationships the infant is capable of 'taking on board'; which relates to the question of whether a key relationship with the mother is of primary importance in relation to a sense of stability of self, or whether the concept of 'mother' can be extended to security of attachment to father and to older siblings (Dunn 1993).

The way in which an individual brings their own 'meaning making' to the complexity of relationships offered to him or her is a matter of controversy among those who study infants, just as it is among therapists of different persuasions. The questions relating to what patterns in the family constitute 'security' for a child, and the degree to which this is invested in the child's relationships with his siblings are of great importance to social workers who have to work with family breakdown as well as with the subsequent formation of foster or adoptive families. It has significant implications for how one might consider the placement of children. What the patterns are that are likely to recur in a destructive manner in a new family or care context needs to be borne in mind; and the question of what needs preserving from the family the child has moved on from (which may be a core part of their identity) needs assessment and discussion with the new family into which the child or children will be moving.

The Carry Forward of Pattern

What may contribute to the carry forward of pattern, the replication of aspects of pattern within new structures of family living? Where the pattern is adverse what acts as a protective factor which in buffering an individual against stress allows sufficient flexibility for new patterns to emerge in a new context? A number of studies have looked at family systems characteristics carried forward through the generations with particular reference to violent patterns such as spouse abuse, marital instability and child maltreatment, and have looked at the way in which young children experience and acquire positive and negative adult interactions (Bel and Pensky 1988, Caspi and Elder 1988, Radke Yarrow et al. 1988). As many other researchers with children and families are now doing, they use the concept of internal working models, a concept originally put forward by Bowlby (Bowlby 1971, Bretherton 1985, Main et al. 1985, 1992). Internal working models are defined as affectively laden mental representations of the self, others and of the relationship derived from interactional experience. Recent work (Sroufe and Fleeson 1988) has looked at the way children learn whole relationships and carry them forward into other contexts in their lives. In focusing on the abusive pattern in the families studied, they note how children repeat both aspects of the abusive behaviour, being able to play the role of both abused and abuser in contexts away from home.

This work is of particular relevance to current family practice since so much of the work now taking place is not with intact biological families who have remained within the same parameters of living over many generations, but with families in the process of ongoing transition. This is discussed further below.

In reviewing the research into family pattern referred to here, Hinde and Stevenson Hinde (1988) make a number of observations and distinctions about the likely transfer of pattern. Concepts of learnt pattern influence future process insofar as they are inside the heads of individual participants. Great care is therefore needed in imputing one internal working model to the family as a whole and more attention needs to be paid to the potential variety of working models held within the family group, as well as to those discrete features of family life which offer sufficient difference for new patterns to be learnt and to develop.

Emde (1988), in thinking about the relevance of research to clinical intervention, addresses the question of individual meaning and the way in which lived experience becomes transformed into represented relationships. How do repeated interactions influence the formations of represented relationships which include ways of looking at the world, affective themes and social value systems? In addition how do configurational patterns begun in families couple with other social systems with which the family interact? Do these offer the opportunity for more flexible development and variety in options, or do they become more stereotypic in their transaction with the family? At which points do children's ways of viewing the world become relatively inflexible and self perpetuating? When do rare events (trajectories or random factors) lead to new learning within systemic patterns (Quinton and Rutter 1984, Rutter 1987, 1989)?

The Therapist as Part of the Pattern; an Extension of Mutual Influence

The study of what has come to be known as 'second order cybernetics', in which the role of the therapist and the therapist's meaning system is considered as part of the 'field' of therapeutic interaction, preoccupied family therapy theorists in the 1980s, following developments from the 'Milan' school of family therapy (Campbell *et al.* 1991). The puzzle of therapist 'objectivity' and 'approximation' in relation to the assessment and measurement of 'reality' has long been known to physicists (Capra 1983) and was part of early family systems thinking as developed by Bateson and the MRI group (Bateson 1973). The famous dictum of Korzybski (1958), 'the map is not the territory' is part of all systems training. However, a reaction to the idea of 'objective' descriptions of family pattern (Colapinto 1991), to the idea of 'neutrality' in the therapist's relationship with his task (Selvini

Palazzoli *et al.* 1980), and to the question of intervention as a one-way process of influence, brought the field back to preoccupations about the way in which the therapist in turn was influenced: a process formerly familiar to psychodynamic family therapists under other terminology such as transference, counter-transference, projection and projective identification (Bentovim and Kinston 1991, Box 1981, Dicks 1963, 1967), and to psychologists under the heading of constructivism (Kenny 1988). The many conversations that have taken place around these topics have considered how a therapist, in construing a problem, by implication becomes part of the problem-determined system in which he or she is creating or constructing the definition of the problem with a family. Von Foerster (1981), in work on neural sets, held that we actively compute our version of the world – the act of observation determines the interpretation of that which is observed. Objective reality is not therefore possible and, in seeking such a definition, we can only look for 'fit' rather than 'match' (Von Glaserfield 1984).

In searching for a position that will make sense within the observable world of human relationships family therapists have turned to constructivism, which includes a recognition that people categorise the world the way they do because they have participated in social practices, institutions, and other forms of symbolic action (for example, language) which give shared meanings to events within relationships. The constructivist paradigm itself has been widely critiqued for failing to take account of the structural imbalances of power in society which controls how such problems are thought about and discussed at both visible and invisible levels. Major critiques have come from women therapists (MacKinnon and Miller 1987, Speed 1991), from different ethnic perspectives, from the wider development of experience of working with power and abuse in sexually abusing families, and from researchers (Shields 1986).

How does Attachment Theory Connect Systemic Theory with the Internal World? Outer and Inner Realities

As I mentioned earlier, there is an ongoing debate between attachment theorists who claim the relevance of this model to the growing adults later 'patterns of attachment', and those who adhere to other studies of infants and their siblings which suggest a more diverse model of attachment in early childhood where older siblings play an important part in the child's daily life (Byng-Hall 1986, 1991). Dunn *et al.* (1991) have shown how children in families where 'feelings' are frequently discussed as part of the family domain of reality show more intersubjective understanding of others. Children are also able to comprehend greater diversity within the relationship with a single person; that is, the inconsistencies of mother in different contexts. Attachment theorists hold that the early established working model developed primarily in relation to mother is projected outwards by the child, and used to guide emotional attachments towards persons outside the immediate family even when these expectations have limited validity. The complexity of 'measuring' attachments has so far prevented many researchers assessing the impact of siblings on the child's developing interactions with the world. Within an attachment theory frame the child displays tenacity in applying an early working model developed primarily with one person to later relationships, even where this may be dysfunctional (Hobson 1993). This obviously poses different questions relating to the importance of other relationships than does a model which allows for the child's wide variety of attachments from the beginning of his life. In an attachment model the child who shows an early sensitivity to individual variation, may come later to ride roughshod over variation that is subsequently encountered. A model that allows for variety also allows the child to keep more options open.

Implications for models of therapy

If the enhancement of reflectiveness captures one of the essential elements of the psychotherapeutic process (Fonagy *et al.* 1991, 1993), the question of how individuals mentally represent their own early relationships with mothers, fathers, siblings and others, and the degree to which these early representations influence subsequent relationships remains a key question which links individual and family therapy. These two approaches can be seen as working towards the same goal from opposite directions, one by exploring the interactional components of family living, both as it is lived and represented; and the other by working primarily with the mental representations of relationships. However, there remain fundamental differences about the contribution of the dynamic process of the developing individual which radically differentiate the way a therapeutic approach is undertaken.

How do Individuals Mentally Represent Their Own Early Relationships with Their Parenting Figures?

One aspect of psychoanalytic object relations theory as it applies to infancy and early childhood defines an infant as biologically predisposed to engage with other people. Primitive modes of interpersonal sharing and conflict are mentally represented in the language of object relations (Fairbairn 1952, Kernberg 1976, Sandler 1978). Infants register when the person looking after them and interacting with them is not appropriately attuned with and responsive to their state of minds, and this has been demonstrated in interactional research (Fivaz-Depeursinge *et al.* 1994, Murray 1991, Stern 1977). If things go well enough children develop an internal world in which schemata, mental representations and phantasies of self-other relationships, are essentially benign (Fonagy *et al.* 1993). On the other hand if early caretaking is inadequate or actively unkind or cruel powerful feelings that are created come to 'people' the infant's mind. Where these persist they affect the potential to evolve positive images of self and self-other relationships. The capacity to hold a number of different views about the self and others may be impaired. As children acquire concepts about the minds of others, their view of these minds may develop increasing complexity or may be channelled by early negative experience into the development of perceptions of self and other which have dominant patterns excluding other more positive possibilities.

In systemic therapy increasing attention is now paid to this concept of dominant and marginalised voices; but these are not only seen as coming from within the individual. They are also seen to be active in the family of which the individual remains a part, and of the wider society which 'privileges' certain voices at the expense of others. Narrative, and the study of 'coherence' in narrative, is now playing a part both in the study of adults and their capacity to be securely attached as parents to their children (Fonagy *et al.* 1993, Main 1992), and in working with individuals in the context of their family setting. From a constructivist stance human beings are seen as the 'self in language'. Ideas form and reform, and offer possibilities for change in images of self. Too often human beings are seen as in a language that describes human traits as stable states rather phenomena in process and change. Too often one description becomes dominant at the expense of a hundred others that are marginalised. This can happen particularly powerfully in families.

The job of the therapist then is to explore the different power accorded to voices in the family and where appropriate to reintroduce the marginalised voices. Where voices are contributing to ongoing negative images of the self, alternative descriptions will be sought within the family, or the family's wider milieu. If more positive or benign descriptions become part of the language spoken about the person then the person's inner images, the voices with which he speaks to himself, will also change (Penn and Frankfurt 1994). In therapeutic conversations whether with an individual or with the family, the inner 'negative' monologue or self-description is invited into conversation, challenged by, and tested out against other more positive views of the self. If the alternative descriptions are heard and accepted they may be incorpo-

rated into the language and interactional pattern of the family and subsequently into the self.

Family therapists, in their study of narrative and the coherence of people's
stories, find themselves at a confluence with attachment research and the
interest in the adult story as a vehicle for reflecting and predicting security
in parenting. However the work in family therapy is more often with the
'family' story rather than with the story of an individual alone. The
introduction of discourse analysis into the work of therapists working with
a number of people in the room over time shows how the therapist
'orchestrates' talk in such a way that overdominant voices are diminished
and marginalised voices are heard more (Aronsson and Cederborg 1994).
As a strategy for opening up new perspectives a necessary precondition is
the establishment of new ways of talking and listening which includes
attention to the dimensions of emotion, perception and description (White
and Epston 1989). Key story points in the life of the family may need to be
de-constructed and reworked as multiperspective phenomena (Aronsson and
Cederborg 1994).

In individual therapy with a systemic perspective the reworking of stories
may also include the use of written material; the active recapturing and
reworking of old versions of the self which can then be scrutinised and
rewritten many times. This may be accompanied by the active reworking of
old stories with family members in later life (Gorell Barnes and Henessy
1994).

In systemic therapy the view that patterns laid down in childhood are
available to be reworked in later life remains of key importance. Child
development research has provided a variety of models for thinking about
how these patterns are constructed and represented within the individual
mind. While a systemic approach to the therapeutic reworking of these
patterns retains some essential differences to an individual perspective there
are now more bridges across the two theoretical perspectives. It will be a
continual challenge to see how these can be further linked in the future to
make therapeutic conversations more relevant and accessible to those who
wish to engage in them.

References

Aronsson, K. and Cederborg, A.C. (1994) *Co-narration and voice in family therapy.*
    Voicing, de-voicing and orchestration. Doctoral dissertation University of Linkoping,
    Sweden.

Bateson, G. (1973) *Steps to an Ecology of Mind.* London: Paladin.

Bel, J. and Pensky, E. (1988) Developmental history, personality and family relationships: toward an emergent family system. In R.A. Hinde and J. Stevenson-Hinde (eds) *Relationships with Families: Mutual Influences*. Oxford: Oxford Scientific Publications.

Bentovim, A. and Kinston, W. (1991) Joining systems theory with psychodynamic understanding. In A. Gurman and D. Kniskern (eds) *Handbook of Family Therapy, Vol. 2*. New York: Brunner/Mazel.

Boh, K., Bak, M., Clason, C., Pankratova, M., Quortup, J., Squitt, G. and Waervers, K. (eds) (1989) *Changing Patterns of European Family Life: A Comparative Analysis of 14 European Countries*. London and New York: Routledge.

Boss, P. and Weiner, P. (1988) Rethinking assumptions about women's development and family therapy. In C.J. Falicov (ed) *Family Transitions: Continuity and Change Over the Life Cycle*, pp. 235– 254. New York: Guilford Press.

Bowlby, J. (1971) *Attachment and Loss, Vol. 1: Attachment*. Harmondsworth, Middlesex: Penguin Books.

Box, S. (1981) *Psychotherapy with families: an analytic approach*. London: Routledge and Kegan Paul.

Boyd, F.N. (1989) *Black Families in Therapy: A Multi-System Approach*. New York: Guilford Press.

Bretherton, I. (1985) Attachment theory: retrospect and prospect. In I. Bretherton and E. Waters (eds) *Growing Points of Attachment Theory and Research*. Monographs of the Society for Research in Child Development Vol.50, 1–2 Serial No. 209.

Burck, C. and Speed, B. (1994) *Gender, Power and Relationships*. London: Routledge.

Byng-Hall, J. (1982) Family legends: their significance for the family therapist. In A. Bentovim, G. Gorell Barnes and A. Cooklin (eds) *Family Therapy: Complementary Frameworks of Theory and Practice*, pp. 213–228. London: Academic Press.

Byng-Hall, J. (1986) Family scripts: a concept which can bridge child psychotherapy and family therapy thinking. *Journal of Child Psychotherapy* Vol.12, 1, 3–13.

Byng-Hall, J. (1991) The application of attachment theory to understanding and treatment in family therapy. In C.M. Parkes *et al.* (eds) *Attachment Across the Life Cycle*. Routledge: London.

Campbell, D., Draper, R. and Crutchley, E. (1991) The Milan systemic approach to family therapy. In A.S. Gurman and D.P. Kniskern (eds) *Handbook of Family Therapy, Vol. 2*. New York: Brunner/Mazel.

Capra, F. (1983) *The Tao of Physics*. London: Flamingo, Fontana.

Caspi, A. and Elder, G.H. (1988) Emergent family patterns: the inter-generational construction of problem behaviour and relationships. In R.A. Hinde and J. Stevenson-Hinde (eds) *Relationships Within Families: Mutual Influences*. Oxford: Oxford Scientific Publications.

Colapinto, J. (1991) Structural Family Therapy. In A.S. Gurman and D.P. Kniskern (eds) *Handbook of Family Therapy, Vol. 2*. New York: Brunner Mazel.

Cook, J. and Watt, S. (1987) Racism, women and poverty. In C. Glendinning and J. Millar (eds) *Women and Poverty in Britain*. Hemel Hempstead: Wheatsheaf Books, Harvester Press.

Cooklin, A. and Gorell Barnes, G. (1993) Taboos and social order: new encounters for family and therapist. In E. Imber Black (ed) *Secrets in Families and Family Therapy*. New York and London: W.W. Norton & Co.

Dicks, H.V. (1963) Object relations theory and marital studies. *British Journal of Medical Psychology* Vol.36, 125–129.

Dicks, H.V. (1967) *Marital Tensions: Clinical Studies Towards a Psychological Theory of Interaction*. London: Routledge and Kegan Paul.

Dunn, J. (1988) Connections between relationships: implications of research on mothers and siblings. In R.A. Hinde and J. Stevenson-Hinde (eds) *Relationships Within Families: Mutual Influences*. Oxford Scientific Publications: Oxford.

Dunn, J. and Plomin, R. (1990) *Separate Lives: Why children are so different*. New York: Basic Books.

Dunn, J., Brown, J. and Beardsall, L. (1991) *Family talk about feeling states and children's later understanding of other's emotions*. Developmental Psychology Vol.27, 448–455.

Dunn, J. (1993) *Young Children's Close relationships: Beyond Attachment*. London: Sage Publications.

Emde, R.N. (1988) The effect of relationships on relationships: a developmental approach to clinical intervention. In R.A. Hinde and J. Stevenson-Hinde (eds) *Relationships Within Families: Mutual Influences*. Oxford: Oxford Scientific Publications.

Emde, R.N. (1991) *The wonder of our complex enterprise: steps enabled by attachment and the effect of relationships on relationships*. Infant Mental Health Journal Vol.12, 3, 164–173.

Fairbairn, W.R.D. (1952) Object-relationships and dynamic structure. In *Psychoanalytic Studies of the Personality*. London: Routledge and Kegan Paul, pp. 137–151. (Original work published 1946).

Fivaz-Depeursinge, E., Stern, D., Byng-Hall, J., Corboz Warnery, A., Lamour, M. and Lebovici, S. (1994) *The Dynamics of Interfaces. Seven authors in search of encounters across levels of description of an event involving a mother, father and a baby*. (Presented at the European Family Therapy Conference Athens 1994).

Fernando, S. (1991) *Mental Health, Race and Culture*. Basingstoke and London: Macmillan, Mind Publications.

Fonagy, P., Steele, M., Steele, Moran, G. and Higgitt, A. (1991) The capacity for understanding mental states: the reflective self in parent and child and its significance for security of attachment. *Infant Mental Health Journal*, Vol.12, 3, 201–218.

Fonagy, P., Steele, M., Steels, H., Higgitt, A. and Target, M. (1993) The Theory and Practice of Resilience. *Journal of Child Psychology and Psychiatry* Vol 35, No.2, 231–257.

Glendinning, C. and Millar, J. (eds) (1987) *Women and Poverty in Britain.* Hemel Hempstead: Wheatsheaf Books, Harvester Press.

Goldner, V. (1985) Feminism and family therapy. *Family Process* Vol.24, 31–47.

Goldner, V. (1988) Generation and gender: Normative and correct hierarchies. *Family Process* Vol.27, 17–31.

Goldner, V., Penn, P., Sheinberg, M. and Walker, G. (1990) Love and violence: gender paradoxes in volatile attachments. *Family Process* Vol.29, 343–364.

Gorell Barnes, G. (1981) Pattern and Intervention: Research findings and the development of family therapy theory. In A. Bentovim, G. Gorell Barnes and A. Cooklin (eds) *Family Therapy: Complementary Frameworks of Theory and practice.* London: Academic Press.

Gorell Barnes, G. (1985) Systems theory and family theory. In M. Rutter and L. Hersov (eds) *Child and Adolescent Psychiatry: Modern Approaches.* Oxford: Blackwell Scientific Publications.

Gorell Barnes, G. (1990) Making family therapy work: the application of research to practice. *Journal of Family Therapy* Vol.12, 17–29.

Gorell Barnes, G. (1991) Stepfamilies in context: the post divorce process. *Association for Child Psychology and Psychiatry Newsletter,* November.

Gorell Barnes, G. (1994) Family therapy. In M. Rutter, E. Taylor and L. Hersov (eds) *Child and Adolescent Psychiatry (3rd edition).* Oxford: Blackwell Scientific Publications.

Gorell Barnes, G., Thompson, P., Daniel, G. and Burchhandt, N. (1992) (in preparation). *Growing up in step-families: life story interviews.* NCPS Cohort 1958. University of Essex, Department of Sociology and Institute of Family Therapy, London.

Gorell Barnes, G. and Henessy, S. (1994) Reclaiming a female mind from the experience of child sexual abuse. In C. Burck and B. Speed (eds) *Gender, Power and Relationships.* London: Routledge.

Hare-Mustin, R.T. (1987) The problem of gender in family therapy theory. *Family Process* Vol.26, 15–27.

Henwood, M., Rimmer, L. and Wicks, M. (1987) *Inside the Family: Changing Roles of Men and Women.* Family Policy Studies Centre, Occasional Paper 6.

Hinde, R.A. and Stevenson-Hinde, J. (eds) (1988) *Relationships Within Families: Mutual Influences.* Oxford: Oxford Scientific Publications.

Ho, M.K. (1987) *Family therapy and ethnic minorities.* New York: Sage.

Hobson, R.P. (1993) *The intersubjective domain: Approaches from developmental psychopathology.* London: Tavistock Clinic, Adult Department.

Imber-Black, E. (1987) Families, larger systems and the wider social context. *Journal of Strategic and Systemic Therapies* Vol.5, 20–35.

Jones, E. (1991) *Working with Adult Survivors of Childhood Abuse.* London: Karnac Books.

Jones, E (1992) *Family Systems Therapy: Developments in The Milan Systemic Therapies.* Chichester: John Wiley and Sons.

Kenny, V. (ed) (1988) Radical constructivism, autoprocess and psychotherapy. *The Irish Journal of Psychology* 9.1.1988.

Kernberg, O. (1976) *Object Relations Theory and Clinical Psychoanalysis.* Northvale, New Jersey: Aronson.

Kiernan, K. and Wicks, M. (1990) *Family Change and Future Policy.* London: Family Policy Studies Centre and Joseph Rowntree Memorial Trust.

Korzybski, A. (1958) *Science and Saints.* Conneticutt, USA: The International Non-Aristotelian Library.

Lau, A. (1988) Family therapy and ethnic minorities. In E. Street and W. Dryden (eds) *Family Therapy in Britain.* Milton Keynes and Philadelphia: Open University Press.

Main, M., Kaman, N. and Cassidy, J. (1985) Security in infancy, childhood and adulthood: a move to the level of representation. In I. Bretherton and E. Waters (eds) *Growing Points in Attachment Theory and Research.* Monographs of the Society for Research in Child Development, Vol.50, 1–2, 66–104, Serial No. 209.

Main, M. (1992) Metacognitive knowledge, metacognitive monitoring and singular (coherent) vs. multiple (incoherent) model of attachment. Findings and directions for further research. In C. Murray Parkes, J. Stevenson Hinde and P. Mains (eds) *Attachment across the life cycle.* London: Routledge.

McGoldrick, M., Anderson, C.M. and Walsh, F. (1989) *Women in Families: A Framework for Family Therapy.* New York and London: W.W.Norton.

MacKinnon, L. and Miller, D. (1987) The new epistemology and the Milan approach: feminist and sociopolitical considerations. *Journal of Marital and Family Therapy* Vol.13, 139–155.

Messent, P. (1992) Working with Bangladeshi families in the East End of London. *Journal of Family Therapy* Vol.14,3, 287–304.

Murray, L. (1991) Intersubjectivity, object relations theory and empirical evidence from mother infant interactions. *Infant Mental Health Journal,* Vol.12, 3, pp 219–232.

Murray, L. and Trevarthen, C. (1985) The infant's role in mother–infant communications. *Journal of Child Language,* Vol.13 (1986).

O'Brien, C. (1990) Family therapy with black families. *Journal of Family Therapy* Vol.12, 3–16.

Parkes, C.M., Stevenson-Hinde and Marris, P. (1991) *Attachment Across the Life Cycle.* London and New York: Routledge.

Penn, P. and Frankfurt, M. (1994) *Creating a Participant Text: Writing, Multiple Voices, Narrative Multiplicity.* New York: Ackerman Institute.

Perelberg, R.J. and Miller, A.C. (1990) *Gender and Power in Families.* London and New York: Routledge.

Quinton, D. and Rutter, M. (1984) Parents with children in care: 1.current circumstances and parents; 2. intergenerational continuities. *Journal of Child Psychology and Psychiatry* Vol.25, 211–231.

Radke Yarrow, M., Richards, J. and Wilson, W.E. (1988) Child development in a network of relationships. In R.A. Hinde and J. Stevenson-Hinde (eds) *Relationships Within Families: Mutual Influences.* Oxford: Oxford Scientific Publications.

Reiss, D. (1981) *The Family's Construction of Reality.* Cambridge, Massachusetts and London: Harvard University Press.

Reiss, D. (1989) The Represented and Practicing Family: Contrasting visions of Family Continuity. In A. Sameroff and R. Emde (eds) *Relationship Disturbances* (191–194). New York: Basic Books.

Robinson, M. (1991) *Family Transformation Through Divorce and Remarriage: A Systemic Approach.* London and New York: Routledge.

Rutter, M. (1987) Psychosocial resilience and protective mechanisms. In S. Rolf, A. Master, D. Cicchetti, K. Muerchterlein and S. Weintraub (eds) *Risk and Protective Factors in the Development of Psychopathology.* New York: Cambridge University Press.

Rutter, M. (1989) Intergenerational continuities and discontinuities in serious parenting difficulties. In D. Cicchetti and V. Carlson (eds) *Child Maltreatment: Theory and Research on the Causes and Consequences of Child Abuse and Neglect,* pp. 317–348. London: Cambridge University Press.

Sandler, J. and Sandler, A-M. (1978) On the development of object relationships and affects. *International Journal of Psychoanalysis,* Vol.59, 295–296.

Selvini Palazzoli, M., Boscolo, L., Cecchin, G. and Prata, G. (1978) *Paradox and Counterparadox.* New York: Aronson.

Selvini Palazzoli, M.S., Boscolo, L., Cecchin, G. and Prata, G. (1980) Hypothesizing, Circularity-neutrality: three guidelines for the conductor of the session. *Family Process* Vol.19, 3–12.

Shields, C.G. (1986) Critiquing the new epistemologies: toward minimum requirements for a scientific theory of family therapy. *Journal of Marital and Family Therapy* Vol.12, 359–372.

Smith, G. (1994) *Systemic Approaches to Training in Child Protection.* London: Karnac Books.

Speed, B. (1991) Reality exists o.k.? An argument against constructivism and social constructionism. *Journal of Family Therapy* Vol.13, 395–411.

Sroufe, L.A. and Fleeson, J. (1988) The coherence of family relationships. In R.A. Hinde and J. Stevenson-Hinde (eds) *Relationships Within Families: Mutual Influence.* Oxford: Oxford Scientific Publications.

Stern, D. (1977) *The First Relationship: Infant and Mother.* London: Fontana Open Books.

Stern, D. (1985) *The Interpersonal World of the Infant.* New York: Basic Books.

Trevarthen, C. (1979) Communication and co-operation in early infancy. A description of primary intersubjectivity. In A. Bulow (ed) *Before Speech: the Beginning of Human Communication.* London: Cambridge University Press.

Trevarthen, C. and Hubley, P. (1978) Secondary intersubjectivity: confidence, confiding and acts of meaning in the first year. In A.Lock (ed) *Action, Gesture and Symbol: the Emergence of Language.* London: Academic Press.

Trevarthen, C. and Marwick, A. (1986) Signs of motivation for speech in infants and the nature of a mother's support for development of language. In B. Lindblom and B. Zetterstrom (eds) *Precursors of Early Speech*. Basingstoke: Macmillan.

Von Foerster H. (1981) *Observing Systems*. Seaside, California: Lukesystems.

Von Glaserfield E. (1984) An introduction to Medical Constructivism in P. Watzlawick. *The Invented Reality*. New York: W.W. Norton.

Weiselberg, H. (1992) Family therapy and ultra orthodox Jewish families: a structural approach. *Journal of Family Therapy* Vol.14, 3, 305–330.

White, M. and Epston, D. (1989) *Narrative Means to Therapeutic Ends*. New York: W.W. Norton.

Chapter 6

From Subjectivity towards Realism
Child Observation and Social Work

Stephen Briggs

Social work theory is largely silent on the subject of observation. Trowell and Miles (1991) point to the capacity social work has had for ignoring the knowledge gained about child development from the work of observers such as Spitz (1945) and the Robertsons (1969). As with many innovations in social work, the recent emergence of observation as an important factor in social work training and practice is the consequence of developments outside the profession. The first of these were the two reports of Louis Blom Cooper into tragic deaths of children in the mid-eighties (Blom Cooper 1985, 1987). He placed great emphasis on the failure of social work practice to keep the children in mind and in sight. His criticism of the way the social worker in the Beckford case 'misconceived her role' emphasised, albeit in rather simple terms, the elements of observation in child care work:

> She averted her eyes from the children to be aware of them only as and when they were with their parents, hardly even to observe their development, and never to communicate with Jasmine on her own. (Blom Cooper 1985)

In other words observation of children should first of all serve the purpose of treating them as individuals; it should be focussed on understanding development; and it should facilitate communication with the child. It is implicit in this statement that such information leads towards assessment of the child's developmental, emotional and social needs, and to the assessment of risk. A link is made, in other words, with the theoretical training of social workers in understanding the development and needs of children.

A second source of influence on the development of observation in social work has been the programme of infant observation begun by the child analyst Esther Bick. Although this training was devised for child psychotherapy trainees and was clothed with the sophistication and complexity of psychoanalytical theory, one aim of the programme, as Bick herself described it, was to ensure that therapists, when faced by their child patients in the clinical setting, would have an actual experience of observation of an infant to support their experiences of relating to the infantile anxieties and object relationships of their patients.

> It would give each student a unique opportunity to observe the development of an infant, more or less from birth, in his home setting and in his relation to his immediate family and thus to find out for himself how these relations emerge and develop. (Bick 1964 p.558)

This statement expresses her belief that extensive and intensive exposure of the student or trainee to the observational procedure can be a central part of the overall training objectives. It is indeed an extensive training method. In the Bick model students are required to observe an infant at home weekly for one hour from birth to two years. Each hourly observation is recorded after the event (note taking at the time is eschewed, as it is felt to detract from the task of observation). These detailed descriptive accounts are then discussed in a small seminar group, usually of five members, and two recordings are normally presented in rotation in each seminar. Considerable emphasis is placed on the importance of description; the observer is encouraged to record as nearly as possible everything that happened in the hour. Theoretical and other forms of speculation are left until the seminar discussion. Bick was clear about the difficulties of 'objective' recording, whilst optimistic that the essential task of separating description from interpretation could be accomplished. She wrote:

> As soon as these facts (i.e. the observational events) have to be described in language we find every word is loaded with a penumbra of implication. In fact the observer chooses a particular word because observation and thinking are almost inseparable. This is an important lesson for it teaches caution and reliance on consecutive observations for confirmation. (Bick 1964, p.565)

The need for repeated observations to confirm assessment is one which justifies the massiveness of the project, namely, the regularly repeated observations over two years. In turn this regularity and the relatively long time scale of observations leads to the development of emotionally powerful relationships between the observer and observed, together with an appreciation of the depth of the relationships between parent and infant. For newcomers to observation, both the discomfort in adopting an observational or non-interventionist role, and the quality of the relationship between parent and infant provides an experience which can be surprising in its intensity.

If the child abuse Inquiries lent urgency and purpose to the social work task of assessing children's needs, particularly in cases of risk, the model of infant and child development developed by Bick offered the method for undertaking the necessary observational training. This is now an extensively used model, forming a central part of the M.A. in Psychoanalytical Observational Studies at the Tavistock Clinic, and incorporated in other Tavistock trainings. In modified form it is a requirement in all substantial social work trainings in the Clinic, including Master's courses. Additionally, this model of child observation is now widely used in DipSW training programmes (Briggs 1992, Trowell and Miles 1991, Wilson 1992), and the Clinic provides training for social work tutors in the task of introducing it on qualifying courses.

It has been found in the course of these developments that the learning provided by observation is essentially pluralistic. The observation provides the student first of all with an extensive opportunity to learn from experience about infants and young children. He also learns how the family members experience the crucial events of the infant's first two years, and the quality and nature of relationships that develop between them. He is subject to the emotional impact of these events and relationships. In learning about this impact, the observer is part of a process in which his awareness and sensitivity are also developed. The observer's role is not that of the 'fly on the wall'; although required to refrain from initiating activity and interaction, he is expected to maintain a friendly and receptive attitude to the family, of whom he is a privileged guest. He is also expected to be active emotionally and mentally, and the observation of the events in the family is coupled with digesting the emotional impact of the encounter. It is in any event not possible to be an observer in a family and go unnoticed, or to have no impact on the family system. Thinking about the quality of this impact, in both directions, that is, on observer and observed, is an important part of the process of understanding the observational material.

Here the seminar discussions have the function of holding or containing the emotional dynamics in which the observer is involved (Rustin 1989a). The observer also has a containing function in the family, relying on the parent to help to define the boundaries of the observation, and to accommodate him in this role, but also being available for the family – both parent and infant – through being emotionally attentive to the interaction in the family.

Infant observation thus has many potential uses, both in terms of developing the sensitivity of the worker and increasing understanding of child development and of the development of parent infant relationships. Additionally, the method has been transferred to other settings. Where the Bick model focuses on mother–infant interactions, recent observational studies also bring in the other family members; father, siblings. Magagna has studied nanny-infant interactions (Magagna 1993). Observations of children also take place in the nursery, or school, where the impact of the group is observed, and the development of play. Mackenzie Smith (1992) has observed elderly people, and there have been adaptations to include observations of institutions, for example in the M.A. in Primary Health and Community Care at Marylebone Centre Trust. There is an international flavour to observational study with courses and conferences established in Europe and America. Observation has thus emerged as a flexible tool for teaching and learning, where the original method has been demonstrably capable of adaptation to different settings, time scales and consumer groups.

The application of Bick's method of observation over forty-five years by numerous students in countless seminars has created a considerable expertise in the method, and a massive accumulation of observation reports. The rigour of the approach and the repeatability of the method suggests, as Rustin (1989b) has noted, that the method has potential as a source of research. Until recently, it was thought that this source had not been tapped, but the contributions of many authors at the 1993 Infant Observation Conference at the Tavistock Clinic revealed a number of theoretical and methodological innovations. These included comparative studies of particular categories, for example, cross-cultural experiences of children and parents, single parents, nannies, and infants at risk. Theoretical innovation and the delineation of concepts suggested that the observational approach may play a significant part in the future of infancy studies as a whole. From the social work point of view, two developments in particular would appear to be of significant relevance to the development of professional practice. These are, first, the production of theoretical concepts which have direct bearing on the social work process of understanding infants and young children and the parent– infant relationship and, second, the development of studies that offer insight into and evidence for the ways in which family situations can be assessed, with a special interest being taken in the assessment of risk.

My own studies in this field have concentrated on these two categories. I have undertaken a study in which five infants at potential risk were observed using the method described by Bick; that is, each infant was observed at home in his or her family for one hour each week from birth to two years. This study therefore involved the observation of a small sample of infants, with the aim of describing in detail the interaction between the infant and his or her parents. The data produced by these observational experiences then provided a basis for thinking about the quality of interactions between infant and parent, observer and observed, the development of the infant, and the means of assessing the degree and quality of risk identified.

  The problems encountered in the process of this work were chiefly that there needed to be a way of assessing the quality of description achieved, and a framework which would render intelligible the quality of relationships and the infant's development. Here I wish to describe this process, emphasising, first, the ways in which the observations were thought about within theoretical frameworks, a process which led to the development of a conceptual framework, and second, to show how this framework could then be used to address problems of professional concern, particularly the degree of concern or risk in each case. I shall then use some examples from the sample of my study to illustrate the outcome of this approach.

Two Paradigms

In the process of observation, description is advanced as the prime task of the observer. Making sense of the description occurs through analysis of the descriptive report. The element of subjectivity which inevitably occurs in description, through the choice of word or the particular way any observer or commentator may choose to study an observational report, is not eschewed. Rather, coherence is given to the reports through the application of an underpinning theoretical paradigm. In the field of infancy there are two predominant paradigms, psychoanalysis and child developmental psychology. In the course of my analysis of my data, I explored the relationship between the observed material and both paradigms, together with a comparison at points of contact between them. It was this process of comparison, in relationship to the data, that developed the theoretical framework. The following is inevitably a very condensed presentation of a long discussion.

  Recent developments in both paradigms suggest areas of convergence, in which the integration of aspects of both has been explored (Alvarez 1992, Murray 1982, Stern 1985, Urwin 1986). For example there is a similarity between the concepts used by Bion (1962) (container-contained), Stern (attunement) and Ainsworth (1985) ('sensitive parent') for describing the activities which parents undertake to meet the needs of infants when in interaction with them. These concepts have emerged from different traditions and from different methodologies. Bion's is essentially reconstructive, based on his work with psychotic adults; Stern's developed from a review of developmental psychology and (North American) psychoanalysis, with an emphasis on micro-technology, and Ainsworth's arose from her experimental application of attachment theory in the 'Strange Situation'. Murray (1988, 1992) adapted Trevarthen's methods for studying what he called 'happy relationships' between mother and infant, to observing what happened when mothers were depressed. Her view was that naturalistic or longitudinal studies could have an important role in describing the area between the kinds of interaction observed when non-depressed mothers relate with their infants, and those encountered amongst a wider population of parents. Convergence of theoretical concepts could then be linked with complementary research methods.

On the other hand, ideas about infancy appear to be diametrically opposed in these two paradigms. Whilst the psychoanalytical tradition, particularly in the work of Bion and Winnicott, posits an infant on the point of incipient collapse in the face of unbearable or overwhelming anxiety, the developmentalists describe a baby who is 'competent', endowed with, in particular, wonderfully tuned perceptual capacities (Bower 1989) which permit complex cross modal communications (Stern 1985), and sophisticated patterns of interaction with mother, heralding language development (Trevarthen 1980). With this wide repertoire of theories of infancy, one approach has been for the proponents of each paradigm to criticise each other. The developmentalists criticise the anxiety-driven model of the Kleinian psychoanalysts; the psychoanalysts in turn point to the neglect of subjective, internal features such as phantasy. A second approach has been to establish the underlying value base on which the studies are based. For example, Bradley (1989) makes a plea for the acknowledgement of the essential misery of human existence, and criticises the developmentalists for idealising the human condition. A third approach is to explore the methodological frameworks of the different accounts and to compare what aspect of the infant is encountered in each case. Thus the developmentalists concept of 'alert inactivity' in which all subjects are 'tested' in laboratory conditions is absent from the psychoanalytical accounts which are reconstructive and concerned primarily with the study of the relationship between well-being and pathology. In contrast, observing infants naturalistically, in the home setting, over time, permits an encounter with a full range of emotional states. Infants are observed, in fact, in 'happy' interactions; neutral states of mind (alert inactivity) and moments or passages of anxiety and distress. A model for understanding the full range of mother–infant interactions observed naturalistically would include all these states of mind, and therefore need to combine elements of both paradigms.

Conceptual Framework

The operationalisation of this kind of model meant that consideration had to be given to the range of concepts used by psychoanalysts and developmentalists. With regard to parental behaviour towards infants, the aim was to choose the most flexible concept. Bion's container-contained fitted this description, and could be operationalised (as indeed it is constantly in infant observation seminar discussion). Bion himself described two kinds of container-contained relationship: one in which the infant's anxiety, communicated to the parent through 'normal projective identification', is modified by the parent's capacity to receive, digest and detoxify these communications. He called this the mother's capacity for reverie. Second, he described a pattern of interaction where the mother and infant misunderstand each other, and the mother blocks the infant's attempts to communicate with her through projective identification. Instead of taking in and digesting the communication, the mother refuses to admit it, leaving the infant with the overwhelming task of attempting to do his own thinking and digesting. Developmentally, this notion fits closely with Trevarthen's perturbation studies where the mother presents a 'blank' fact to the infant, and the impact (usually distressing) of this is then studied. Murray's work links this 'blankness' or 'blocking' with maternal depression.

These two categories of Bion's, when explored in conjunction with the observed material, lead to a formulation of the type of containment a parent offers the infant when in interaction with her or him. These were categorised in terms of shape, so that the aspect of the parent in the mode of 'reverie' was described as 'concave' container, suggestive of the availability of the mother to admit the infant's communications. Similarly, the 'blocking' or 'blank' aspect of the mother was categorised as 'flat' container, suggesting the unavailability to admit the infant's communications. The effects of these two types of container for the emotional life of the infant and the parent–infant relationship are:

the concave – which identifies and mediates the emotion the flat – which ignores or diffuses (flattens) the emotion.

Descriptions of interactive sequences between mother and infant can then be followed, in terms both of the type of container being offered by the parent, and the effects of this on the emotional quality of the interaction.

That is, the infant's responses to a particular kind of container can also be observed and identified.

However, the observed material repeatedly pointed to a third type of container, which was not described by Bion, and this category embraces that aspect of parental interaction, frequently observed in naturalistic observation, where the parent initiates rather than responds to communication. In the sample of infants I observed, this frequently had a negative, intrusive or distressing impact, but this need not always be the case. Further, this kind of container activity, which I have called convex container, can also be observed in terms of the transmitting of emotionality to the infant. It is here that it has significance clinically and in assessing risk. The notion of the convex type of container holds a sense of the parent 'putting into' the infant an aspect of the parent's preoccupations and/or state of mind. It is the opposite of the concave type of container and gives the infant an additional emotional experience with which to contend.

The second part in this model building process concerned the infants' modes of relating to their parents. Infants showed a wide range of responses and activities in the face of the kind of container experience to which they were subject. They also demonstrated a range of capacities for, as it were, mitigating the experiences of the parental behaviour, particularly in its 'convex' form, and for initiating interaction. Very often this was observed through the bodily movements of the young infants; the ability to make contact through the range of perceptual and bodily functions. This accords with the tradition in infant observation of paying close attention to the movements and gestures displayed by small infants. These behaviours appeared to be in the service of maintaining contact and relationship with the parent, turning away from contact with parents and self-comforting. In all modes, the infants made a grip on another (animate object) or themselves. Since the content and purpose of the behaviour was to make contact with another person or thing, or themselves, these behaviours have therefore been called 'grip relations'. It was possible to identify not only the mode of relating used (the sense or part of the body used), and the object of the 'grip' but also the intensity of the grip employed. The level of intensity carried a sense of the quality of emotionality involved. Through the course of their development, the characteristic form of grip was observed to become a pattern of behaviour and then, with the development of symbolic functioning in the second year, the patterns of grip became identifiable in the quality of symbolic communication employed, where the content of the phantasy behind the behaviour could be described.

This notion of grip relations combines the idea of Klein (1952) that infants object-relate from birth, and that of developmentalists like Bower (1989) who emphasise the importance of perceptual qualities in the young infant. The study of patterns of grip relations led to the possibility of describing patterns of relationships and relatedness and qualities of defensiveness. In other words there was a language for the study of early 'object relations'. The following extract from an observation demonstrates the sequences of container type and the qualities of grip relations taking place in the interactions between a mother and her infant. The infant is Hashmat, a Bengali baby, aged 14 weeks.

Hashmat, sitting in his bouncing chair looked alertly around the room and in my direction, his head shaved and his very dark eyes looking out. His legs kicked a little and his arms moved also, his hands touching each other lightly.

1. Alert inactivity. Eyes seeking grip. Light hand grip.

2. Moment of convex container.

Mother pulled Hashmat, in his chair, towards me, quite abruptly, so that Hashmat was at my feet. He looked up at me and seemed unsure.

He kicked his legs making small and vigorous staccato movements with his feet, and his hands gripped each other quite tightly. I was struck by how tightly they gripped. He continued to look up at me, smiled, and he started to make a high pitched noise; a continuous shriek or scream that had three tones, and then repeated.

3. Tight hand grip; agitation. Large motor movements contrast earlier gentle activity. Eye grip with me. Voice and mouth confusion (shriek and smile).

The sequence clearly shows the change in quality of Hashmat's 'grip' before and after the 'convex' moment of being abruptly moved, namely that it become more intense, tighter and shows some confusion. The intense grip on himself and activity relates to psychoanalytic notions of the way in which the infant attempts to make a skin for himself, in the absence of parental containment (Bick 1964). In developmentalist terms, the intensity of reaction is due to an overload of stimulation, from which he attempts to 'tune out' (Stern 1985).

Applications

In my study I wished to follow this work of conceptualising and following sequences of interaction with an application of this way of thinking about the observed material to the task of making assessments of risk. To apply the model in naturalistic family settings it was necessary to take into account the role and function of the observer in each case. Particularly I needed to assess the impact of the observer on the family and vice versa, and to characteristic the role and function the observer played. As I have suggested above, the observer offers an inevitable and inescapable role of containment. This function is brought about by the observer's attention to the family members. In the families in the sample of this study, the observer's containing function was heightened by the relatively low levels of attention available from the parents for their infants. The features of the observer's role included support for the parents, and perhaps more surprising, a containing role with the infants. These have been categorised as 'parental container' and 'auxiliary parent' respectively. The following two examples provide an illustration of both.

Example 1. Hashmat: The observer as object for grip relations – 'auxiliary parent'
Hashmat has given cause for concern because he frequently vomits feeds; he has developed defences of a withdrawn kind and he has been periodically attacked by his siblings. His early patterns of grip relations show a particular way of relating with his hand which is multifunctional and which carries a notion of three-dimensionality, that is of container contained. When he was alone with me at 4 months 2 weeks he showed distress.

'Rani rubbed his back more, and then she picked him up and put him in a bouncing chair and went out and Hashmat made high pitched noises. He seemed about to cry and I leaned forwards and touched his foot. His hand reached down so I put my finger in his hand and he held on to it tightly and pulled my hand towards him. He made a range of noises, from content to distress, with a suggestion of a smile'.

Following this he noticeably made more eye contact with me, conveying the sense that I was someone with whom he could communicate his inner states. This in itself indicated the observer played the part of an additional parent, maintaining the infant's willingness to 'object relate'. For example he looked at me in the following sequence.

'Hashmat sat and looked at me with a long look. His eyes focused on me steadily, with his face on the brink of tears. His hands moved on the table and he had a small hard plastic whistle which he held. He cast his eyes in the direction of the door where Rani, the mother, had gone out. I felt there was something very delicate in his mood, so that he could shift easily from smiling to crying. The look he was giving me was held on a gossamer thread. He made a little shrieking noise and I made a soothing one in return. He put his finger in his mouth, and he poked with it behind his top gum, his mouth wide open and his eyes constantly on mine' (Hashmat at 6 months 3 weeks).

The function of the observer's responses was to acknowledge Hashmat's solitary struggle to communicate and share his internal subjective world, in the face of limited attention from mother. The observer, through the act of careful attention, always offers a containing role in the family. Here the role is directly between the infant and observer, and follows the observer's linking with the kind of grip relations the infant demonstrates. To the act of careful attention the observer adds the more active aspects of the containing process, namely naming and differentiating and emotionally resonating (Sorenson 1993).

Example 2. Hester: The observer as aid to mother's containing role – 'parental container'

In this example, the observer links with the parent who employs the observer to help her be more containing of her infant. Struggling with depression, which has led her to prematurely wean the infant Hester from the breast, the mother Yvonne has conveyed to the observer the difficulty she has in maintaining alone the internal resources to provide a receptive (concave) space for thinking about the needs of her baby. The observation was then used as a time when Yvonne could think aloud, as it were, with the observer listening to her.

'Hester started to cry and punched her arms towards Yvonne's face a few times. Yvonne said "what's the matter? Are you hungry?" She took the pacifier out of Hester's mouth and put the knuckle of her finger in her mouth. Yvonne looked at Hester's response and said "she's not hungry". Hester arched her back and cried strongly. Yvonne held her upright and said "maybe she's wanting to go to the toilet – powder milk leaves her constipated". I asked if there was anything Yvonne could do about it and she shook her head and said "nothing". Yvonne thoughtfully looked at Hester and wondered if her nappy was too tight. She laid her on her back on the changing mat and Hester cried. She undid the babygro quickly – without tenderness – and then more tenderly she loosened the nappy, holding and slightly rubbing Hester's tummy. Yvonne sat looking at Hester and smiled at her. Hester quietened.

Yvonne took Hester's feet out of the babygro and took her nappy off. Hester cried for a moment and then let her legs kick around. Yvonne said she liked having her nappy off and she added that she guessed all babies do. She said Hester was very heavy for her age and added "look at her legs, they are really chubby". I was in fact enjoying Hester moving her legs around in the air, describing un-leg-like circles. Yvonne said how chubby her face was, "look at those double chins". I said she seems more cuddly than anything else and Yvonne said she is cuddly, and how nice that is. Yvonne asked me if I thought Hester had grown and whether she seemed big to me. I said she had grown over the weeks, and Yvonne told me about a woman in the hospital who had kept comparing her second baby unfavourably with the first one. She thought for a moment and "you're not so delicate with your second baby anyway, you're more confident'" (Hester at 7 weeks 2 days).

The observer in this example is called upon to be a focus for mother's thinking aloud, which is also in the service of augmenting her perception of the baby as cuddly and lovely, rather than big and indelicate. Her own reflections on her parenting at the end of the sequence show her capacity through this process to gain a more positive – or confident – sense of her parenting. These features of the observer's role help to provide containment for the parent.

Assessment and Prediction of Risk

Finally, I should like to give an example from the sample of how the combination of observation, the conceptual framework applied to sequences of interaction and the containing function of the observer can together provide assessment of risk, which has predictive value.

Example 3. Michael failing to thrive

Michael was the third child of a single mother. The example combines appreciation of the emotional difficulties in the mother–infant relationship, and the impact of these on subsequent developmental problems. I shall select three features from an observation of Michael. The sequence occurs when he is three weeks old.

'Mary, the mother, asked me if I would continue to hold Michael because that stopped him crying. Michael sat in my arms holding tightly on to my finger; his eyes looked ahead, unfocussed. We sat like this for some time, and I got him comfortable by holding him quite close and tight. In the background I could hear Mary feeding Darren, his 11 month old brother. I then had the feeling of wanting to throw him across the room and I was puzzled and disturbed by this feeling. Mary came in with Darren who ran around the room with some toys and Mary said how she could kill the children's father if she saw him. She was very angry and really could kill him. He knew she could be violent; she did not lose her temper very much but when she did it was very strong' (Michael at 3 weeks).

I choose this extract because within it are three levels of evidence: the subjective experience of the observer (counter-transference); the verbal reporting of mother and the observed behaviour of the baby. The three features to which attention should be drawn are, first, the feeling of the observer when holding Michael; second, the report of the mother of murderous feelings towards the father; and third, the strength of Michael's grip on my finger.

There are two themes that link the sequence. First, the feeling of wanting to throw away the baby which is mirrored by the murderous wish of the mother towards the father. Second, there is a parallel between the strength of Michael's hand grip and mother's self-reported temper. Through her comments, the mother makes her feelings clear. In fact the baby is particularly unwanted and might have been aborted had she been aware of her pregnancy in time. She asked me to hold the baby indicating she had not enough space in her mind to calm him herself. Darren's appearance is vivid evidence of mother's other preoccupations. Her wish that Michael is quiet puts me in mind of her repeated comments that she 'just wants them to be quiet.'

At one month Michael is reported by mother to cry for long periods. In observations his distress appears to be relieved by sucking the pacifier. He has begun to regurgitate feeds; though he makes eye contact there is a distant look in his eyes. Both his sucking and crying indicate his wish to (object) relate; the distant look in his eyes and the regurgitation of feeds hint at unsatisfactory experiences in relating. At three months his physical development is markedly backwards. He can lift his head but seems disinclined to do so. He sleeps a lot, cries a lot and he continues to regurgitate feeds. He still sucks the dummy both awake and asleep; when he makes a grip on another, either by making eye contact with Mary, or by holding my finger, it is noticeable that he lets the pacifier fall from his mouth. The tightness of his grip on my finger contrasts the slackness of his mouth when the pacifier falls. Two particular observations are important to describe. Firstly I watch him for a long time when he is awake but peers through barely open eyes, lying quite still. Secondly as I watch him in this state I hear the sound of his older brother approaching and he shudders quite visibly. He barely seems to be there.

With some understatement Michael's development and behaviour at this stage could be categorised as 'unadventurous'. His substitution of one mode of grip for another, in an either-or way, suggests the reverse of amodal transfer is taking place (Stern 1985), and Michael is in a subtracting rather than adding state of relating. The implication is that the images being built, the internal representations, are forming in an unintegrated way. Moreover, the purpose of his mouth grip appears to do with self-comfort and the relationship with the bottle is one where Michael rejects through regurgitation. This relationship with food suggests both an unwillingness to firmly take the side of growth, and to introject from mother. The outcome of these features would lead to a prediction that the following problems would be present in later development: difficulties in learning, difficulties in developing a sense of self-protection, difficulties in feeding. In fact all these were present when Michael was 15–18 months.

(1) DIFFICULTIES IN LEARNING

In one of the observations when Michael was 11 months I had the opportunity to administer an 'unofficial' object constancy test. Despite my gaining his full cooperation he failed to look for an object which was hidden. He seemed either not to have a concept of absence, or to be uninterested in absent objects (O'Shaughnessy 1964). The task is one which is accomplished by an infant of 7–9 months, and Michael appeared in this instance quite developmentally delayed. He developed a striking slack-mouthed expression, which makes him look 'stupid', which again appeared related to his poor mouth-teat grip. Assessments at one year, 15 months and 18 months showed his language development to be minimal. The overall picture was therefore of slow, or delayed, development towards symbolic thinking.

(2) DIFFICULTIES IN SELF-PROTECTION

Michael was frequently bruised and mother reported him constantly falling down. This tendency to 'fall over' was apparent in observations where he appeared to have very little awareness of his physical capabilities or limitations. I became very actively involved during observations in his second year in preventing him from falling or walking off a table, bumping into doors and cupboards. His lack of proprioceptive awareness appeared to give some indication of the qualities of his internal world, particularly the internationalisation of the anti-containing (convex) quality of mother's relating to him.

(3) FEEDING DIFFICULTIES

Michael had difficulties retaining his food and in putting on weight. Even when he did not regurgitate food, his lack of weight gain suggests he failed to metabolise the food he did take in. He was a borderline 'failure to thrive'. At one year his weight was less than two-thirds the average for a baby of his birth weight. At nearly 14 months I described him in these terms:

'He looked thin, wearing a vest babygro which seemed to hang off him and emphasised the thinness of his arms and legs'.

Michael's dispensing of food is the physical counterpart of his emotional and mental development. The experience of containment at an emotional level becomes experienced on a physical level in the relationship between Michael, food and mother. The experience of both the lack of attention and the sense of intrusion come together, as it were, in the case of an infant like Michael who seemed porous or very prone to receive the projections in the environment, to create a failure to thrive pattern. Sadly, in the event, the analysis of patterns of grip relationships, as they were observed in the first three months of Michael's life, had the capacity to predict the quality of future development over the next 12 to 15 months.

Conclusions

The need for purposeful observational study in social work training and practice has coincided with the expansion of Bick's observational method, from its origins as a part of the training for child psychotherapists, into a many faceted form of study. It has begun to develop as a research methodology, with a particular place in relationship to the theoretical frameworks of psychoanalysis and child developmental psychology. It has been applied to a wide range of professional trainings, and has become useful in studying subjects other than infants and young children.

In this chapter I have described these developments and then paid particular attention to a study where the aim of assessing the development of infants at potential risk led to concentration upon the development of concepts for describing the observed infant, a process which made use of the developments in the main paradigms used for thinking about infancy.

The emergence of a vocabulary for describing the observed infant has the effect of liberating the subject. In turn, this provides the possibility of delineating the containing function of the observer. I have then described both the qualities of this function in the sample of families, and the quality of interaction between parents and infants. Predictive assessment appears possible within this framework. That observation has a significant role to play in social work appears to be the outcome of studies such as the one I have described.

References

Ainsworth, M. (1985) Patterns of Infant Mother Attachments. *Bulletin of New York Academy of Medicine*, Vol.61, 9, 772–791.

Alvarez, A. (1992) *Live Company*. London: Routledge.

Bick, E. (1964) Notes on Infant Observation in Psychoanalytical Training. *International Journal of Psycho-analysis*, Vol.45, 558–566.

Bion, W. (1962) *Learning from Experience*. London: Heinemann.

Blom Cooper, L. (1985) *A Child in Trust*. London Borough of Brent.

Blom Cooper, L., Harding, J. McC., Milton, E. (1987) *A Child in Mind*. London Borough of Greenwich.

Bower, T. (1989) The perceptual world of the new born child. In A. Slater and G. Bremner (eds) *Infant Development*. London: L.Eribaum.

Bradley, B.S. (1989) *Visions of Infancy*. Cambridge: Polity Press.

Briggs, S. (1992) Child Observation and Social Work Training. *Journal of Social Work Practice*, Vol 6, 49–61.

Klein, M. (1952) Some theoretical conclusions regarding the emotional life of the infant in *Envy and Gratitude and Other Works 1946–63*. London: Virago.

Mackenzie Smith, S. (1992) A psychoanalytic observational study of the elderly. *Free Associations* Vol.3, 3, 27, 361–396.

Magagna, J. (1993) The nanny in infant observation. Paper given to International Infant Observation Conference, Tavistock Clinic 1993.

Murray, L. (1988) The effects of postnatal development on infant development in I.F. Brockington and R. Kumar (eds) *Motherhood and Mental Illness*. London: Academic Press.

Murray, L. (1992) The Impact of Postnatal Depression on Infant Development. *Journal of Child Psychology and Psychiatry*, 33, 3, 543–561.

O'Shaughnessy, E. (1964) The absent object. *Journal of Child Psychotherapy*, Vol.1, 2.

Robertson, J. and Robertson, J. (1969) *Studies in Brief Separation: John*. Concord Films.

Rustin, M.E. (1989a) Encountering primitive anxieties. In L. Miller, M.E. Rustin, M.J. Rustin and J. Shuttleworth, *Closely Observed Infants*. London: Duckworth.

Rustin, M.J. (1989a) Reflections on methodology. In L. Miller, M.E. Rustin, M.J. Rustin and J. Shuttleworth, *Closely Observed Infants*. London: Duckworth.

Sorenson, P. (1993) The containing process. Paper given to International Infant Observation Conference, Tavistock Clinic.

Spitz, R. (1945) Hospitalisation; an enquiry into the genesis of psychiatric conditions in early childhood. *Psychoanalytic Study of the Child,* Vol.1, 53–74.

Stern, D. (1985) *The Interpersonal World of the Infant.* New York: Basic Books.

Trevarthen, C. (1980) The foundation of intersubjectivity in D.R. Olson (ed) *The Social Foundation of Language and Thought.* London: Norton.

Trowell, J. and Miles, G. (1991) The application of child observation to professional development in social work. *Journal of Social Work Practice,* Vol.5, 51–60.

Urwin, C. (1986) Splitting the difference. Developmental psychology and psychoanalysis in M. Richards and P. Light (eds) *Children of Social Worlds: development in a social context.* Cambridge: Polity Press.

Wilson, K. (1992) The place of child observation in social work training. *Journal of Social Work Practice,* Vol.6, 1, 37–47.

Chapter 7

Anti-Racism and Modernism

Ilan Katz

This chapter will consider some anti-racist theories of identity development in black and mixed parentage children. It will examine them in the light of post-modernist social theories and will draw conclusions about social services policy and practice relating to interracial families.

Post-modernism is a concept that has entered the discourses of many disciplines such as architecture, art, literature, philosophy and sociology but has limited influence in social work (Rojek *et al.* 1988). The most commonly used definition is provided by Lyotard (1984), who defined the post-modern as: '…incredulity towards metanarratives' (p.xxiv).

Post-modernism is a reaction to 'Modernism', a way of seeing the world characterised by 'grand-narratives' or 'meta-narratives'. These are explanations of the world that try to unify and explain all human experience, establish political systems that will liberate all humans from oppression, or explain all scientific and natural truths. They include the philosophies of humanism, Marxism, positivism, feminism and Christianity (Lyotard 1992), and although very diverse, they have some things in common:

- **Totalisation** – they are holistic, and attempt to explain the whole human condition or the condition of whole societies either philosophically, psychologically or socially. They emphasise 'sameness' rather than 'difference'.

- **Teleology** – they see societies, individuals and theories progressing towards an ultimate goal such as liberation, emancipation or maturity. Modernist theories see individuals and/or society as starting from some form of primitive existence and progressing through stages to a higher level of being.

- **Essentialism** – the belief that people, cultures, and society as well as natural phenomena have an 'essence' or true nature that is, in principle, able to be discovered by Science.

Post-modernism theorists attack these tenets.

Totalisation is attacked because of its 'hidden agenda' of terrorism or totalitarianism. According to post-modernist theory Stalinism and Nazism are not aberrations or retreats from modernism. They are the consequences of a view of the world that can easily move from describing people's similarities to forcing people to be the same.

Totalisation therefore either incorporates 'the other' into 'the self' or excludes 'the other' from 'the self'. Western philosophy, especially Humanism, is attacked because of its assumption that humans are basically the same (Barthes 1973, Young 1992). Humanist philosophies imply that people who are not part of the 'good society' become identified with 'the other' and therefore become dehumanised (Derrida 1978).

Post-modernists attack teleologies because of their tendency to totalise. Teleological theories aim at a future in which human beings will all be the same, and their essence revealed, whether the goal or *telos* is the liberation of 'man', the coming of the Messiah, or the dawning of a new socialist age. Teleological theories view the past as a precursor of the inevitable achievement of the *telos*. But each *telos*, and the totality it implies, is seen as the only truth and the right way forward. In modernist thinking the goal has usually been the reproduction of male, western, bourgeois ideals. Those with different ideals are resisting the inevitable advance of history as irrational, immature or marginal. They become part of the dehumanised 'other' who needs to be resisted or eliminated (Bernstein 1991).

Essentialism is attacked because Modernist theories of the truth or essential nature of human beings or societies rely on universal and everlasting truths. However, post-modern theorists believe that this version of 'truth' is constructed by Western society and imposed by violence on other cultures or dissenters. In modernist thought the subject is central: biology is seen as prior to and more fundamental than society, the individual over the collective, and the conscious 'self' over the unconscious or the group. Post-modernists 'decentre the subject', seeing truth and 'human nature' as bound by culture, time and place. Human nature is a product of culture, rather than cultures being different ways of expressing human nature.

Post-modernism views societies and cultures as conflictual, irrational and changing. Their development is contradictory, discontinuous, and agonistic. The totalising beliefs which hold societies, cultures, individuals and families together are seen as myths or metanarratives which need to be constantly deconstructed so that their role in legitimating power structures be uncovered. Bhabha (1990a) contrasts this post-modernist notion of 'difference' with the modernist notion of 'diversity' – the liberal view that sees culture as a superficial addition to essential human nature.

Modern anti-racism started in the 1960s with the 'colour blind' approach. This approach saw the task of black people as integrating into British society, and the role of social work as facilitating assimilation. Then came multi-culturalism. Instead of creating a melting pot of individuals who would all become British, multi-culturalism envisaged a melting pot of cultures, whose ideal was a society in which people of different cultures would live together. Teachers and social workers were expected to help individuals to understand and live with each other's cultures.

Anti-racism claims that both these stances omitted the oppressive forces prevailing on all black people in British society. Dividing black people into ethnic or cultural groups denies their common historical subjection to colonialism and racism and also the institutional nature of racism in society (Dominelli 1988, Husband 1991). More recent anti-discriminatory theory sees racism as one of several oppressive forces, including sexism, disabilism and ageism (Thompson 1993), and has developed the notion of 'multiple oppressions' or hierarchies of oppression.[1]

At first glance anti-racism appears to be a post-modernist attack on modernist liberal ideals. Anti-racism attacks the totality of 'Britishness' and shows how notions of 'Britishness' are racist (Gilroy 1987, Husband 1991). Attempts to integrate black people into British society carry an underlying assumption that British culture is superior to their cultures and that any rational person would want to become fully 'British'. The anti-racists show how British society and culture has always treated black people as the 'other' and even radical white activists have excluded them and colluded in their oppression (Dominelli 1988, Harris 1991). Additionally, the notion of 'institutional racism' can be seen as an example of 'decentering of the (British) subject', that is, racism is not seen as individual pathology, but is rather part of a web of cultural, political and institutional practices (Ballard 1989, Husband 1991).[2] The notions of 'black identity' and the 'black family' embraced by anti racists are close to the 'incommensurability of discourses'

---

1   See Dominelli (1988) or Rattansi (1992) for a more comprehensive history of British anti-racism.

2   But contrast Husband's rather unidimensional decontruction of new-right racism with the much more complex work of Saggar (1993), illustrating the poverty of the social work discourse.

posited by post-modernists, because of the claim that there is little in common between black and white British identity.

Post-modernist anti-racists such as Rattansi, Cohen, and Gilroy point out, however, that instead of deconstructing racist ideologies and practices, modernist social work anti-racists have simply inverted them. Instead of one way of being British, there are now two – 'black' and 'white'. Modernist anti-racism views 'culture' and 'race' in essentialist terms and imposes its own teleology. For modernist anti-racists, black children have a right to their 'roots' and 'culture' which are transmitted to them by the 'black family'. The 'black family' itself is seen as having strengths that have allowed it to survive through the tests of racism. According to the post-modernist anti-racists, these essentialist notions are a simplification. They note that the relationships between, race, culture, class and gender are complex and fractured, rather than hierarchical (Brah 1992). They see culture as being constantly reconstructed rather than being 'transmitted' to new generations.

Racism too, is seen as a much more complex phenomenon than multiculturists or modernist anti-racists are prepared to acknowledge. Rather than seeing a totalised, unitary institutional racism that is stitched into society, they see different racisms which are local, context-bound, and time-limited. Anti-racism, they claim, must therefore address racism on a local and appropriate level (Cohen 1992). Rattansi says:

> Race can produce simplified interpretations of complex social, economic and cultural relations for anti-racists as well as racists. (1992 p.29)

Gilroy (1987) believes that anti-racism and racism share the same discourse of totality and exclusion. He shows that the definition of 'black' in modernist anti-racism means that other groups such as Jews, Irish etc. are excluded from the anti-racist analysis (see also Alderman, 1993). Individual black people are included only in regard to being black; other aspects of their identity are disregarded. Gilroy maintains that instead of having an identity imposed by anti-racist theorists, blacks in Britain should be, and are, developing their own common identity through 'street culture' and forms of local political action.[3]

Gilroy's critique shows some difficulties in modernist anti-racism's view of black identity, especially 'positive' black identity. The 'modernist' view,

---

3   Ironically, Modood (1988) criticises Gilroy for marginalising Asian Britons, who are seen as possessing 'Black British' identity only in so far as they participate in Afro-Caribbean inspired 'street culture'.

although it has largely been superseded in educational anti-racist discourses, is still part of social work orthodoxy, both here and in the United States, and has been confirmed by such recent authors as Ahmad (1990), BAAF (1987), Banks (1992a, 1992b), Macdonald (1991), McMahon and Allen-Meares (1992) and Maximé (1993). These modernist accounts continue to see black identity as something that is essential to all black people, including mixed-race children. A positive black identity is seen as consisting of positive identification, self-esteem and pride. Many of these authors point out, like Dominelli (1988), that whites are able to, and encouraged to, question, doubt and challenge their own identity. White identity is seen as fragmented, contradictory and contested whereas black identity is proud, unified, and essential. Maximé says:

> Racial identity represents the ethnic/biological dimension of the person. (1993 p.177)

This pushes even further the modernist view of black identity as an essential and genetic property of black people. A 'positive identity' rather than being descriptive of well-adjusted black people becomes prescriptive, those whom they define as 'black' and whose identities differ from their notions of 'positive' are seen as pathological. Ironically, Maximé's conceptions of racial identity along with that of Small (1986) echo the biologically based 'eugenic' racists of the early twentieth century whom Park (1964) and Stonequist (1937) set out to counter in their marginality studies. Black people are seen as having a (modern) identity in which metanarratives are not challenged, where a black 'essence' underlies superficial cultural differences. Whites, in contrast, have a 'post-modern' identity that incorporates difference, challenges metanarratives and disseminates meanings. There is little possibility for meaningful interaction in interracial families. Harris says:

> ...the Black child can only experience bonding in a Black family. The phenomenon experienced by Black children in a White family is merely 'sham bonding' which soon dissipates once the issue of colour and race becomes a factor for the child. (1991 p.143)

It is this totalising view of black identity which is criticised by post-modernist anti-racists. Maximé does not differentiate between the black identity of a child living in a close-knit, Urdu-speaking Muslim community, and a child of mixed parentage living in a multi-ethnic environment. All 'black' children are seen to have the same kind of black identity irrespective of gender, class, culture and family type. Post-modernists acknowledge that there are times when people are treated as faceless 'blacks', for example in racial attacks, but believe there are other circumstances when culture or gender are the salient markers.

Banks' two articles (1992a, 1992b) are similar, illustrating his technique of 'Cognitive Ebonisation'. The first, however, describes it as a technique of working with 'mixed ethnicity' children and their mothers. The second describes it as a technique for direct identity work with black children. So although he makes a distinction between mixed ethnicity and black children in his first article, he does not actually acknowledge one. He sees his technique as applying universally to black children with 'identity confusion'. Banks takes an ambivalent stance towards the concept of 'race'. Citing Small (1986), he vigorously denies that race has any 'real' meaning, but his technique is designed to elicit pride in exactly the concept whose reality he denies!

Many anti-racist texts make the point that 'race' is socially constructed, and therefore not a biologically valid 'marker'. Post-modernist thought shows this as a spurious point. It is rooted in the Anglo-Saxon assumption that the biological is primary, and that biological differences are more real than social differences. It implies that there are other categorisations that are 'valid' bases for discrimination. Feminists (Nice 1992, Walkerdine 1985) and disability theorists (Oliver 1990) show that 'biological' differences such as gender and disability are also socially constructed. The claim that 'race' does not exist in reality is thus a rhetorical point and not part of a coherent anti-racist argument.

Banks further asserts that all Afro-Caribbeans are 'mixed-race', all having white ancestors, and therefore the group we are discussing are 'directly mixed'. Along with Small (1986) and Maximè he confuses the *biological* with the *social* meaning of race, resulting in his echoing of eugenicist arguments.

Banks bases his views of identity development on that of Erikson whom he calls the 'pioneer of the concept of identity'. He challenges Tizard and Phoenix's view that mixed-race children can have a range of identities, saying:

> The Eurocentric foundations on which (such) psychological perspectives are based need a significant perceptual shift to even begin to be relevant to considering the identity needs of black children and adolescents. (1989)

But what is Eurocentric and what is not? Why is it that Tizard and Phoenix's views are considered to be Eurocentric, whereas Erikson and Piaget's are not? This is doubly ironic, because Erikson's theory is based on Ego Psychology, which has been attacked by European theorists such as Lacan (see Sarup 1992) and Løvlie (1992) as being a product of Western, and particularly Anglo-Saxon, conceptions of the self and identity. Banks is therefore using an 'Anglocentric' theory to challenge the 'Eurocentric' assumptions of those whom he opposes. Piaget has similarly been attacked for ethno-centrism (Donaldson 1978).

Further difficulties appear when considering Banks' technique of 'Cognitive Ebonisation' in detail. Part of this technique, for example, involves telling:

> ...imaginative stories...which attempt a subliminal reversal of the negative connotations of blackness and hence black people. A brief example would be: 'Basil was a beautiful shiny black beetle. All the other animals wanted to look like him. "We love your glossy black coat," said the white pelican, "I wish I had one as nice as you". Basil was very proud indeed, no other animal looked as smart as him and he was very happy to be so handsome'. (1992b p.22)

Although on the surface the story is meant to counteract negative connotations of blackness, the 'hidden agenda' is that:

> The most important attribute of people is the colour of their skin.

> People should be judged according to a hierarchy in which skin colour is the main determinant of their position.

> Skin colour should be associated with pride and envy.

Cohen (1989, 1992), Rattansi (1992) and Troyna and Hatcher (1992) have all shown that simple reversals of racism in stories and didactic techniques are largely ineffective in anti-racist teaching. Rattansi says:

> Both multi-cultural and anti-racist critiques ignore the actual literary and pedagogic devices involved in the construction of subject position for the child/reader in school texts. They neglect *how* texts construct meanings, as opposed to *what* they supposedly mean. (1992 p.35)

Other aspects of Cognitive Ebonisation involve the use of books with black heroes, positive labelling of black features etc. Citing Piaget, Banks advises parents:

> ...until the child has reached an appropriate development for understanding of its abstract political meaning...rejection of the term 'black' may be due to a child's literal or concrete understanding of colour labels rather than a rejection of group identity or denial of political affinity. (p.22)

He advocates:

> Blackness as a positive aspirational goal to be achieved can also be
> useful with statements such as 'When you understand more about the
> world you will like being black'. (p.23)

There are major difficulties here. First, Banks' use of Piagetian theory to
explain the child's misidentification is rather disingenuous. Unless he means
very young children (that is, under the age of four), he is simply mistaken.
Even early theories of racial development such as Goodman (1964) and Katz
(1976) acknowledged that by the age of four children have a sense of identity
and can describe their colour. Secondly some of Banks' own teenage
subjects[4] talked of themselves as 'brown' and not 'black'. Brown does not
have the same abstract political connotation as black, so is Banks saying that
these teenagers had not yet developed an abstract understanding of the term?

All this points to a simple view of black identity possessed by all black
children, no matter what their background, which needs nurturing. Any
self-definitions by the children contradicting the identity worker's view are
seen as a result of either identity confusion or immaturity. How cultural,
gender and class identities interface with this essential black identity is not
described by Banks, or Maximé. Presumably these other identities are
non-problematic and do not require an identity worker.

Banks' view of black identity is the mirror image of a supposedly 'positive'
white identity which represents the kind of essentialism which Gilroy, Cohen
and Rattansi wish to transcend.

My purpose for providing this critique of Banks' and Maximé's theories
is not because I think they are wholly wrong or inadequate. Pride, self-esteem
and positive identity are surely important for all mature identities. I do
believe, however, that prescriptions for healthy identity should not be
decreed by 'experts', and that troubled children's own definitions of their
problems should be the starting points of therapy, and not the preconceived
theories of 'experts'.

From Park and Stonequist onwards, marginality and hybridity have been
seen as either pathological states with dire psychological consequences or
alternatively as a celebration of difference and a sign of breaking down
barriers. I believe that neither is the case. Different families deal with different
issues and there is no one 'mixed-race' family, just as there is no one 'black'

---

4   His research with Afro-Caribbean adolescents showed that 83 per cent rated themselves as
     'black' or 'brown' whereas only 8 per cent of white adolescents described themselves as
     'white'.

family. Interracial families may be harmonious, conflictual or both. When conflict does arise it may be around race, cultural values or be a personality clash. It may well involve a complex combination of all these. Conflict may be open and easily expressed, or subtle and implicit. The degree of damage to children is impossible to predict. When children do show signs of distress, it is likely to have multiple interrelating causes, as does most psychological damage to children.

Gilroy (1987) believes that black people in Britain are moving away from a definition of themselves purely as victims. They are involving themselves in political and cultural activity and developing new conceptions of identity which transcend the old totalising categories of race, class and nation. But this is not easy. Painful choices confront these parents and children, and they may go through traumatic phases in which external and internal forces will combine to undermine their stability. Marginality or 'hybridity' is not simply a celebration of difference. Bhabha says:

> The marginal or minority is not the space of a celebratory or utopian self-marginalisation. It is a much more substantial intervention into those justifications of modernity – progress, homogeneity, cultural organicism, the deep nation, the long past – that rationalise the authoritarian 'normalising' tendencies within cultures in the name of the national interest or the ethnic prerogative. (1990a p.4).

Children of mixed parentage are on the margin of the margins, challenging fixed notions of identity and culture.

A major study has recently been published by Tizard and Phoenix (1993) who studied 56 teenagers who had one Afro-Caribbean and one white parent. The subjects were 15 year olds from inner and outer London. They separately interviewed 16 parents.

Tizard and Phoenix found that less than 50 per cent of their subjects considered themselves to be 'black'; most saw themselves as 'mixed-race' or 'brown'. Most had suffered from racism, and had developed strategies to cope with this. Most had high self-esteem and positive identities, although there were a small number who showed marked identity problems. Having a 'black' identity did not correlate with being 'positive' or with high self-esteem. Parents had helped with the strategies. Black and white parents used similar strategies wilth similar effects on the children.

Tizard and Phoenix's findings are similar to those of Wilson (1987). Neither study found evidence that identity confusion is widespread, nor that interracial families show marked pathology or marginality. Interracial families sometimes face problems, especially hostility from both communities and a lack of role models in the media with which to identify. Nevertheless there is no interracial family 'type' and the families are more diverse than similar. Class background and nationhood are the main forces which seem to determine how the families see themselves and cope with their lives.

Other recent research, for example, Back (1993), Bennet *et al.* (1991), Stopes-Roe and Cochrane (1990), Troyna and Hatcher (1992) and van Dijk (1987) all found that racism is a constant threat to many of their subjects, but that patterns of racism, racial identity and culture are not straightforward. They neither conform to modernist anti-racist categories nor are amenable to simple didactic solutions.

I would like to turn to the modernist anti-racist portrayal of mothers in interracial families. Two views emerge from the literature. One view is that these mothers are racist, with the implication that they are the cause of the psychopathology in their children (Banks 1992a, Maximé 1993). Some theorists, using a psychoanalytic framework, go further and explain their racism in terms of their early relationships with their fathers and their association of 'blackness' with 'badness' (Holland and Holland 1984). In this view, the mothers' low self esteem is caused by poor bonding with their fathers. They feel unworthy of white men like their idealised father, and the relationship with the black man symbolises their anger with both their fathers and themselves. Children are a concrete symbol of this anger and ambivalence, and so the anger towards the black partner is projected on to the children.

Other theorists see the mothers as being mature, civilized or rational in their ability to overcome difference (see Rustin 1991). This dichotomy reproduces the modernist anti-racist debate and its totalising celebration of either homogeneity or heterogeneity. Neither position acknowledges that both love *and* fear of difference may have motivated the mothers. Holland and Holland see their patients as depressed women, rejected by their parents, spouses and children. All white mothers are seen as having similar motivations and pathologies, with similar consequences for themselves and their families. None of these articles shows how a successful interracial relationship might be achieved. They assume that the 'blackness' of their partner is the only significant factor about him, and treat it either in an idealised or denigrated way. They also deny that a partner or child might symbolise many things other than blackness and badness. This point is highlighted by the television series *The Buddha of Suburbia* by Hanif Kureshi, portraying an Asian/English family. This is one of the very few portrayals of interracial families in the media, and shows how complex race, racism and sexuality can become. However, even here the white mother is portrayed as a passive foil to the father and son. The accounts in Alihbai-Brown and Montague (1992) and Tizard and Phoenix (1993) also show the complex motivations and relationships in interracial families, and the video *Coffee Coloured Children* shows how painful external racism can be to children of mixed parentage.

These accounts have an even more disturbing message than mere patholo-gisation of the interracial situation. They imply that the children's problems are solely the mother's responsibility. Fathers, both black and white, are absent from Banks', Maximé's and Holland and Holland's accounts, except occasionally as 'role models'. The implication here is that fathers, as long as they are present and black, are by definition positive role models for their children. Mothers, on the other hand are subjected to intense scrutiny to discover the 'roots' of their racism. White fathers are not considered impor-tant at all because all the theories see the mother as the primary carer, and the father is therefore given little responsibility for his children's identity development. Black mothers are assumed to provide adequate parenting.

Walkerdine (1985) shows how damaging these assumptions are for women, whose role is seen as producing and nurturing children to facilitate their 'natural' ability to become productive, autonomous, rational and happy adults. Mothers are seen as 'irrational' and their own feelings and desires are suppressed and discounted. This applies especially to working class mothers, whose disciplining style is seen as harmful and pathogenic. This view of motherhood is extended by the modernist anti-racists to seeing the mother's role as nurturing the natural 'black identity' of her children (see especially Maximé on this point). Since the mothers' choice of black partners is already seen as a sign of pathology, they cannot be 'efficient producers' of children with a positive black identity. Nice (1992) shows how black mothers are similarly pathologised by modernist social theories, either by being seen as overbearing or having unlimited capacity to parent with no support.

It is true that some mothers are racist, and most will have some racist beliefs or feelings, but their motivations are complex, and sometimes con-flicting. Conflict is likely to produce racialisation, but even this connection is not ubiquitous. Over time relationships change, so individuals may have different, perhaps conflicting, motivations and feelings, depending on their situations. To reduce their motivations for partner selection to a single cause is to dehumanise both partners, many of whose choices are probably no different than 'normal' motivations for partner choice; a combination of pathology, irrationality and maturity. Most women in Alihbai-Brown and Montague's and Tizard and Phoenix's books chose partners of similar educational and class backgrounds. But why should this choice of 'sameness' be any more natural or rational than the choice of 'difference' in cultural or racial background? Rationality is equated by these authors with 'normality' which for them means 'conformity'. Those who challenge the natural order are seen as pathological. Bhabha says:

> Hybridity is the perplexity of the living as it interrupts the representation of the fullness of life; it is an instance of iteration in the minority discourse, of the time of the arbitrary sign...through which all forms of cultural meaning are open to translation because their enunciation resists totalization. (1990b p.314)

Hybridity challenges orthodox notions of culture, and those who see it as their task to uphold cultural values (that is, maintain sameness as opposed to difference) seek to pathologise and further marginalise those who cross boundaries. But Bhabha is not merely celebrating difference. This is not a naïve 'melting pot', assimilationist or multiculturalist discourse. Difference is a form of disjuncture, interruption and fracture, as well as of celebration.

Interestingly, Holland and Holland, as well as Banks, refer specifically to working class women. Perhaps choices are more limited for working class children and mothers, although Maximé specifically denies this, saying all 'black' children have the same identity issues to face. Nevertheless I still doubt that all working class white women in this situation are racist, or that their racism has a single, common psychological cause. Psychoanalytic accounts tend to see racism as a manifestation of the psychotic defenses splitting and projective identification, with black people given the negative 'split off' atributes of the racist (see Young 1990 for a good account of this process) But if racism is multi-faceted, local and context specific, why should it always be associated with one particular psychological process?

Another problem with modernist psychoanalytic explanations is that they provide a sequence of significant events which predate the 'pathology', in which cause and effect are determined. Adorno *et al.*, Holland and Holland and Rustin see the roots of racism in early life, just as Stonequist, Park and Maximé see the causes of pathology for people of mixed parentage as being in early parenting. What is never considered is that later events, such as becoming a fascist or having a mixed-race child might affect how early family life has been reconstructed, and that the context in which the story is told also plays a part.

Narrative analysis, however, sees causation in a more circular way than does psychoanalysis, so that effects and causes are more difficult to uncouple from each other (Sass 1992).

What is interesting about modernist anti-racist accounts is that their discussions of race and racism contain the metaphors of disease. Like the eugenicist racists and the cultural racists who saw black immigration as a 'disease' affecting indigenopus culture, these anti-racists treat racism as a disease. It is this metaphor which leads to the pathologisation of interracial families, and leads most authors to become social 'doctors' who can cure society of the infection. But Cohen, Gilroy, and others show how inadequate this metaphor is, and how misguided it is as a basis for anti-racist action. Foucault and Lyotard also show that 'power' and 'difference' can be seen as much more complicated and multi-faceted phenomena than 'social diseases'.

I am not here abandoning modernist theories of development, racism and racial identity in favour of post-modern theory. I believe that totalisation is sometimes absolutely necessary. It is self-indulgent and morally unacceptable for social work not to support the anti-racist forces which are attempting to unite black people. A white person has no right to tell black people how to organize their resistance. However, solidarity with anti-racism should not be equated with an uncritical acceptance of social work's anti-discriminatory orthodoxy. Racist discourses have an unnerving capacity to adapt and disseminate to meet the challenges of a changing world. I believe that if anti-racism does not do the same then the anti-racist gains made in social work, already under threat, will be reversed (Rooney 1993).

Gilroy's (1992) point about this similarity of racist to anti-racist discourses is graphically highlighted by recent debates about single parenthood, education and crime, in which the 'British family' and 'British culture' are being portrayed as the panacea for all social ills, which is being threatened by alien forces. British family and culture is described by the new right in almost mystical terms, virtually identical to social work anti-racist's 'black' families and culture (Jones and Novak 1993, Saggar 1993), leaving little room for variety, and confusing description with prescription. The danger of emphasising 'sameness' which is rightly criticised by all anti-racists is counterbalanced by the danger of emphasising 'difference' or incommensurability, because it invites the racist's argument that 'different' peoples are too exotic and unlike British people to fit into this society.

I believe that post-modern discourses can add to many debates in social work, not only anti-racism. Some of these concepts are already being used by a few authors (for example, Harris and Timms 1993, Rojek *et al.* 1988, Sands and Nuccio 1992). Social work, however, is developing a culture in which professional judgement is being increasingly devalued, where policy makers and academics do the thinking and social workers use checklists, and where good practice is equated with efficiency and economy. Post-modernism provides a potent rebuttal of this approach, as well as to traditional Marxist and Feminist approaches (Rojek *et al.* 1988, Sands and Nuccio

1992). It shows that any construction of social situations and problems is contextual, temporary and ideologically framed, that every inclusion is also an exclusion and that opposites can be identical.

References

Adorno, T.W., Frenkel-Brunswick, E., Levinson, D. and Sanford, R.N. (1950) *The Authoritarian Personality*. New York: Harper.

Ahmad, B. (1990) *Black Perspectives in Social Work*. Birmingham: Venture Press.

Alderman, G. (1993) The Jewish Dimension in British Politics since 1945. *New Community* Vol.20 1, 9–26.

Alibhai-Brown, Y. and Montague, A. (1992) *The Colour of Love: Mixed Race Relationships*. London: Virago.

BAAF (British Agencies for Adoption and Fostering) (1987) *The Placement Needs of Black Children*. Practice Note 13. London: BAAF.

Back, L. (1993) Race, identity and nation within an adolescent community in South London. *New Community, 19*, 2, 217–235.

Ballard, R. (1989) Social Work with Black People: What's the Difference? In C. Rojek, G. Peackock and S. Collins (eds) *The Haunt of Misery. Critical Essays in social work and helping*. London: Routledge.

Banks, N. (1992a) Techniques for Direct Identity Work with Black Children. *Adoption and Fostering* Vol.16, 3, 19–25.

Banks, N. (1992b) Some considerations of 'Racial' Identification and Self Esteem when Working with Mixed Ethnicity Children and their Mothers as Social Services Clients. *Social Services Research* Vol.3, 32–41.

Barthes, R. (1973) *Mythologies*. St Albans: Granada.

Bennet, M., Dewberry, C. and Yeels, C. (1991) A Reassessment of the Role of Ethnicity in Children's Social Perception. *Journal of Child Psychology and Psychiatry* Vol.32, 6, 969–982.

Bhabha, H.K. (1990a) DissemiNation: time, narrative and the margins of the modern nation. In H.K. Bhabha (ed) *Nation and Narration*. London: Routledge.

Bhabha, H.K. (1990b) Narrating the nation. In H.K. Bhabha (ed) *Nation and Narration*. London: Routledge.

Bernstein, R.J. (1991) *The New Constellation*. Cambridge: Polity Press.

Brah, A. (1992) Difference, diversity and differentiation. In A. Rattansi and J. Donald (eds) *'Race' Culture and Difference*. London: Open University and Sage.

Cohen, P. (1992) 'Its Racism what dunnit': Hidden narrative in theories of racism. In A. Rattansi and J. Donald *'Race' Culture and Difference*. London: Open University and Sage.

Cohen, P. (1989) Reason, racism and the popular monster. In B. Richards (ed) *Crises of The Self: Further Essays on Psychoanalysis and Politics*. London: Free Association Books.

Derrida, J, (1978) *Writing and Difference*. Chicago: University of Chicago Press.

Dominelli, L. (1988) *Anti-Racist Social Work.* London: Macmillan.

Donaldson, M. (1978) *Children's Minds.* London: Fontana Press.

Erikson, E. (1963) Youth: fidelity and diversity. In E. Erikson (ed) *Youth: Change and Challenge.* New York: Basic Books.

Gilroy, P. (1987) *There Ain't no Black in the Union Jack.* London: Routledge.

Gilroy, P. (1992) The end of Antiracism. In A. Rattansi and J. Donald *'Race' Culture and Difference.* London: Open University and Sage.

Goodman, M.E. (1964) *Race Awareness in Young Children.* Cambridge, Massachusetts: Addison-Wesley.

Harris, R. and Timms, N. (1993) *Secure Accommodation in Child Care: Between Hospital and Prison or Thereabouts.* London: Routledge.

Harris, V. (1991) Values of Social Work in the Context of British Society in Conflict with Anti-Racism. In Curriculum Development Project Steering Group (ed) *Setting the Context for Change. Anti-Racist Social Work Education 1.* Leeds: CCETSW.

Holland, R. and Holland, K. (1984) Depressed Women: Outposts of Empire and Castles of Skin. In B. Richards (ed) *Capitalism and Infancy: Essays on Psychoanalysis and Politics.* London: Free Association Books.

Husband, C. (1991) 'Race', Conflictual Politics and Anti-Racist Social Work: Lessons from the past for action in the 90s. In Curriculum Development Project Steering Group (ed) *Setting the Context for Change. Anti-Racist Social Work Education 1.* Leeds: CCETSW.

Jones, C. and Novak, T. (1993) Social Work Today. *British Journal of Social Work* Vol.23, 3, 195–212.

Katz, P.A. (1976) *Towards the Elimination of Racism.* New York: Pergamon.

Løvlie, L. (1992) Postmodernism and Subjectivity. In S. Kvale (ed) *Psychology and Postmodernism.* London: Sage.

Lyotard, J-F. (1984) *The Postmodern Condition: A Report on Knowledge.* Manchester: Manchester University Press.

Lyotard, J-F. (1992) *The Postmodern Explained to Children Correspondence 1982–1985.* London: Turnaround.

McMahon, A. and Allen-Meares, P. (1992) Is Social Work Racist? A Content Analysis of Recent Literature. *Social Work* Vol.37, 6, 533–539

Macdonald, S. (1991) *All Equal Under the Act?* London: REU, NISW.

Maximé, J.M. (1993) The Importance of Racial Identity for the psychological Well-being of Black Children. *ACPP Review and Newsletter* Vol.15, 4, 173–179.

Modood, T. (1988) 'Black' Racial Equality and Asian Identity. *New Community* Vol.14, 3, 397–404.

Nice, V.E. (1992) *Mothers and Daughters: The distortion of a Relationship.* Basingstoke: Macmillan.

Non-Aligned Productions (1988) *Coffee Coloured Children* (Video). London: Albany Video Distribution.

Oliver, M. (1990) *The Politics of Disablement: Critical Texts in Social Work and the Welfare State.* Basingstoke: Macmillan.

Park, R.E. (1964) *Race and Culture.* New York: Free Press.

Rattansi, A. (1992) Changing the subject? Racism, culture and education. In A. Rattansi and J. Donald (eds) *'Race' Culture and Difference.* London: Open University and Sage.

Rojek, C., Peacock, G. and Collins, S. (1988) *Social Work and Received Ideas.* London: Routledge.

Rooney, B. (1993) Questioning Anti-Racist quality. *Community Care* 7 October Vol.12.

Rustin, M.J. (1991) *The Good Society and the Inner World. Psychoanalysis, Politics and Culture.* London: Verso.

Saggar, S. (1993) Black Participation and the transformation of the 'race' issue in British Politics. *New Community* Vol.20, 1, 27–42.

Sands, R. and Nuccio, K. (1992) Postmodern Feminist Theory and Social Work. *Social Work* 37, 6, 489–494.

Sarup, M. (1992) *Jaques Lacan.* Hemel Hempstead: Harvester Wheatsheaf.

Sass, L.A. (1992) The Epic of Disbelief: The Postmodernist turn in Contemporary Psychoanalysis. In S. Kvale (ed) *Psychology and Postmodernism.* London: Sage.

Small, A. (1986) Transracial Placements: Conflicts and Contradictions. In S. Ahmed, J. Cheetham and A. Small (eds) *Social Work with Black Children and Their Families.* London: Batsford.

Stonequist, E.V. (1937) *The Marginal Man: A Study in Personality and Culture Conflict.* New York: Russel and Russel.

Stopes-Roe, M. and Cochrane, R. (1990) *Citizens of This Country: The Asian-British.* Clevedon: Multilingual Matters.

Tizard, B. and Phoenix A. (1989) Black Identity and Trans-Racial Adoption. *New Community* Vol.15, 3, 427–38.

Tizard, B. and Phoenix, A. (1993) *Black, White or Mixed-Race? Race and Racism in the Lives of Young People of Mixed Parentage.* London: Routledge.

Troyna, B. and Hatcher, R. (1992) *Racism in Children's Lives A study of Mainly-White Schools.* London: Routledge.

Thompson, N. (1993) *Anti-Discriminatory Practice.* London: Macmillan.

van Dijk, T.A. (1987) *Communicating Racism: Ethnic Prejudice in Thought and Talk.* Newbury Park, CA: Sage.

Walkerdine, V. (1985) On the Regulation of Speaking and Silence: Subjectivity, Class and Gender in Contemporary Schooling. In C. Steedman, C. Urwin and V. Walkerdine (eds) *Language, Gender and Childhood.* London: Routledge and Kegan Paul.

Wilson, A. (1987) *Mixed Race Children.* London: Allen and Unwin,.

Young, L. (1990) A Nasty Piece of Work: A Psychoanalytic Study of Sexual and Racial Difference in 'Mona Lisa'. In J. Rutherford (ed) *Identity: Community, Culture, Difference.* London: Lawrence and Wishart.

Young, R. (1992) Colonialism and Humanism. In A. Rattansi and J. Donald (eds) *'Race' Culture and Difference.* London: Open University and Sage.

Chapter 8

Creativity and Child Protection Social Work

Rose Stanford

In the course of research into social workers' and police officers' joint investigations of suspected child abuse, a problem was found to exist with social work practice: this was the capacity of social workers to be creative within the organisational and legal boundaries of their work.

The intention that had led to the research – which included individual interviews with specialist social workers in child protection, and their colleagues in the police Child Protection Team – was to reassert the importance and interest of 'professional practice' at a time and in a field where managerial expertise and regulation were dominant. These seemed to me to fail to grasp the nature of child abuse related work, which was thought to be better understood and ordered by an emphasis on practice. To this end, I asked the social workers and police officers about their experiences of working with their own and the other agency in police and social work joint investigations of cases of suspected child abuse. The understandings held by the participants were investigated in terms of their moral and ethical beliefs and the way in which these informed and responded to practice. The moral theory of Alasdair MacIntyre (1985) was drawn on here. This framework was complemented by those aspects of psychoanalysis that are concerned with meaning, symbol formation and social system defences. These approaches were found to illuminate key themes of professional practice in the area of child protection that included justice and discretion, identity and identification, the institutional bounding of practice – and the problem of creativity.

The causes that led to the inhibition of creative professional practice were seen to be complex. Reinforcing the organisational and political environment and in part at least influencing that environment, is the nature of the work content itself: child abuse.

In the accounts given by social work participants in this research a profound confusion was expressed by nearly everyone. They were convinced that creativity was essential, and that they were creative in some of their practice, but they maintained that their creativity was continually vitiated or waylaid when working in child protection. Their very language and manner of expression illustrated their sense of puzzlement. Remarkably rich and 'emotionally full' symbols and imagery characterized these passages in the interviews. But these episodes would falter, and be patched with almost a breakdown of coherence, even sometimes of speech itself. The researcher perceived this at the time as a 'kind of clawing at meaning'. In the margins and perhaps the source of the linguistic richness and confusion was the case material, the experiences of the children. Evident in these accounts is a kind of attack on thinking and making links, an absence of the assured use of autonomy and discretion, and a persistent undercurrent of unacknowledged cruelty and passiveness that seem to block rather than generate creative movement.

Signs of the inhibition of creative response are the absence of spontaneity and humour, and the 'ordeal by seriousness' to which the topic of child abuse and the professional practitioners are subjected. Intense guilt felt by the professionals about the fascination and even envious emotions that child abuse excites in adults leads these feelings to surface in curtailed and disguised forms. Current theoretical and ideological frameworks for understanding and handling child abuse work can be seen partly as narratives developed to give form to essentially disruptive phenomena. These stories we tell ourselves about child abuse are in effect defensive manoeuvres.

The substantial literature testifies to the difficulty of practice, of working together with other professionals, of even thinking and acting when engaged in practice in cases of child abuse.

I will argue that professional responses to child sexual abuse and child abuse attempt to domesticate the disquieting cruelty and hostility inherent in child abuse by placing around them acceptable structures. The narratives bestow a form: beginning, plot development, dénouement; characters and characterisation; varying sets of moral assumptions. Role triads of victim, persecutor, rescuer emerge, differing only in the sophistication with which they are expressed.

The domesticating narratives of child abuse are various: legal-administrative, therapeutic, feminist. The hallmark of each of these is that despite the vigour and liveliness of the originating theory or institution, once applied to child protection it becomes reified and insipid.

When practice is pursued by several people, in collaboration with other professional groups or with colleagues, themes that become apparent may include repression of forbidden feelings; the re-enactment of case material; wishes for differentiation and fantasies of merging. The effects of the case material, organisational contingencies, and individual and group characteristics may either interfere with or enhance listening, thinking and acting.

Dori Laub (1992) writes of the dangers when acting as either an interviewer or a psychoanalyst for a Holocaust survivor who tells of their experiences. 'Listening defences' include a sense of paralysis; a sense of outrage and anger directed at the victim; withdrawal or numbness; awe and fear, endowing the victim with a kind of sanctity; foreclosure through an obsession with fact finding; hyperemotionality, which superficially looks like compassion and caring.

Acceptance of the first three of these defences is widespread, but the sanctity of the victim and the foreclosure of fact finding are less openly discussed. Arguably, the first of these is evident in some of the feminist analyses of child abuse, and the second, in juridification. All of the listening defences may be carried through into social work practice, and may distort the worker's capacity to recognise the reality of the client and the situation.

Such themes were evident in the accounts of their practice given by the social workers and in the language and symbols in which these were conveyed. In these accounts, what emerged as central to the workers' practice was their identification with their clients, and their efforts to draw out and hold onto intelligibility from the mass of experiences and emotions with which they were confronted. Critical in this process was the setting provided by the agency and the conceptual, administrative and legal frameworks determining the social work intervention. To attain a sense of intelligibility that could emerge from and in turn foster creativity, the social worker needed the capacity to think, articulate and make links: to move between thought, expression and action.

This chapter looks at some of the social workers' experiences that are relevant to these points, and examines them in relation to psychoanalytic ideas about identification and containment, and the effects of these on the social workers' capacity to think. It will be argued that the domesticating narratives are implicated in the problems of identification and containment in the work of child protection, and come to serve both as defences against and barriers to thinking, so hindering creative practice.

Social Work: Identification and Intelligibility

The themes of identification and the seeking and imposition of intelligibility were suggested by the social workers to be central in their efforts towards creative practice. But herein lies the tension in social work practice in child protection. If the worker proceeds through empathy, or identification with his/her client, then there is at least momentarily a suspension of independent thinking at the time of the imaginative merging with the experience of the other. To then detach and gather oneself back into the thinking and acting professional is precarious and uncertain. It is made even more so if defensive manoeuvres are resorted to in order to cope with the profound anxieties evoked by the subject matter of cruelty and sexuality, including infantile sexuality. A social worker may, by the use of empathy/identification, have felt some of the feelings of the child, abuser, or other carer, but then had to reject or distort some of the more unacceptable aspects of those feelings, whether or not those feelings are consciously felt by the child/abuser/carer. In such a case, the worker's capacity to reflect on and think about the full experience of the client and the abuse constellation will be impaired.

In 'working alongside' the client, the worker's identification is transformed by professional ethics and discipline into 'empathy'. The earliest form of empathy is how Hannah Segal characterizes projective identification: 'the phantasy of entering the object with the whole or part of the self which may lead to an altered perception of the self and object in relation to each other' (Moustaki 1981). As an attempt at communication, someone may unconsciously project impulses and parts of herself into another so the latter may feel and understand those experiences.

A functional use of such identification is described by one social worker:

> If you're picking up strong feelings of fear or depression or anything like that, then it's a good indication of how people in that house are feeling. If you're sitting there feeling, this person is on a tight fuse and I'm scared that I'm going to say the wrong thing...that child is running the gauntlet more than you are. Because you can go.

But the aggression from the courts which several social workers reported experiencing seems to embody a less functional process of identification. This occurred in the data where reference was made to care proceedings, in contrast to criminal proceedings. In the latter the workers are angry or unhappy about what the child has been subjected to by the court process, but the distress remains placed with the child. In accounts of care proceedings (and case conferences) where the child does not give evidence or speak, and indeed is probably absent, then it seems from the social workers' accounts that, in speaking for the child and their interests, the worker becomes identified with the child in the eyes of the court and in their own eyes. They describe instances of being 'strung out to dry' where they have felt vulnerable and attacked.

> The last time I went to court on a child protection issue I felt it was really 'kill the messenger'. We got a *hammering* from the magistrates. The court was hostile. The clerk of the court was hostile to us. He kept quoting precedents which said that the place of a child was *always* with the parents. The case was found proven, and they still only gave us a supervision order on it!

These seem to be examples of the particular form of projective identification as a defence to get rid of unwanted or unbearable parts of the self to the point where it comes to be used as a means of control. The social worker has projected into her the feelings associated with powerlessness, cruelty, and anger that others in the setting cannot bear to think about. The ancient phrase 'kill the messenger' exactly explains this phenomenon. The social worker becomes controlled and bullied by the processes and procedures in a way normally unthinkable. The workers' difficulty in retaining their separateness from all this is caused by the temporary loss of differentiation between self and object that occurs in projective identification, involving a loss of the sense of self.

Where the capacity to retain some sense of separateness is weakened by excessive use of projective identification, fantasy and reality become confused to such an extent that the person's 'capacities for verbal and abstract thinking are crippled.' This is looked at in the section below on tenacity and making sense.

The problematic aspects of projective identification are intensified by the nature of child abuse. Main (1957) describes in his classic paper 'The Ailment' the chaos in a psychiatric hospital when the staff became prey to their own fantasies and the projections of themselves and the patients. Ideas and feelings about the roles of victim, persecutor and rescuer may influence the use made of identification by the social worker to establish communication. Social work interventions in child abuse cases are likewise affected, and it may be that they correspond in their particular features to the patterns of projective identification in operation.

There is a particular vulnerability here to the juridification narrative of 'empowerment' and 'partnership' which may be adopted by the agency in an unthinking way. Empowerment and, particularly, partnership have come to refer to the methods and aims of working with parents. A dynamic is set up in which the powerful agency or family proceedings court identifies itself with the powerful abuser, and this leaves the child and the social worker who identifies with that child with a sense of angry powerlessness and isolation. This forms part of a complex identification process that denies the violence and cruelty of child sexual abuse and the abuser. The worker is burdened with the identification with the child, and feels the sole witness to this violence to the child.

The power of identifications in this area is commented on by Isabel Menzies in her classic study about nursing:

> The objective situation…bears a striking resemblance to the phantasy situations that exist in every individual in the deepest and most primitive levels of the mind. The intensity and the complexity of the nurse's anxieties are to be attributed primarily to the peculiar capacity of the objective features of her work situation to stimulate afresh these early situations and their accompanying emotions. (Menzies 1961 pp.5–6)

These anxieties, likely to be evoked as much by child abuse as by illness, relate to damage, death and injury, reparation and aggression. The fusion of aggression and sexuality, resulting from the abuse of power by the sexual abuser, is further complicated by the implications of the Oedipal metaphor as described by two feminist commentators, Mary MacLeod and Esther Saraga.

> The collective anxiety, panic and confusion set off by discussion of child sexual abuse can be seen as the unsurprising response to the challenging of a founding idea of our civilisation: that incest is the boundary between stability and chaos. (MacLeod and Saraga 1988)

A female social worker recalled that

> One parent was threatening to kill me. He threatened to kill me to two different third parties who didn't think it important enough to let me know.

> He came to a case conference and told the chairperson beforehand that if I said anything he didn't like, he was going to hit me. He sat in the conference and I went merrily through, giving my report, thinking, there's something that doesn't sit right with me, but there

again, that's nothing new and it was only afterwards when the chair said, 'By the way...'

There is an avoidance here of the violence and sexuality inherent in child sexual abuse that is underscored by the gender of the protagonists in the scene. This is a complex area, and one where feminists have been led to overstate their case in their justified challenge to the previous orthodoxy of 'the collusive mother' and even collusive child. But the inherent danger in the new orthodoxy is one which besets the social worker: the victim role and its associated denial of strength and power to a point that approaches complacency. Social workers will use identification with their clients in order to help, and this identification with outsiders in society will reinforce their scapegoat role. But social workers are not their child clients: they are adults, and professionals, and have considerable statutory clout. Their persistent sense of being cruelly treated and misunderstood is, of course, largely realistic. However, the way in which this feeling of weakness and impotence is sometimes clung to suggests there is an investment that has not been acknowledged by social workers, and perhaps can be illuminated by the recent and more sophisticated feminist analysis of sexual politics.

Jessica Benjamin (1988) writes of the tendency of feminist thought to construct the 'problem of domination as a drama of female vulnerability victimised by male aggression' where an analysis of female submission is not undertaken for fear that in admitting women's participation in the relationship of domination, the onus of responsibility will shift from men to women. She attempts rather to clarify the needs that are fulfilled for both dominator and dominated, and what binds people into sexual relationships of cruelty.

The underlying pattern is seen to be a culturally induced failure to attain mutual recognition and to acknowledge the impulses of both women and men towards both differentiation and merging. The failure leads to splitting, a polarisation of subject and object, idealisation and repudiation, good and bad, doer and done-to.

Such an analysis permits the ownership of sexual and aggressive feelings by both women and men, adults and children. It challenges the valorisation of the victim and so opens a way to freer reflection about child abuse.

Time and the Organisation

If the disturbing and complex content of child protection social work is to be susceptible to thinking and creativity, then the work needs to be bounded or contained in some way to allow time and psychic space for this creative thought and action to proceed. Only if sufficient security is provided can the worker then enter into 'identification and feeling mad oneself' in order to gain a realistic grasp of not only the experiences of the protagonists – including the professional 'networks' – but also their relationships and interactions.

The effects of juridification are evident in the structures and procedures developed by the agencies, deliberately or by default, in order that the social work fit in with the requirements of a process shaped and ordered by the law. Although the law can be a source of containment and discipline for creative practice, the role and approach of the civil courts seem to have 'juridified' child protection. Juridification is a concept developed by Jurgen Habermas (1981) to describe the increase of legal regulations and a resulting 'pressure towards the redefinition of everyday life situations'. This entails a process of 'compulsory abstraction' of these situations: cognitively necessary so that everyday life situations can be subsumable under legal categories, and practically necessary so that administrative control can be exercised. The reifying influence of juridification is felt in such areas of life as family relations, education, old age, and physical and mental health and well-being. In juridification, the law assumes a constitutive character, constituting new spheres of action or redefining existing ones. Habermas sees a growing commodification of private life in which we are presented with 'new and more extensive pre-selected packages of behavioural, psychological and sexual scripts'. Such scripts can be seen in current approaches based on 'empowerment', 'working in partnership' and which are regulated and constituted by court procedures, profoundly extended by the Children Act.

Time and space that allow and encourage creative practice do not appear to emerge from the time scales and the pace of the workings of the legal and agency systems.

Social workers saw the process of joint investigations of suspected child abuse with the police both as dragged out: 'it took so long!', 'In the end *you* lose interest, you forget things!' and as too rushed, with the police and social services agendas forcing the pace of the social workers.

Time is seen as hostile to the social work practice and its goods. Pressure to hurry is experienced as impingement and demand; delay robs the work of interest and meaning. Either way, an inherent rhythm appears to be threatened. David Bohm's image of listening to music as a metaphor for the implicate order may help to explain what the social workers accounts seem to imply:

> At a given moment a certain note is being played but a number of the previous notes are still 'reverberating' in consciousness. Close attention will show that it is the simultaneous presence and activity of all these

reverberations that is responsible for the direct and immediately felt sense of movement, flow and continuity. To hear a set of notes so far apart in time that there is no such reverberation will destroy altogether the sense of a whole unbroken, living movement that gives meaning and force to what is heard. (Bohm 1980 pp.198–199)

'Space' and a sensitive pacing of time – freedom from 'intrusive identification'(Meltzer 1986) – act as a container for the symbolic work necessary in child abuse investigations in order that the worker may preserve and articulate what is learned in the course of the investigation.

A social worker talks of how

a decision never quite gets taken and there has to be a series of discussions and meetings and other people involved, and you discuss the same issues over and over, without ever coming to a decision. Or if you do, it can be three different decisions on three different but similar cases.

The social workers' accounts suggest that the Social Services Department lacks the capacity to act as a container for the complex and powerful dynamics of identification, projections and reflections. Its bureaucratic nature, reinforced by the effects of juridification, means rather that it is peculiarly vulnerable to fragmentation and to the kind of impoverishment conveyed in its empty vocabulary: characterised by Ziman (1991) as 'pallid' and 'desiccated...where robust, pungent language would cost heads'.
Isabel Menzies' observations of the nursing social defence mechanisms are pertinent to the social workers descriptions. She enumerates such features as the denial of the significance of the individual and their de-personalisation; the attempt to eliminate decision making by 'ritual task performance'; the reduction of responsibility by checks and counterchecks; purposeful obscurity in the formal distribution of responsibility; the reduction of responsibility in its delegation upwards; and avoidance of change. These all assist in the toleration of anxiety – but they do not help the worker completely to avoid it, and secondary anxieties emerge.

The defences inhibit the capacity for creative, symbolic thought, for abstract thought, and for conceptualization. They inhibit the individual's understanding, knowledge and skills that enable reality to be handled effectively and pathological anxiety mastered. (Menzies 1961 p.35)

Elisabeth Hadjiisky (1987) summarizes some of the common defences that child abuse work may feature: denial, for example, may free us from 'an unbearable reality' but a sense of unease will persist. So omnipotence or 'total knowledge' may be resorted to with the professional – or agency – believing she may be able to face everything alone. She 'forbids' further abuse and so if it recurs she cannot afford to recognize it as this would undermine her omnipotence. 'Magic powers' are granted to the worker's 'good relationship' with the parents and the forgotten child may continue to suffer. The professional or agency cannot realize what she/it sees; 'her thought processes are suspended and any links between what she sees and what she hears are severed'. Hence the court clerk who maintained that a child's place was always with his parents, the case conferences where the clinging to the principle of parental participation obliterates the capacity of the chairperson to hear and deal with unambiguous threats of violence. Hadjiisky goes on to describe 'banalization': 'the best antidote to dramatic reality', where incidents of abuse are played down, 'the affective and imaginative capacity is switched off' and there is a flight to generalisation, to the commonplace, conformity, relativism which result in the abuse being placed in a normative framework.

Making Sense: Thinking and Symbols

If the attempt to secure intelligibility in the face of chaos is a feature of social work practice in child protection, then the ideas of Wilfred Bion as explored by Donald Meltzer (1986) may illuminate the processes involved. They will also help to account for the very difficult and painful struggles the social workers describe when trying to hold onto what they recall observing or hearing. To repeat the comment of one worker:

> I think when you're battling against a lot of the negative that is coming against you, I think it clouds your thinking. I think very often you're uncertain, you begin to think, did I hear?

The repeated use of the word 'think' or 'thinking' in this comment emphasizes the effort being expended on holding on to the cognitive process against the onslaught of very powerful voices, emotions and arguments that 'it was not so'.

Bion would characterize the task for the worker in terms of the 'alpha function' or the process of symbol formation, which always attempts

> to find representations for our emotional experiences if we can tolerate them. But the structure of personality, with its heavy armouring of conventional responses, often intervenes to prevent this from happening. (Meltzer 1986 p.11)

This is particularly the case in the area of child abuse where conventions and the sensibilities of others as well as one's own, are challenged by some of the material which confronts the worker. In the face of this uncomfortable material, the worker needs to handle the ensuing pressure of thoughts and

> to restrain (themselves) from action in order to contain the processes by which the teeming thoughts are organized and developed in thinking. (Meltzer 1986)

Action follows when communication and thought have reached their limit. A distinction is made between what results from the alpha process and the empty though spuriously logical consequences of 'proto-mental processes'. Meltzer describes the distinction thus:

> the capacity of the mind to form symbols for the purpose of representing the meaning of emotional experiences so that they may be stored as memory (rather than held as recall), used for thinking (rather than merely being manipulated by computation and logical operations), and transformed into a variety of symbolic forms for the communication of ideas (rather than being transmitted as bits of information). (Meltzer 1986 p.13)

Reliant on this process are equitable judgement requiring complex and subtle reflection and the re-thinking of safe and conventional responses, imagination and resourcefulness, and creativity and empathy. 'These areas of activity and relationship that require emotion, symbol formation, thought, judgement, memory and decision as the background to action' need the quality of tenacity to protect them from the incursion of 'non-symbolic mindlessness' (Meltzer 1986).

The problem of creativity in the deadening carapace in which child protection social work exists becomes clear when the conditions necessary for 'alpha functioning' are considered.

First, there must be an authenticity to what the participant is going to say: where a person does not mean what they say or say what they mean, then meaning itself becomes impoverished and shallow. There needs to be, as in Wittgenstein's image, 'something coupled to those words which would otherwise run idle' (Meltzer 1986). This is directly related to the points made by Meltzer in his development of Bion's thought (see below), and in Ricoeur's ideas about emotionally full and empty language and symbols.

The second condition relates to the various attacks on reality, thinking and linking that may follow from the impingement of seriously disturbing phenomena which constitute aspects of child abuse work. Sexual abuse in particular may be seen as representing a loss of the separateness which makes thinking possible. How this may affect symbol formation and therefore adequate communication to the researcher, is described by Meltzer. Thinking about an emotional experience is necessary for learning and starts with the unconscious operation of the alpha function upon the observations of the emotional experiences. The resulting symbolic representations may then be transformed into words or other symbolic thoughts as well as to levels of abstraction. But if the assimilation of the experiences is diverted by, for example, their disturbing nature, then what results is essentially a story or fiction, suffused with received meaning, often requiring the distortion of facts to fit. This 'construction' can be recalled in a mechanical way but such recollections have a sense of dogmatic certainty. This would be an instance of the emotionally empty, reified narratives which structure so much child protection social work.

This can be contrasted to those emotional experiences which, distilled for their meaning, become learning experiences which may alter the personality. They are not recalled factually but may be reconstructed with a sense of uncertainty about the facts, which are 'stripped of litigious significance and not valued in themselves but in the meaning distilled from them' (Bion 1987a). Thus the social workers' accounts were marked in many passages by such uncertainty, reflection, and suppleness of thinking.

To follow Bion's argument further: if reality is felt to be so intolerable that it must be avoided and attacked, then this has implications for 'verbal thought' on which psychic reality is dependent. Verbal thought 'synthesizes and articulates impressions and…is essential to awareness of internal and external reality' (1987b p.60). The order provided by space and time is obliterated by the chaos and aggression of sexual abuse and the echoes evoked in the workers/agencies inhibits thought and 'attacks linking'.

> The primitive matrix of ideographs from which thought springs contains within itself links between one ideograph and another. All these are now attacked till finally two objects cannot be brought together in a way which leaves each object with its intrinsic qualities intact and yet able, by their conjunction, to produce a new mental object. Consequently the formation of symbols, which depends for its therapeutic effect on the ability to bring together two objects so their resemblance is made manifest, yet their difference left unimpaired, now becomes difficult. (Bion 1987b p.50)

As the person has rid himself of

that-which-joins, his capacity for articulation, the methods available
for synthesis, are felt to be macilent; he can compress but cannot join,
he can fuse but cannot articulate. (Bion 1987b p.52)

This may account for the carapace that constricts much child abuse work
and the paralysis of the exploration and movement, so that creative practice
is frustrated.

The capacity to lend alternative perspectives is central to Paul Ricoeur's
concept of symbols (Ricoeur 1970). The power of the symbol to capture
several views of something, to face both inwards and outwards, both contains
the anxiety producing stimuli (injury, sexual cruelty, chaos) and is a response
to it.

The richness of the concept of justice as constructed by the participants
in my research interviews and as they described it in their practice was a
particular example of containing the powerful emotions evoked by sexual
abuse. Issues of reparation and punishment, the recognition of wrong doing,
the problems in recognizing the latter and responding to it, the risks of
abusing professional and statutory powers: these all contributed to a highly
elaborated and complex symbol that represented justice. An important
influence for me were the conceptions of justice worked out in Aeschylus's
Oresteia where the initial opposition of private vengeance and impersonal
justice become reconciled and mutually dependent. Euben notes that 'the
instinctive passions of the Furies invigorate dreams of ideality, equity and
balance' (Euben 1990). And so, in a reaction to the disorder and 'upside
down' perversity of, for example, sexual abuse, 'justice' serves as a symbol
that contains both the original impulse, and the attempt to transcend it. This
is evident in the conclusion to the Oresteia of Aeschylus where the newly
established justice contains and transmutes the avenging Furies into the
Eumenides (the 'Kindly Ones'), who nevertheless 'never cease to be the Furies
too' (Fagles 1977). Such justice as is available in professional responses to
child sexual abuse would seem to be better obtained from the creative
responses of the practitioners than from reified legal-administrative structures.

Conclusions

Empty thinking and symbols, hostile to creativity, constitute the domesticating narratives provided by simplistic ideas of empowerment and crude
distortions of feminist perspectives on child abuse, and invite the colonisation
of this particular part of the life-world by juridification. Juridification and
the other debased narratives that have come to determine child protection

interventions, are the antithesis of a truly communicative rationality which makes possible an ethical and creative practice.

References

Benjamin, J. (1988) *The Bonds of Love.* London: Virago.

Bion, W.R. (1987a) Development of Schizophrenic Thought in *Second Thoughts.* London: Heinemann/Karnac.

Bion, W.R. (1987b) Differentiation of the Psychotic from the Non-Psychotic Personalities in *Second Thoughts.* London: Heinemann/Karnac.

Bohm, D. (1980) *Wholeness and the Implicate Order.* London: Routledge and Kegan Paul.

Euben. J.P. (1990) *The Tragedy of Political Theory.* Princeton: Princeton University Press.

Fagles, R. (1977) Introduction to Aeschylus, *The Oresteia* (tr.Fagles). London: Penguin.

Felman, S. and Laub, D. (1992) *Testimony.* London: Routledge.

Habermas, J. (1981) *The Theory of Communicative Action,* Vol.2. Boston: Beacon Press.

Hadjiisky, E. (1987) On First Contact with Abuse and Neglect, *Journal of Social Work Practice.* November.

MacLeod, M. and Saraga, E. (1988) Challenging the Orthodoxy: Towards a Feminist Theory and Practice. *Feminist Review* No.28, January.

MacIntyre, A. (1985) *After Virtue. A study in Moral Theory.* London: Duckworth (2nd edition).

Main, T.F. (1957) The Ailment. *Medical Psychology* Vol.XXX, pt.3, pp.129–145.

Meltzer, D. (1986) *Studies in Extended Metapsychology.* Clinical Applications of Bion's Ideas. London: Clunie Press/Roland Harris Educational Trust.

Menzies, I.E.P. (1961) *The Functioning of Social Systems as a Defence against Anxiety.* Tavistock Pamphlet No.3. London: Tavistock. Reprinted (1970) London: Tavistock Institute of Human Relations.

Moustaki, E. (1981) A Discussion and Application of Terms. In S. Box, B. Copley, J. Magagna and E. Moustaki (eds) *Psychotherapy with Families, an Analytic Approach.* London: Routledge and Kegan Paul.

Ricoeur, P. (1970) *Freud and Philosophy. An Essay on Interpretation.* New Haven, London: Yale University Press.

Ziman, J. (1991) Shelflife. In *Times Higher Education Supplement* 6th December.

Part Three

Learning Processes and the
Learning Environment

Chapter 9

Who Cares if the Room is Cold? Practicalities, Projections and the Trainer's Authority

Lynette Hughes and Paul Pengelly

Introduction

No course which invites social workers to consider any aspect of their work can be free of the powerful impact of the organisational context which they bring with them. This is particularly true in the turbulent environment within which social workers today go about their tasks. A course which fails to address this impact – which fails to contain the anxiety and anger engendered and to challenge course members to consider their own involvement in the organisational dilemmas of which they complain – will also fail to help them to work more effectively, be they practitioners, supervisors or senior managers. In this chapter we shall argue that social workers' approach to details of course content, structure and process is constantly affected by their experience of the dynamic issues in their work places, and in particular by their attitude to the exercise of managerial authority. We shall further argue that it is only as far as trainers recognise themselves as 'managers' of all aspects of their courses, and in particular address the ways in which authority is used between trainers and participants, that they will enable effective learning to take place in a way that facilitates its transfer to the work setting.

In exploring the main points underlying our argument, we shall focus first on how course participants' assumptions about managerial authority may emerge on courses. We shall then concentrate on the tasks, responsibilities, and experiences of trainers as they 'manage' their courses. We shall illustrate our argument with material drawn from our experiences of running courses of various lengths and sizes, based both outside and inside employing agencies, making the alterations necessary to maintain confidentiality. We shall also describe briefly concepts which we have found helpful in our work as 'managers' of courses.

Training and the Work-place

Every trainer has experienced at one time or another the following contrasting reactions from course participants – on the one hand a course is idealised as a wonderful, protected ivory tower, in which members find relief from the demands of a non-understanding work-place; on the other, it is angrily criticised as useless because so removed from the realities of everyday work. For trainers faced with such extreme reactions, the powerful temptation is either to collude or to be furious.

We would argue that these dynamic issues of idealisation and denigration and the question of how to respond as a trainer are present in some form in most training courses, both in-house and external, not least because of the conflict in most of us between wanting to learn something new and the discomfort of having to question old assumptions. However, when idealising and denigrating are both presented as above in terms of the 'distance' between the course and work-place, the issue broadens into a key training question of how course learning can in reality be transferred from the learning context into the context of work (Whittington 1986).

This perennial training question has a new urgency in today's climate of rapid organisational and task changes. It lies at the heart of much recent debate about the relationship between social work managers and trainers in the planning and delivery of social work training. Many issues fuel this debate – concerns about unsafe practice (Department of Health 1992); the need to monitor staff training, ensuring that it is sufficient to fulfil specialist tasks (Department of Health 1991); the emphasis within a training continuum on assessing competencies in daily practice (CCETSW 1990, 1991, 1992) and the move towards a contract culture in welfare organisations. It is not our aim in this chapter to discuss the broad organisational, structural, political and academic issues involved, nor the importance of trainer/manager co-operation in planning training within organisations (Riches and Obibuaku 1993). Instead, we shall focus on how a trainer, face-to-face with course participants, may best use her or his authority to promote a learning that will prove relevant to day-to-day work in its organisational context.

Five Points

Five assumptions underlie our argument.

(1) Trainers are 'managers' of the courses they run, and effective training requires that this aspect of their role is seriously considered and utilised. The responsibilities of course 'managers' can be described in terms similar to those of work-based managers. They set tasks and define aims; evaluate outcome; manage technical and practical resources; relate aspirations to realities; select and allocate membership; manage time, place and confidentiality boundaries; clarify which decisions are open to negotiation and which are not; set rules for basic practice and take responsibility for deciding what to do when rules are found lacking or are broken.

(2) Current organisational issues are so pervasive in their impact on practice at all levels that they will be to the fore in participants' minds on any course they attend.

(3) With time and resources available for only the most urgent statutory work, social workers are increasingly preoccupied with issues of their own authority, and with the tension between its various sources – professional, statutory, agency and personal.

(4) The idea of partnership with service-users, embodied in the NHS and Community Care Act 1990 and the Children Act 1989, requires that social workers be empowered by their own training and management (Stevenson and Parsloe 1993). The way in which authority is viewed and used between people lies at the heart of the concept of partnership. Tunnard and Ryan's observation about partnership under the Children Act is equally relevant to staff empowerment:

> Partnership is not about equal power, but about people working together towards a common goal. It is about empowerment, about families having sufficient information to be able to understand and contribute to planning, and having some power to influence the outcome. (1991 p.67)

We would add that it also requires clear definitions of what is and is not negotiable.

(5) Course participants' anxieties, conflicts and satisfactions in their own organisations can become replicated in the temporary organisation of the course itself. In particular, trainers as the managers of courses will at times become the recipients of the powerful feelings and beliefs

which participants experience towards the role of management in their work setting.

The Trainer as Manager: Course Participants' Perceptions

The following two very different situations illustrate how issues of management and authority from the work setting may come alive in a course, regardless of the behaviour or action of the trainer. They parallel the ways in which managers in the workplace may be perceived and treated by staff according to their previous experience of figures in authority – idealised or denigrated, mistrusted or trusted, resisted or welcomed for the change they may bring. The illustrations suggest how the interactions that ensue on a course may be converted into a learning experience. We shall describe them in the first person and shall distinguish which of us is involved only when this is relevant to the issue under consideration.

Illustration A

It was the first day of a short course for first-line managers which I was running with an internal trainer as part of an agency's in-house training. Participants had initially shared their work experience of having no time to stop and think, of not being listened to by senior managers and of being left to 'carry the can'. The course was welcomed as a space where they could think and they worked hard.

The last session of the day was designed as an opportunity for participants to reflect on any issues about their work or the course that had emerged during the action-packed day. I led the session. It quickly felt awful. An uncomfortable silence prevailed, broken only by my repeating, on request, the explanation of the purpose of the session, some attempts by my co-trainer and myself to explore what was happening, and a few perfunctory responses. I felt useless and anxious, unable to say anything that made contact with the participants, and then I felt angry at them for withdrawing. The session ended with my fearing that the good experience of the earlier part of the day could be wiped out unless some shared understanding was reached of what had taken place. My co-trainer and I later discussed at length our similar responses and tried to understand what had gone wrong. For the rest of the evening my mind kept returning to this experience which had so got under my skin.

I began the next day by inviting comments on any unfinished business from the previous day, saying that my colleague and I had been left with a strong feeling of things left unsaid. The response was thoughtful and illuminating. The participants had talked together about the session as they had left the previous day, and some had resolved to raise the matter if we had not. They had all been extremely suspicious of the purpose of the session and had assumed that the stated open agenda concealed some manipulative purpose of my own, that I had a secret expectation of what they should reveal in the group which I was deliberately not revealing to them. My colleague was seen as acceding to my plans as I was leading the session. I was very taken aback by the power of their thoughts about me. They had also been struck, however, by their own passivity, by their failure to confront us in the session, reserving all discussion until afterwards. I now had to explain, and was believed, that we had had no such secret purpose. The question remained of how my colleague and I, who earlier in the day had been perceived as enabling, had so rapidly come to be seen as manipulative.

Gradually an understanding emerged, based on thinking about their initial comments on their work situation. We had been perceived in the way many of them had described their managers, unwilling to listen, withholding the real agenda from them and interested only in their 'carrying the can' in any difficult situation. Precisely when we had offered, in the last session of the day, the space they ostensibly wanted to think about work, it had been impossible to accept that we might be offering anything good and silence had seemed the only way of avoiding blame. One participant suddenly related this to his experience of departmental meetings, chaired by his line manager, where he and his peers never said what was really on their minds, but saved this for informal chats afterwards. Others quickly came in with similar experiences. In departmental meetings as in the group, it seemed, these first-line managers wiped out their own legitimate authority and instead attributed a persecuting manipulative power to the 'senior manager'. We discussed how this prevented them from experiencing any normal anxiety about asserting their authority and revealing their views in a 'space' that was unprotected by busy-ness. In the group, while they treated my colleague and myself as an all-powerful duo, they had ensured that we, not they, had the experience of anxiety, of being left to 'carry the can', and of fury.

A follow-up session some weeks later confirmed that for a number of participants this powerful experience of their attitude to authority had provided the most important learning of the course. An additional twist to the story emerged when my co-trainer mentioned in passing how the unstructured session had been so difficult that I had decided to end it thirty minutes early. The course members confirmed my belief that I had not done so. We considered what form discussion might have taken between the participants and their supervisees or supervisors had such a basic and unexpected conflict of perceptions occurred at work. We struggled ourselves to appreciate the powerful impact anxiety could have on perception and communication, understanding that my co-trainer had in effect attributed to me the way of managing the anxiety of the session that she herself would have preferred to employ.

Illustration B

As part of a large, college-based course, I ran a weekly work-discussion group for child care practitioners and managers from a variety of settings. All group members and I as facilitator were women. An emerging theme had been the struggle to explore difference (expressed in terms of race, gender and setting) in the face of a pull towards consensus and sameness. Some months into the course, participants mentioned in passing some criticisms about confusing aspects of recent course requirements, adding that the course director (also a woman) had a very difficult job and was clearly extremely busy.

I addressed supportively some of the queries raised and then found myself remembering that, in many of their work presentations, participants had complained angrily of the lack of understanding, clear leadership and emotional availability of their middle and senior managers, all of whom had been men. I drew attention to the difference in their attitude to perceived deficiencies in these male managers and the female 'senior manager' of the course. This prompted a lively acknowledgment by the participants of their annoyance about the course, and of their difficulty in expressing this anger towards a senior woman, particularly as she was seen as the victim of poor administration and of too much work arising from her emotional availability to her colleagues. The link to members' difficulties in ever perceiving women as the perpetrators or men as the victims in their work in the field of child sexual abuse was vividly made. The participants explored their own fear of being persecutory towards the female course director if they expressed their annoyance. Whatever the real differences between the functioning of the work-based managers and the course director, the experience highlighted participants' own part in creating their perception of their managers. By using the difference of gender as a way of avoiding their own difficult feelings, they had denied themselves their own legitimate, professional voice and had maintained themselves in a victim position.

In addition, it became clear that my own management role in the course was being denied. Albeit only a 'first-line manager' in relation to the course director, I was the representative of course management within the group. The participants preferred to externalise the bad aspects of authority on to the more distant director manager, protecting me from their anger by treating me as a supportive member of the group, who could be at one with them. The parallels with the relationship between social workers, team leaders and senior managers in their work settings were usefully explored.

Some Practical Concepts

The way we have presented both examples illustrates our use of certain theoretical ideas to help us in our training roles. We shall outline briefly our understanding of six concepts and consider their application to the two training situations described.

Open systems

In both illustrations, our interventions as trainers were clearly derived from the thought we tried to give to our experience of interacting with course participants. Our stance draws on the work of a tradition of group and organisational consultants (Bion 1961, Menzies Lyth 1989, Miller 1989) who developed ideas about the dual position of consultants in work-focused groups. The consultant is on the one hand part of the group and influenced by it, and on the other is outside it enough both to be able to use the experience to think about the functioning of the group and to maintain a 'cultivated ignorance' (Bain 1982) that allows a questioning of group assumptions. In relation to the theme of this chapter, it is relevant that mediating this tension between belonging and being outside the group is, of course, a major task of managers. In the illustrations, the pressure to join (illustration B) or be pushed right out (illustration A) was powerful.

This stance relates to an open systems formulation of organisational functioning (De Board 1978) which stresses the inter-relatedness of the individual, group, organisation and environment, with the management function being essentially management of issues at the boundaries between these. In the situations in illustrations A and B, this theoretical perspective helped us to be alert to the question of how the participants' functioning in the small training groups related to issues in the larger organisations, be the latter the whole course (illustration B) or their employing organisations (illustrations A and B). For the development of service-delivery at work and of learning on courses to take place, boundaries need to be permeable. However, in times of turbulent environmental change, there is a tendency for the boundary between various entities either to be obliterated (as in illustration A, where at one point no distinction could be made between the perception of trainers and of managers) or to become defensively rigid (as in illustration B, where there was a wish to keep the disturbing issues of difference out of the course and isolate them in the work-place).

Training triangles

We have also found it useful to adapt Mattinson's (1981) thinking about supervisory triangles to the training relationship. Just as in any two-way supervisor/supervisee relationship there are in fact three 'participants' whose interests require consideration – the supervisor (representing the agency requirements), the worker and the client/user, so any training event could be depicted as follows:

Trainer
(Standing for the primary task of running the training course in such a way as to fulfil the stated aims.)

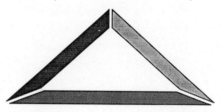

Participants
(Standing for individual learning needs, competencies and weak spots.)

Employing organisations and senior managers
(Standing for the competencies required for staff to do the work and for maintaining service-delivery during staff training.)

Figure 1 Training triangle

It is the trainer's responsibility to ensure that the three corners of the triangle are attended to. The fact of only two 'corners' usually being present in the training room exemplifies the difficulty of bearing all three in mind. The saying 'two's company, three's a crowd' has a special meaning in this context. Illustration B exemplifies Mattinson's point that it is the corner of the triangle causing most anxiety that is most likely to be left out, as shown by the wish to exclude from the rather cosy training relationship the anger felt towards senior managers at work. On the other hand, the training triangle will be deadly and not developmental if the trainer attempts to keep it rigidly 'equilateral', with equal attention carefully measured out to each corner and no one corner ever allowed more attention than the other two. For example, in illustration B, if I had not empathised strongly with the participants' struggles at work (the participants' corner) to the extent of running the risk at times of losing sight of the aims of the course (the trainer's corner), it is unlikely either that I would have been close enough to their concerns to have been able to bring in the relevant work-setting issues (employers' corner) on this occasion, or that my challenge to participants in doing so would have been listened to.

Reflection process

Mattinson's (1975) earlier observations on the appearance and usefulness of the reflection process in supervision can also apply to training. Both our illustrations provide examples of the way in which interactive dynamic issues which originated in the work-setting become replayed (reflected or mirrored) in the course interaction. Mattinson, elaborating on the work of Searles (1965), argues that in work with disturbed clients/users, particularly those who cannot tolerate experiencing their anxieties but try to expel them through action (as in child abuse), workers who allow themselves to get sufficiently emotionally close to their clients to be useful will inevitably, from time to time, find the difficult dynamics have so got under their skin that they too become caught up in the enactment and unable to think about what is happening. We would add that in these days of turbulent pressures within the organisations of welfare services, such dynamic issues and anxieties are as likely to originate from the organisation as from the client/user. The replaying of these dynamics in training or supervision may involve a pressure on the supervisor or trainer to join in, as, for example, in illustration B, when for a time the trainer joined in the cosy exclusion of negative feelings. Identifying such apparent malfunctioning in the training relationships provides a valuable tool for understanding the parallel malfunctioning in the work-based relationships. As a trainer, it is of course easier to recognise a reflection process operating in dynamic interactions which are uncomfortable or seen as being at odds with one's view of oneself. For example it was easier for the trainer to be alert to a mirroring dynamic when seen as negative and persecuting in illustration A than when regarded as supportive as in illustration B.

Victim/persecutor/rescuer triangle

The difficult dynamic issues most available for mirroring may differ according to the nature of the client/user group, profession or organisational structure (Furniss 1983, Will and Baird 1984, Woodhouse and Pengelly

1991), but we have been struck by the frequency with which, in these days of crisis statutory work and organisational change, the triangular dynamic of victim/persecutor/rescuer prevails (Karpman 1968). In both illustrations, for example, participants sought to preserve their victim role and attributed all hostile and potentially persecuting intent to others (the trainers in illustration A and the male managers in illustration B).

Projection and projective identification

Such processes of projection and projective identification are highly familiar and recognizable in their effects. These two closely-linked concepts refer to the mechanisms whereby vulnerable, hostile or otherwise difficult feelings may be disowned by an individual and attributed to another, by whom the feelings may then, as the result of the interaction, be experienced. The terms have received considerable attention and definition in psychoanalytic litera-ture (for example Klein 1946, Ogden 1979), but it is sufficient in this context to highlight two related and usually unconscious purposes of the processes involved. The first is to get rid of difficult feelings that cannot at that time be tolerated by attributing them to another. The second is to communicate the importance of these feelings by expelling them into another, in the inarticulate hope that this person will be able to struggle with the feelings in a way that can make them available for consideration in a more bearable form in the interaction between the people involved (Skynner 1964). In training courses both purposes require attention. In illustration A, for example, the participants, by their behaviour, projected into the trainer the powerful feelings of anxiety and hostility that they could not at that point acknowledge in themselves. By this indirect communication to the trainer of some of their core work issues, they provided the possibility that these issues might receive attention on the course, but the struggle for them and the trainer was to find a way of thinking about their experiences together rather than blindly continuing to enact their feelings (Britton 1981).

Containment

Bion (1962) used the term 'containment' to describe the active capacity, outlined above, to be open to a depth and range of feelings and experiences in interaction with others, to think about the meaning of these feelings and, usually, to find words to give shape to and communicate this understanding. While Bion develops the term specifically to describe the stance of a mother with a baby and of a therapist with a patient, his discussion of the role of a group consultant (Bion 1961) focuses on the same capacity for rigorous containment. The view of the trainer as providing such a containing function underpins the other ideas outlined here.

The Trainer as Manager: Tasks and Responsibilities

The test of the value of theoretical ideas to trainers is whether they help to provide a framework for tackling the most practical and common training tasks. Having earlier suggested ways in which course participants may project onto trainers aspects of their own attitudes to managerial authority, our purpose in this section is to explore the impact on participants of the ways in which trainers may attend to their inescapable managerial tasks and responsibilities. These will be discussed under three headings: providing practical resources; contracting, consulting and negotiating; confronting difficulties and valuing initiative.

Providing Practical Resources

Management is experienced most directly through the provision of practical facilities and resources. A significant indication of how managers of an organisation are viewed by staff is whether they are deemed to be concerned for the physical conditions of employees' work and to understand the effect physical conditions may have on the capacity of staff to work. Social workers on our courses increasingly refer to the considerable disruption to their work caused by such factors as inadequate interviewing rooms, changes of office or closure of canteens. Most trainers are well aware of the training equivalent of this, for example the effect of prompt and well-provided refreshments in promoting an atmosphere conducive to taking in and digesting new ideas. The following example about the availability of comfortable physical space highlights the relevance of such considerations to the management role of trainers.

Illustration C

Towards the end of a four-day course, in a plenary session aimed at reviewing the event, participants expressed for the first time their fury at the freezing temperature of the room where they had had their refreshments throughout. None of our staff group of three had gone into the room, the refreshment breaks being designated as staff meeting times.

We found it hard to listen to their protest. We felt we had struggled with a climate of complaint from the start of the course and that nothing would be experienced as satisfactory. Our initial, private, defensive reactions (we discovered later) were that if the room had been warm we would have been blamed for its being too hot. Fortunately, we managed to keep this to ourselves. Gradually, we let ourselves face the impact of our negligence in not checking that the room was comfortable, in not calling in during breaks to ensure all was well. Staff meetings during breaks had never previously prevented our doing so. Laying emphasis as we did on the importance of detail in any interaction, we felt ashamed. We acknowledged we were in the wrong and apologised, adding that, as a staff group, we would need to think hard about how we had acted so negligently. (In a later staff meeting, we realised how affected we were at the time by the current stresses in our own employing organisation. This had made us less open to engaging with the stresses of the course and had prompted our retreat into a small, safe, staff group).

The atmosphere lightened and we were then able to explore participants' responsibility for not raising this serious matter with us on the first day. It became clear that our absence and their suffering had served to confirm the deeply-felt belief of many, based on their perceptions of their work-places, that staff in senior managerial positions would care little for their well-being. We then pointed out that our current interest might be seen as challenging this assumption. In their interaction with us, the question of participants' contribution to their perception of their managers' continued neglect could not be ignored.

This interaction also highlighted three further points – that mistakes and bad practice are inevitable from time to time; that they can be a source of learning and development; and that acknowledgement of being in the wrong is an essential component of good management, not least because it contributes to the empowerment of staff by helping them to distinguish between, and acknowledge, their own strengths and weaknesses.

Contracting, Consulting and Negotiating

The dilemma about how much detail to distribute on paper and how far to rely on face-to-face interactions is as important to trainers as to managers. Too much paper may be ignored or viewed as an imposition; too little gives participants no real opportunity to consider their course application or prepare for an event. Written aims and expectations also need to be specific enough to provide a reference point against which the course may be evaluated. Additionally, the task of providing clear written information can help a trainer to clarify his or her thoughts and prompt exploration of the basis for certain decisions, for example whether membership is to be allocated by managers or open to individual, voluntary choice. Early contact with course participants, whether in writing or face-to-face, needs to clarify the respective responsibilities of trainers and participants, including defining any aspects of the programme which are intended to be open to negotiation. We would argue that empowerment requires knowing about the limits as well as the extent of the authority of one's role in an organisation.

Managers succeed or fail, however, by their attention to how plans and procedures are in reality translated into action. This managerial task of trainers lies at the heart of our argument, bearing directly on how the ideals of training may be related to the reality of work. The issue is frequently posed for trainers in the struggle to decide whether to stick to an established course programme or to change plans in the face of the reaction of participants. As resources of time and staff skills are always limited, and as considerable hope, commitment and thought have usually gone into planning a programme, pressure by participants to change a course structure or content, or criticism of either, is never easy to manage, especially as most trainers like to feel their courses are valued by participants. The temptation is to react in one of two ways.

First, it is tempting to stick rigidly to the programme. A course structure, intended to provide a containing and enabling framework, may thus be used defensively instead, in order to avoid the anxiety and uncertainty of thinking about participants' views, in much the same way as procedures and guidelines in health and welfare agencies may be mechanically applied to avoid grappling with the powerful complexity of the work (Menzies Lyth 1959). In this way, in illustration C regarding the cold room, we had used our staff meeting defensively to avoid thought and contact and not, as intended, to develop our capacities. Similarly, any training technique may become rigidified as an end in itself rather than used as a means to learning. For example, ground rules worked out with participants may be treated as a panacea rather than merely a reminder of the areas that will continue to need to be struggled with. Similarly the useful technique of keeping out chairs as an important reminder of absent participants may be rigidly adhered to without consideration of the impact on the learning of those present.

The second temptation is to give in to suggestions and criticisms to avoid a possible confrontation, in the mistaken belief, not only that total agreement can be reached, but that it is a goal to be aimed for. In such contexts, altering a programme may be a flight into the panacea of reorganisation when what is needed is consistent management that can provide a continuity of purpose in the face of difficulties in applying plans. However, the decision whether to change or continue is never easy. In all our illustrations, had time not been taken to address the powerful dynamic issues operating, they would have prevented continued learning taking place, but the time given to such discussion was often at the expense of time allocated to other topics.

Criticisms about the way in which a course addresses anti-racist and anti-discriminatory practice, with suggestions for change during the course, are in our experience particularly difficult to address openly so as to arrive at a thoughtful decision about how to proceed (Brummer and Simmonds 1992). The reasons are not surprising. Criticisms in this area hit at the basis of our professional and personal identity, where despite our best efforts most of us are conscious of our need for continuing development. Such criticisms are also therefore readily available for misuse as vehicles for expressing a range of grievances about the use of authority and power. It is also an area especially prone to defensive certainties or fears of disagreeing, where real difference in all its complexity is difficult to explore (as, to some extent, over gender in illustration B) and it is easier to become paralysed in the fixed position of victim, persecutor or rescuer than to struggle with the mixed feelings and responsibilities involved (Baldwin, Johansen and Seale 1990 p.30).

In all the situations raised in this section, we would argue that the question is rarely one of making the right decision, but rather of trying as honestly and openly as possible to explore with participants the basis on which to make a decision amid uncertainty, then to make the decision and to live with the pros and cons of the consequences. This requires the trainer not only to struggle to listen to what is said, however uncomfortable, note the communication in the behaviour of participants and be attentive to the practical realities, but also to give attention to his or her own feelings and experiences which may give clues to what has been left unsaid. All our illustrations highlight the emergence of a discrepancy either between what was said and what was done and experienced or between what was said at different times. In illustration A, for example, participants longed for space but could not use it; they experienced the trainers as enabling then manipulative, and the course was perceived as being different from work but then suddenly the same. In illustration C, the contradictions lay between our words and our actions regarding the cold room and between participants' assumption that we did not care and our actual responses to being told about the room. The 'cognitive dissonance' between staff emotions and beliefs and their pre-scribed tasks and behaviour, which Schorr (1992) describes vividly as 'a source of malaise and disempowerment in the personal social services, largely unattended to especially by senior managers', seems a highly relevant parallel.

Confronting Difficulties and Valuing Initiative

All course participants carry some responsibility for confronting the difficult behaviour of a fellow participant, but clearly the trainer carries prime responsibility and, like the manager in the work-place, provides a model of empowerment for staff. Most of our illustrations convey the trainer's struggle to combine acknowledging participants' efforts, anxieties or achievements in difficult situations with challenging them about their assumptions, mistakes and their own contribution to their difficulties. In this, the trainer's role as manager is crucial to participants' own struggle to combine the care and control functions of their roles. The pressure in such situations to be either authoritarian (as in illustration C) or collusive (as in illustration B) is familiar to most social workers. While at times it may be necessary to confront a participant in order to put an end to behaviour which clearly interferes with the learning of others, at other times a trainer may have difficulty in distinguishing between such disruptive behaviour and the legitimate challenge posed to the trainer's own comfortable assumptions by creative, independent thinkers. Whatever the context, the constant purpose of challenge is to enable participants to take more responsibility for their own actions and thoughts.

For example, on many courses trainers have to decide how to deal with participants' late arrival for sessions. We refer particularly to repeated lateness after refreshment breaks by all or most participants, when punctuality has been defined as a ground rule of the course. The meaning of this behaviour will clearly vary, but trainers who continue to turn a blind eye to lateness do so at the expense of course members' learning. A decision has to be made about whether to take over the responsibility being denied by participants for implementing the course rules, for example by chasing them up and reminding them of the rules, or whether to draw the situation to the attention of participants and explore with them their experience of lateness and breach of rules both on the course and in their work.

In a number of our illustrations, the task of the trainer became one of questioning participants' perception of themselves as the victims of persecutory or neglectful management. In our experience, participants, particularly if they are first-line or middle managers, are likely at some point to present themselves in a way similar to that described in a recent exploration of the future of the personal social services: 'I heard managers say "management should communicate", reflecting a traditional failure to see themselves as part of the section of management that needs to communicate' (Harding 1992 p.47). Practitioners and managers seem to attribute the problem mainly to whoever is one step above them in their pecking order. A principal task of the trainer then becomes challenging participants to reconsider their self-defined role as innocent victims of a persecutory management. By refusing either to collude with their perspective (to rescue them) or blame them (to persecute them), the trainer's activity then seeks to empower by challenging participants' passivity.

A brief example will illustrate further the link between challenge and empowerment.

Illustration D

In the weeks between two parts of a course, experienced participants had been given material to read so that the next session on theoretical concepts would take the form of discussion rather than input. The session felt flat and uninspired. I felt useless in my failed attempts to generate a lively discussion and became increasingly active, giving more and more theoretical input. It was only during the subsequent break that I was able to wonder whether my frantic activity and sense of failure had been my attempt to avoid exploring with these experienced workers the reason for their silence, for fear of exposing them in some way. I remembered that most of their presentations of their own supervisory work had been about how to challenge the practice of experienced staff. When I was later able to share with them my observations about my own behaviour and my questions about their part in it, the participants were able to acknowledge their sense of failure and shame at not having prepared adequately and at not being familiar with the theoretical ideas. From this point, a more lively exploration of the theoretical ideas began to take place, and participants were surprised at how well they in fact understood them. It was clear that acknowledging their sense of failure had freed them, and myself, to discover the strengths they had. More specifically, our shared experience allowed us to think more deeply about the difficulties they encountered in confronting their own ostensibly experienced staff.

Conclusion: Taking Authority for Learning

We have attempted in this chapter to consider the interaction between the trainer's inescapable managerial role and the way in which she or he will be perceived as 'manager' by course participants. We have not attempted to explore all the variable factors which affect the experience of managing a course, such as the nature of the content, structure and overall methods, the number of trainers and their relationship, and whether or not the course participants know each other or work in the same organisation. Whatever the conditions, however, attempting to grapple with the management issues of running a course can be a painful, powerful and exhausting experience, and will need at some point to be so if the course is to be rewarding or useful. Experiences of omnipotence and powerlessness follow each other in rapid succession and it is hard to know what is 'good enough'. Maintaining a 'managerial' stance confirms the trainer in a separate, isolated role, not relying on the gratitude or friendship of the participants for her/his own gratification, but the trainer also needs to be involved closely enough with the participants to respond to their needs. This, of course, is a reminder of the difficult role of managers at all levels.

Trainers' capacity to maintain a thinking and containing stance in such a role will depend on a number of factors, not least their own attitude to managerial authority, bearing in mind that many trainers have chosen a training career path as an alternative to continuing in the managerial hierarachy. As with managers, the influence of their own work setting is crucial in determining what energy and mental space they have available to consider thoughtfully their own use of authority. Serious turbulence in their own work environment will limit their capacity to attend responsibly to the needs, discomforts and criticisms of course participants (as was seen in our failure to attend to the cold room). The availability of practical help and adequate resources for trainers (for example in providing refreshments, flip charts, putting out chairs, etc.) will also significantly influence their capacity to take seriously the needs of participants. Finally, trainers need to ensure sufficient time for their own thinking. Timetabling of staff meetings, both before and during courses, needs to have as much priority as fixing training dates. While to arrange staff meetings during course refreshment breaks may be experienced by some participants as excluding, explaining the need for such meetings may provide a model of legitimising professional thinking time and self-care, and may also question views of management as being omnipotent or negligent.

Trainers need to give considerable thought to what backing they need to enable them to face the full extent of their managerial authority and of the potential impact of this on the functioning of participants. The more they know about their own authority, the less are they likely either to deny it and collude with participants in avoiding powerful learning experiences or to wield it unthinkingly and impose rigid, unresponsive courses. Our argument has been that the more open trainers are about the extent and limits of their own authority, the more open they can be to the professional and personal authority of course participants.

Staff who learn on courses to take more responsibility for their successes, weaknesses, actions and feelings, and to relate their course functioning to their work context, are in fact developing competencies that are readily available for transfer to their work-settings. At worst, staff thus empowered may offer a challenge too threatening to be coped with by an unempowered organisation and management structure (Menzies Lyth 1959, Stevenson and Parsloe 1993). At best, they can become a stimulating and thoughtful resource for their agencies.

References

Bain, A. (1982) *The Baric Experiment: The Design of Jobs and Organisations for the Expression and Growth of Human Capacity.* Tavistock Institute of Human Relations. Occasional paper No. 4. London: Tavistock.

Baldwin, N. Johansen, P. and Seale, A. (on behalf of the Black and White Alliance) (1990) *Race in Child Protection: A Code of Practice.* London: Race Equality Unit: National Institute for Social Work.

Bion, W. (1961) *Experiences in Groups and Other Papers.* London: Tavistock Publications.

Bion, W. (1962) A theory of thinking. *International Journal of Psycho-Analysis* Vol.43. (Reprinted in *Second Thoughts* (1984). London: Karnac Books).

de Board, R. (1978) Human behaviour and general systems theory. In *The Psychoanalysis of Organisations.* London: Tavistock Publications.

Britton, R. (1981) Re-enactment as an unwitting professional response to family dynamics. In S. Box, B. Copley, J. Magagna and E.Moustaki (eds) *Psychotherapy with Families.* London: Routledge and Kegan Paul.

Brummer, N. and Simmonds, J. (1992) Race and culture: the management of 'difference' in the learning group. *Social Work Education* Vol.11, 1, 54–64.

CCETSW (1990) *Paper 29: Requirements for Approval of Assessment Centres and Award of Qualifications by CCETSW.* London: CCETSW.

CCETSW (1991) *Paper 30: Rules and Requirements for the Diploma in Social Work (revised edition).* London: CCETSW.

CCETSW (1992) *Paper 31: The Requirements for Post-Qualifying Education and Training in the Personal Social Services: A Framework for Continuing Professional Development (revised edition).* London: CCETSW.

Department of Health (1991) *Working with Child Sexual Abuse: Guidelines for Trainers and Managers in Social Services Departments.* London: H.M.S.O.

Department of Health (1992) *Choosing with Care: Report of the Committee of Inquiry into the Selection, Development and Management of Staff in Children's Homes.* (Warner Report). London: HMSO.

Furniss, T. (1983) Mutual influence and interlocking professional-family process in the treatment of child sexual abuse and incest. *Child Abuse and Neglect* Vol.7, 207–223.

Harding, T. (ed) (1992) *Who Owns Welfare? Questions on the Social Services Agenda.* Social Services Policy Forum Paper II. London: National Institute for Social Work.

Karpman, S. (1968) Fairy tales and script drama analysis. *Transactional Analysis Bulletin, 26*, 39–44.

Klein, M. (1946) Notes on some schizoid mechanisms. *International Journal of Psycho-Analysis* Vol.27, 99–110. Reprinted in *The Writings of Melanie Klein* Vol.3. (1975). London: Hogarth Press.

Mattinson, J. (1975. 2nd edition 1992) *The Reflection Process in Casework Supervision.* London: Tavistock Institute of Marital Studies.

Mattinson, J. (1981) The deadly equal triangle. In *Change and Renewal in Psychodymanic Social Work: British and American Developments in Practice and Education for Services to Children and Families.* Massachusetts and London: Smith College School of Social Work/Group for the Advancement of Psychotherapy in Social Work.

Menzies Lyth, I. (1959) The functioning of social systems as a defence against anxiety. In *Containing Anxiety in Institutions: Selected Essays* Vol. 1. (1988). London: Free Association Books.

Menzies Lyth, I. (1989) A psychoanalytic perspective on social institutions. In *The Dynamics of the Social: Selected Essays* Vol. II. London: Free Association Books.

Miller, E.J. (1989) *The 'Leicester' Model: Experiential Study of Group and Organisational Processes.* Tavistock Institute of Human Relations. Occasional Paper No. 10. London: Tavistock.

Ogden, T.H. (1979) On projective identification. *International Journal of Psycho-Analysis.* Vol.60, 357–373.

Riches, P. and Obibuaku, O. (1993) Mind your Step. *Community Care,* 9th September.

Schorr, A.L. (1992) *The Personal Social Services: An Outside View.* York: Joseph Rowntree Foundation.

Searles, H.F. (1965) The informational value of the supervisor's emotional experience. In *Collected Papers on Schizophrenia and Related Subjects.* London: The Hogarth Press and the Institute of Psycho-Analysis.

Skynner, A.C.R. (1964) Group analytic themes in training and case-discussion groups. In J. Schlapobersky (ed) (1989) *Institutes and How to Survive Them.* London: Methuen.

Stevenson, O. and Parsloe, P. (1993) *Community Care and Empowerment.* York: Joseph Rowntree Foundation in association with Community Care.

Tunnard, J. and Ryan, M. (1991) What does the Children Act mean for family members? *Children and Society* Vol.5, 67–75.

Whittington, C. (1986) Literature review: transfer of learning in social work education. *British Journal of Social Work* Vol.16, 571–577.

Will, D. and Baird D. (1984) An integrated approach to dysfunction in interprofessional systems. *Journal of Family Therapy* Vol.6, 275–90.

Woodhouse, D. and Pengelly, P. (1991) *Anxiety and the Dynamics of Collaboration.* Aberdeen: Aberdeen University Press.

Chapter 10

Learning through Supervision
A Systemic Approach

Judy Hildebrand

Introduction

This chapter describes my thinking and practice as a supervisor in family therapy working from a systemic perspective. The material is based on personal experience of supervising groups of postgraduate trainees from a variety of disciplines on Advanced Clinical and MSc. Family Therapy Training courses (Byng-Hall and Whiffen 1982). Throughout supervision I take into account the interrelationships between supervisor and trainees, between the trainees themselves and between trainees and the families they work with. In addition, supervisors and trainees need to recognise the effects on them of their family of origin, their current relationships, their professional context, and not least of the training itself (Aponte and Winter 1987). In this chapter, the emphasis is on the effect of these interrelationships on the trainees' learning and their approach to therapy, as manifested in the supervision group, rather than on the process of therapy itself (Liddle, Breunlin and Schwartz 1988).

> The supervision group comprises three to four trainees and their supervisor. During academic terms, they meet for four hours per week over a period of two years in order to concentrate on clinical practice. During this period they will be expected to provide therapy for families and to take part in skills training and discussion. Supervised clinical practice is one of the major components of an integrated family therapy course which also includes theoretical input and research modules leading to accreditation as family therapists, and a diploma in teaching Family Therapy.

My aim in supervision is to create a containing, enjoyable and stimulating context in which trainees learn to become good family therapists. I encourage them to link theory and practice, to experiment with new techniques, and to question their assumptions. Since they work with families who come from many different cultures, who have different belief systems, and who are at different points in their life cycle, it is essential that trainees learn to recognise both their strengths and their limitations in terms of their own personal and professional experience. It can take time to learn how to use this awareness constructively. People are often surprised to discover that even what they do not know can be used positively in therapy.

> A young trainee used her inexperience to stressed parents of a new baby and an 18-month-old. 'I can't imagine what it's like never to know when you are going to get a good night's sleep again; how do you manage so well?'

Despite their experience and wider knowledge of the field, supervisors are also inevitably subject to their own limitations. Indeed, a major drawback for supervisors in family therapy is that to date very few have actually had any formal training for this role.

Systemic Supervision

The use of technology

In many forms of social work and psychotherapy, traditional methods of supervision have relied on the retrospective and subjective presentation of an interview by the trainee. In contrast, family therapist trainees have always been supervised 'live' during actual interviews with their clients. Either a supervisor sits in on the interview, or one member of the supervision group becomes the family's therapist, whilst the remaining trainees and supervisor act as her team behind a one-way mirror. This 'barrier' was intended to help the team be more objective and less emotionally involved.

In the early days many family therapists used this procedure rigidly. The team seated behind the one-way mirror remained enigmatic, unseen and unheard. It is now usual for clients to be offered an opportunity to meet the team; it is interesting that when they do wish to do so, they nearly always opt to do this at the end rather than at the beginning of the session. This more open approach is consistent with the movement towards open access policies in both social work and family therapy. It is to be hoped that it is also indicative of a lessening of the 'them' and 'us' approach, and a realisation that most of our clients are struggling with issues which can affect us all. For ethical, practical and therapeutic purposes, we need to work together openly (Andersen 1987).

The use of video equipment has led to further openness, and to an opportunity for more precise observation and learning in supervision. There are unexpected bonuses in supervising families 'live' rather than hearing a posthoc report.

> For example, you can observe at first hand how anxious trainees can use time-honoured, delaying tactics just as a family is about to arrive. There is the sudden dash to the lavatory, the sudden realisation that they have not adequately prepared the room for children, tapes have gone missing or the video will not work. Sometimes, even the supervisor unwittingly colludes in the delay by getting involved in a literally diverting discussion just before a session.

Video also makes it possible for trainees and supervisor alike to analyse the detail of what actually occurs in an interview without relying on subjective recall. The use of the video is explained to clients at the beginning of the interview: if the video is vetoed by them, the interview is continued without it. In the very rare event of clients also refusing to be viewed by the team, via the one-way mirror, other arrangements are made. This usually involves a second member of the team joining the therapist in the room with the family, not as a co-therapist but as an observer who will then consult with the therapist. Video can be a powerful teaching tool:

> At the end of an interview we were videoing a trainee as she repeatedly ran in and out of the room to get the diary, to check a date with the team behind the one-way mirror, and to discuss a proposed intervention with her supervisor. Once the somewhat bewildered clients had left I replayed this video sequence on fast forward which proved hilarious.

This demonstrates the way in which video itself can be humorously and spontaneously used to make an important teaching point by intensification, repetition and by dramatising a situation.

In reviewing videotapes I often stop the tape and ask the team to consider a variety of alternative approaches the therapist could have made. This encourages them to think more widely and to learn that there is more than one way of tackling an issue in therapy. Sometimes clients watch extracts of their sessions on video, which demonstrate their patterns of communication. This can have a very powerful impact indeed. An additional use of video is for a trainee therapist to review the first session on videotape, before embarking on their last meeting with the family. This process often demonstrates the considerable changes clients have made during the therapy, thus confirming them and their therapist. Where little change is discernible this information itself can become the focus of the final session. Technology also allows supervisors to communicate with trainees or to give instructions during a session by the use of an ear-bug or telephone. The ear-bug is a device like a hearing-aid which is worn by the therapist; it is wired to the observation room, and can be used by the supervisor without being over-heard by the client. Its use is always discussed with the family. It can be especially useful in the early stages of therapy when trainees may feel out of their depth and need immediate help. A supervisor can use the ear-bug to provide immediate information, for example she may have noticed that the therapist is ignoring the children or has not spotted a particular piece of interaction between family members.

> I telephoned in with an instruction that the trainee did not like; instead of saying so directly or taking a break to discuss it, she kept saying it was not clear or she could not hear. I got more and more frustrated and must have raised my voice because finally the client turned to the therapist and said 'I think you'd better do what she says!'

Sometimes technology can be inappropriately used:

> A trainee pointed out that in my enthusiasm to be helpful via the ear-bug 'comments came so thick and fast it was hard to do any thinking of my own! I think it is important for the bug to be a word in the ear rather than a cartridge in the brain!'

The main disadvantage of using technology is that it makes some clients feel embarrassed, exposed and inhibited. As a supervisor I remain concerned about the potentially intrusive nature of the one-way mirror, the video, the ear-bug and indeed the team itself. However, overall the use of these methods has undoubtedly improved the quality of supervision and the speed of learning; video recordings provide accurate data about the therapist, the family and their interactions during the session. In my experience, the vast majority of clients do adapt to the technology, and while they do not necessarily forget about it, it seems to become less significant and intrusive over time. However, we need research to support our assumptions and experiences as to the general efficacy of our methods.

The Supervision Group

Preparation

I have now trained many family therapy supervision groups and each has been quite different because of the unique combination of personalities, and the personal and professional experience of its members. Whilst there may be some constant factors due to both my style and method of supervision and to the demands of the course, the pace, the timing of introducing new ideas and the interplay between us all is never the same. The dynamic, the interactions and the use of feedback are inevitably idiosyncratic, the whole being greater than the sum of its parts. Nonetheless, despite these differences, there are issues that regularly come up in these groups. Trainees worry about whether their supervisor will be sympathetic to their individual concerns, whether they can cope with their own anxiety about being observed when seeing families, about the quality of their work in comparison to that of their peers on the course. During the first two to three weeks, I therefore concentrate on reducing the general anxiety level by clarifying my expectations of the group and by eliciting their expectations of me, by presenting the 'ground rules', and by providing an atmosphere and context in which we can get to know each other.

Ground rules

These must be established from the start and include: an acknowledgement of my accountability to the course and responsibility for the supervision group; the responsibility of each trainee for her or his active involvement in the group, in sharing ideas and expertise, and seeing a required number of cases; issues of confidentiality; constructive rather than negative framing of comments about other trainees' performance; punctuality, and timing of sessions; the use of language including psychiatric labels; and checking assumptions about what clients mean or may have understood.

Genograms

To hasten the process of getting to know each other, each trainee is asked to draw up a family tree or genogram within the first few weeks of supervision, prior to any families being seen. I am particularly curious about how their history and current situation may affect trainees' clinical work and how they can use the group as a learning context (Heinl 1987, Lieberman 1979). This exercise also indicates how much insight and awareness they have of their own situation and whether they can think systemically and make links between their private and professional worlds (McDaniel and Landau-Stanton 1991). Having to do this task also encourages them to think about how their clients might experience exposing themselves in this way in therapy. Useful information about how to help trainees learn is often uncovered during open discussions about the genograms, when I might ask: 'What kind of feedback did your family of origin give you?' 'What helps or hinders you from considering new ideas?'

Moving Into the Work

Having become a coherent group and learnt the ground rules, the trainees are now ready to start the clinical work. From approximately the third or fourth week of the first term, they start interviewing clients, with the supervisor and the rest of the group behind the one-way mirror forming the 'team'. Trainees take on two cases each and for the rest of the time act as a member of the supervision team. All new cases are discussed during the supervision slot and I attempt to match complexity of cases with the experience of the trainees. During the course I want them to have worked with a variety of family structures and generations, and with a number of different cultures and ethnic groups. Throughout their clinical practice they are expected to maintain an awareness of the relevance of gender and of life-cycle stages, and to recognise connections between symptomatology and other aspects of family life.

Behind the One-way Mirror: Interventions in the Interview

Most supervisors experience a tension between intervening in the therapy session, and giving trainees sufficient time to settle down, get used to being observed, and work at their own pace. This is not surprising given that the supervisor has two interdependent tasks: first, to supervise the actual therapy, for which she is ultimately responsible and, second, to train the therapist.

During the session most supervisors comment on what they observe and some make further teaching points to the team sitting behind the one-way mirror observing the session. These will be integrated into the discussion held during the break when the therapist comes out, or be considered further at the end of the session. In the early stages of training I would expect the less experienced trainee to carry out my interventions promptly during sessions; towards the end of the training; however, I give the trainee the benefit of the doubt as to the timing and manner in which this is done.

It is important to discuss the way in which supervisory feedback will be given to the trainee during the break. First and foremost the trainee needs to talk about her experience in the room with the family and to ask for the kind of help she wants. The team usually want to give their opinions too, so it can become a juggling act between the needs of the trainee, the enthusiasm of the group, and above all trying to discern in a short time what would be most helpful to the clients. A trainee may experience pressure from both the family and the team, and it is not helpful during the break to float too many ideas about how to proceed lest the trainee get swamped and lose confidence and direction. Therefore, once we have agreed on the direction and method of therapy to be used, we summarise the main points succinctly and the therapist writes them on the board. This is a way of checking that she has understood the ideas which have been reinforced through repetition. I often suggest that the trainee then goes out for a minute or two to digest the ideas before resuming the interview. A fuller discussion takes place after the session has ended. During these post-session discussions I often discover gaps in the trainees' repertoire of skills and confusion about certain therapeutic approaches: if there is insufficient time to explore ideas and practice techniques immediately, a space is reserved for this during a future supervision slot. Supervisors should avoid becoming over helpful by doing too much of the work for the trainee, that is by too frequently sending in instructions and thereby reducing her confidence as a therapist and eventually disabling her. Some supervisors get seduced by their own sense of urgency, fearing that the therapy will only proceed properly if trainees work at a particular pace and in the particular style or model that the supervisors themselves favour. This can sometimes lead to the supervisor actually going into the interview and, in my view, all too often undermining the trainee and confusing the family. Supervisors should resist the temptation to take over the role of therapist and instead find other methods of helping the trainee to help the family (Jenkins, Hildebrand and Lask 1982).

Supervisors should vary their style according to the experience and confidence of the trainee in the room; so sometimes I am challenging and give a punchy directive or comment: 'Just look at how you are both sitting!' This was to a male therapist whose body language was as inappropriately intimate as the client's. On another occasion, when it was not clear what direction an inexperienced trainee was following, I made a suggestion and added the rider, 'if it is useful'. I encourage groups to think laterally and to voice their 'crazy associations' since these associations very often act as a positive trigger for a good intervention.

> An 8-year-old twin boy in a newly separated family took on the grandfather role and was constantly taking charge of what needed to be done and telling the parents how to manage, including deciding

which school his much older brother should go to. A trainee expressed concern about this heavy load of worry, and suggested 'what he needs is a set of worry beads'. To our mutual astonishment, another trainee produced some and these were then given to whichever family member was carrying the worry load at any one time. When the parents became aware of what was happening they insisted on having their fair share. The 8-year-old hesitated and then handed the beads over to his father and started to play more age-appropriately with his twin brother.

Group Training

The trainee group

In the early stages of training the team members observe each other in the role of trainee therapist; I listen both to their comments and to their responses to mine, in order to gauge their level of clinical experience and sophistication. I give them time to see how I work and assign specific observational tasks. I might suggest that they focus on one aspect of the therapy such as the patterns of communication between family members, or the congruence between what the family says and their effect. As they become more confident, I introduce more for them to focus on, such as the difference between the content and the process of a session, or the way in which family and therapist respond to each other. Still later, I encourage each trainee therapist to ask the group for help with a specific concept, situation or technique, which they find difficult to manage. In this way they take on more responsibility for their own practice.

> One trainee asked the group to keep a note of opportunities she missed to address the whole family, rather than just talking to the adults. She then reviewed the videotape of the session and looked for the specific examples of those missed opportunities.

Finally, in the last two terms I expect the team to be thinking about how they would manage the supervisor's role. When they come up with good ideas, and are able to express them succinctly, they are asked to deliver interventions directly to the trainee therapist during the session. During the last two months of their training they act as supervisors to each other and I take on the role of consultant to the supervisor. I often experience a similar tension to that mentioned previously, that is between giving the novice supervisor the opportunity to learn from experience – the training task –

and my wish to ensure that the trainee therapist provides as good a service to the clients as possible – the clinical task.

The supervisor's idiosyncrasies

Trainees are reminded to respond to each family's 'culture' and mood rather than imposing a ponderously serious attitude which they often identify as 'being professional'; we can be respectful to clients and still allow for humour and a timely lightness of touch. As group members become more experienced and confident I feel freer to express and use ideas and phantasies that come to mind, and to introduce other, different theoretical hypotheses to compare and contrast with the systems approach.

As a supervisor I make my trainees work very hard; as one put it,

> We were pushed to take risks, to extend our repertoire, to try something different. I valued this 'pushing' as I realised that given half a chance, I would sit back and coast…

My task is to help trainees develop their understanding and their skill. In this context, I define the latter as the art of applying techniques appropriately. Part of this process means challenging them on issues they avoid, as they challenge the families they work with. In some cases, avoidance may be due to a lack of knowledge, or a phantasy of ignorance, or plain inhibition.

> In one case, a trainee complained that although he was sure sexuality was a relevant issue, the couple refused to discuss it at all. The wife persisted with a request for separate bedrooms and raised the possibility of eventual separation, whilst her husband wanted to carry on as a married couple. The couple resolutely spent the whole session discussing whether or not to invest in a deep freeze or a microwave oven, resisting many attempts at deflection by the therapist, who thought they were avoiding the issue.

This example drew my attention to the fact that most family therapy trainees were avoiding both direct and metaphoric discussion of sexual material; I therefore arranged a teaching seminar and a session in which they could practice discussing sexual matters. The former proved less useful than the latter, suggesting that the avoidance had more to do with personal inhibition than a lack of knowledge. Another example demonstrates the need to 'push' a trainee through a personal barrier.

> A 35-year-old male trainee was talking to a woman of about 70 about the imminent death of her husband. This couple had survived the second world war in prison camps far from each other and had then

been reunited and been together for 40 years. During the interview break the trainee steadfastly avoided any discussion of impending death and loss just as he had in the interview. I finally suggested that he, rather than the client, was side-stepping the real issues. He then said that perhaps that was because his grandfather had died twelve minutes ago. He 'meant', of course, twelve years ago; this slip of the tongue was enough to explain his avoidance of a painful connection.

It may take some time to discover what triggers powerful emotional responses in a particular trainee. The effect of a trigger situation is that the trainee can neither think clearly during the session nor maintain a reasonably objective position, because the issues the family present are too much like their own (McGoldrick and Gerson 1985).

Where a trainee finds it difficult to empathise with certain people I ask the team to role-play the family with the trainee taking the part of the person he or she has found most difficult.

A young therapist had over-identified with a difficult teenager and her wishes. He became increasingly impatient with what he described as her parents' 'inept' efforts to stop their daughter running away and not going to school. He seemed out of touch with their desperation and fears until he role-played each parent in turn. He was then able to appreciate the parents' mixed feelings and sense of powerlessness.

This experience helped the trainee to appreciate the complexity of each individual's feelings and the complicated interactions within the family system and the wider network. From time to time we all get caught up in a family's dynamics. We may stereotype people, make assumptions or be prejudiced. I try to encourage trainees to look at their various biases by being frank about mine, and then move on to discuss how this can affect our work with clients.

One trainee was terrified of working with a couple, both of whom had announced themselves at the point of referral as having Ph.D.s. She had assumed that they would be able to manage their own emotional issues and that she would be proven useless. In fact she met two anxious, caring parents who needed support and wanted advice. Incidentally this trainee herself had four degrees!

This combination of challenging and encouraging trainees to improve their self-awareness in order to raise the level of their clinical practice is typical of my style of supervision. It is also syntonic with the way I teach and do therapy. As a result the trainees learn both through content and the process of supervision.

Issues within the Group

Groups or individual supervision

In my experience, working with a group of trainees and supervising them on a systemic approach to therapy has many advantages over individual supervision. Three to four trainees in a group provide a variety of different ideas, share their different personal and professional experiences, and create a very rich and complex resource. It is also much easier to challenge one's supervisor from within the safety of a group. But there are also drawbacks such as competition for the supervisor's attention and approval. Generally I deal with this by looking at how this affects the clinical work: by bringing the matter into the open, often with humour; and by not concentrating on one trainee or making personal interpretations.

> One trainee complained that I intervened more often during his interviews. Initially I was unsure whether to focus on the significance of this in relation to his position in the group, or in his family of origin, or on the clinical issue itself. I decided to focus on his work with the family and using a positive reframe pointed out that as he was experienced in such cases, he could grasp the thinking behind my interventions and therefore apply them promptly. This helped the whole group to take a more positive view about my interruptions. The issue of what could be termed sibling rivalry was ignored until further similar incidents occurred when I joked about it in the group.

Each supervisor is bound to have some trainees whom they experience as difficult to teach.

> In one instance, I initially shied away from actively supervising a trainee whose famous intellectual family background had already made quite an impact on the course staff and I erroneously credited him with an equally daunting standard of clinical expertise.

Instead of trying to avoid the issue, it would have been more productive to encourage the group of trainees to discuss their differing experience and the strengths which they each brought to the course. Tensions in our own personal and professional relationships have to be constantly kept in mind and linked with our personal history. In the example above it is clear that I have higher expectations of men's intellectual prowess than may always be reasonable. In several instances mature women trainees have also underesti-mated their life and work experience and have deferred to their much younger male counterparts because of the latter's academic achievements. Some women need permission to be clever. As time goes on I would expect a group to acknowledge, indeed to welcome differences, to be less competi-tive, and to be able to offer timely and constructive criticism to each other in a context of mutual support. This is most likely to occur where supervisors do not need to prove to trainees that 'anything you can do, I can do better',

Despite the cohesion of the group, there are times when trainees need help with personal issues, since major life events erupt all too regularly during courses. These may include the gain or loss of a partner, illness, bereavement, divorce, the birth of a child, mental or physical illness or the change or loss of a job, moving house or, as in one recent case, actually moving abroad to a new job and commuting to the course weekly. The effects of these events on individuals and the repercussions on the group have to be openly acknowledged and discussed in general terms within the group, so that appropriate allowances can be made. For example, in times of serious stress I would discourage a trainee from taking on new families. If asked to do so, I do occasionally talk to trainees privately, but when they need ongoing help with their difficulties, I suggest that they discuss the matter with their course tutor and/or seek external therapeutic help. In this way a boundary is kept between the pastoral and supervisory functions which helps to maintain an appropriate level of self-disclosure. In the past when supervising individuals from a non-systemic point of view, I found this harder to manage because of the exclusive, private nature of the one-to-one contact which seems to invite personal revelation.

> In one case a trainee who spoke little about herself told me of her personal problems; possibly because I did not offer regular discussion, she turned to the group who were very sympathetic, supportive and provided containment.

Trainees and therapy

Unlike psychotherapy where personal therapy is a prerequisite of training, family therapists in general have so far failed to deal with the fact that we train people to provide a therapeutic service which we do not expect them to have experienced themselves. Although many family therapy trainees have been in individual therapy, and I believe this can be helpful both conceptually and experientially, it is not the same experience as being in family therapy. It is strange that despite being systemic therapists we have also compounded the issue by ignoring the emotional, practical and social repercussions for members of the trainee's immediate circle. It is extremely rare for a trainee's family to be directly included at all. One approach to resolving this is reflected in the Oldenburg University Family Therapy Course. One of their major criteria for selection for family therapy training is the prospective trainee's willingness to commit themselves to a brief intensive exploration with their family or partner.

An individual interview along systemic or psychodynamic lines can of course be very fruitful but it simply does not have the same complexity and intensity as being interviewed 'live' as part of a couple or family group. Neither is there an opportunity to share the experience and learn from each other's responses. Perhaps not having had such an opportunity themselves explains, in part, why trainees often try to rush on with problem-solving, forgetting that to make emotional adjustments needs time and patience.

'Doing it My Way'

To summarize, the distinctive features of supervision as it has developed in systemic family therapy are its direct observation of the trainee at work with a family, the routine use of video recording, the contribution made by the whole team to supervision, and the technical means developed for communicating with the therapist during the session. Live supervision of this kind (apparent both to family and therapist) is very different from most social work or therapeutic supervision, which is usually retrospective and relies on the therapist's account. Throughout their time with me I look for evidence to confirm trainees' ability and their efforts; in other words I look for and emphasise their strengths as I expect them to do with families. This is often combined with a challenge to greater understanding and experimentation, often expressed humorously. As in therapy, laughter is always 'with' people and not 'at' anyone's expense; it serves a secondary function of keeping us all engaged and stimulated. I believe that in therapy as in supervision, it is effective to change the usual format and produce a few surprises. I therefore often change tack from giving information, or eliciting discussion, to moving into experiential exercises so as to link the content of the discussion with its application. This is also a useful method for pre-empting the tendency of some trainees to avoid 'dealing with' by 'talking about' a difficult technique or situation. Similarly I encourage them to respond to clients by a change of level, especially when the session has become stuck. This could be by introducing lightness or by a very direct comment or question about underlying feelings: 'Why do you stay together?' My methods are not prescriptive: they reflect one style of teaching, supervising, learning and to a large degree my own approach to therapy. I remain stimulated and enthusiastic about the supervisory role and also recognise a need for active participation and feedback, a sense of progress being made and a safe and enjoyable context and place of attachment, which the trainees and I can develop together and in which we can genuinely learn from each other. There is an evolutionary process of co-construction between group members and the supervisor whereby the latter, even though holding the authority vested in her role, is progressively seen as only one of many sources of valid ideas.

Evaluating Supervision

As supervisors we have to evaluate our trainees' progress and prepare them for accreditation, yet our own supervisory input is not subject to evaluation. In fact, in many institutions there seems to be little external quality control and little organised exchange or regular sharing of new ideas. It is left to the individual supervisor to monitor her own work and assess whether or not she is keeping up with new concepts, reading and practice or whether she relies on providing more of the same. This may be good enough to ensure that our trainees reach an acceptable standard but supervisors could be missing an opportunity to extend their supervision skills. After years of experience supervisors have much to share, but they may also run the risk of losing some of their original excitement and energy, and of becoming predictable. From the trainees' point of view, it is arguable that they would get a more varied experience if they spent one year only with one supervisor and then in the second year moved on to another group as happens on some courses, for example at the Family Therapy Institute in Mexico. The counter-argument is that many trainees seem to consolidate their learning towards the end of their course and need the second year to become both confident and capable in any one approach. Whilst the former offers trainees greater variety, this arrangement would still not address the quality of supervisory input. The Oldenburg University course which has been both courageous and adventurous, unfortunately vests pastoral, supervisory and therapeutic functions in one person, and the difficulty of evaluation is therefore compounded.

One way of judging how one is doing is to ask the trainees, and this kind of direct evaluation of teaching and supervising should now be routine. At the end of their course trainees are invited to write a report on their experience of my supervision and what they found the most and the least helpful aspects. They may also choose to use an evaluation form. Despite the fact that the trainees are dependent on my assessments if they are to pass their clinical work, this does not appear to constrain them from making some general comments or from asking for specific help.

One trainee wrote:

> I would have valued more opportunity to supervise myself during the year, and have more in-put on the supervisory process itself. I also would have valued more opportunity for video-review and detailed analysis of snippets of work with families.

As a result, I introduced the practice of booking one afternoon a term for video analysis; that is, each trainee shows a few minutes of their work to demonstrate a difficulty or a learning point; this is followed by a detailed analysis. We discuss alternative interventions the trainee could have made and sometimes use role-play to try them out. These afternoons at first seemed daunting but then proved very popular. From my point of view they give opportunities for discussing the minutiae of skills practice, which can get lost when the focus is on the family in a 'live' session.

Another way in which trainees can be helpful to the supervisor, and at the same time feel empowered, is to act as a supervisory team behind the one-way mirror when the supervisor is working with a family:

> On one occasion, I was asked to interview a bereaved family and I invited the supervision group to act as my team behind the one-way mirror. They made helpful comments during the break and supported me in relation to an extremely painful family session.

To demonstrate that as a supervisor you can be vulnerable and use help can be very reassuring and a good model. Being willing to acknowledge one's own fallibility is not always easy, but when a supervisor is willing to do so, it makes it much easier for trainees to follow suit. On one occasion a trainee acknowledged her embarrassment at being attracted to a client and didn't know how to cope with it. I told them of my experience with a couple.

> I found the man very seductive and probably responded in kind, albeit at a verbal level. After a period of linguistic sparring I suddenly looked at the downcast wife and realised what was going on – and stopped. At the end of therapy some weeks later they thanked me on leaving and he said, 'what a pity you couldn't come and stay with us for four or five days so you could see what we are really like!'

No doubt this dispelled some of the myths about supervisors 'always getting it right' and, one hopes, suggested a model of being open about one's 'mistakes' and therefore how to learn from them.

Trainees also have phantasies about other supervisors and what goes on in their supervision groups on their course. Mutual observation visits may satisfy curiosity and minimize rivalry between groups. However, it is not only trainees who have phantasies about what happens in other groups. Supervisors do too, and exchange visits enable them to explore their similarities and differences.

> I have always been concerned about being too intrusive during 'live' sessions, and imagined that other supervisors would be less so. I frequently weigh up the advantages and disadvantages of interrupting an interview to give an intervention. In fact I learnt that I was intervening less frequently than some other supervisors – at least on the days on which they were visited by my supervision group. Needless to add, I was then concerned that I was not pushing the group hard enough!

What has become absolutely clear is that supervisors are unlikely to be the most suitable or accurate assessors of their own supervision. We have as yet no evidence to demonstrate parity of standards of supervision between or within family therapy institutes. Given the importance of our task and the effect of our supervision on the next generation of family therapists, we urgently need a rigorous method of assessing supervisory input. I am aware that it may not be possible or desirable to measure skills like therapy or supervision in existing scientific categories. For 'in order to deal with human ambiguities, one must bypass the rigid corridors of reason, science and logical analysis and concern oneself with imagery, dreams, symbols and metaphors' (Papp 1984). If this is the case, we must be more creative and devise other methods to ensure our trainees are well supervised in the art and privilege of therapy.

After fifteen years I remain one of the many experienced family therapy supervisors who has never been taught how to do the job. Being a good practitioner has often been thought a sufficient prerequisite for being a good supervisor, but I challenge that assumption. Indeed, I question the nature and quality of any form of supervision which is essentially based on a self-monitoring process.

Paradoxically, those of us who have supervised longest may well be the very people who have to make the greatest shifts to bring our work up to date. Major changes in society have occurred and brought to our notice problems which we neither recognised nor understood even a decade ago. As supervisors and trainers, we can no longer assume that what we provided even five years ago is still 'good enough'. Those of us who supervise on accredited trainings should be considering whether there is parity and a high enough level of supervision being provided so that our trainees and we ourselves are making the most of their potential and our own. We should press for research to evaluate more accurately and less subjectively not only the trainees' performance but also our own. .

References

Andersen, T. (1987) The reflecting team: dialogue and meta-dialogue in clinical work. *Family Process*, Vol.26.

Aponte, H. and Winter, J.E. (1987) The person and the practice of the therapist: treatment and training. *Journal of Psychological Therapy and the Family*, Vol.3.

Byng-Hall, J. and Whiffen, R. (1982) *Family Therapy Supervision: recent developments in practice*. London: Academic Press.

Heinl, P. (1987) Visual geneogram work and change: a single case study. *Journal of Family Therapy* Vol.9, 281–291.

Jenkins, J., Hildebrand, J. and Lask, B. (1982) Failure in Family Therapy. *Journal of Family Therapy*, Vol.4, 3.

Liddle, H.A., Breunlin, D.C. and Schwartz, R.C. (eds) (1988) *Handbook of Family Therapy Training and Supervision*. Guilford Press.

Lieberman, S. (1979) Transgenerational analysis: the geneogram as a technique in family therapy. *Journal of Family Therapy* Vol.1, 51–64.

McDaniel, S.H. and Landau-Stanton, J. (1991) Family of Origin Work and Family Therapy Skills Training: Both-And. *Family Process*, Vol.30, 4.

McGoldrick M. and Gerson R. (1985) *Genograms in family assessment*. London: W.W.Norton.

Papp, P. (1984) The Creative Leap. *Family Therapy Networker*, September/October.

Chapter 11

Working Together in Child Protection
Some Issues for Multidisciplinary Training from a Psychodynamic Perspective

Judith Trowell

Introduction

The caring professions involved in child protection comprise a range of disciplines located in a variety of settings, including the rapidly expanding voluntary sector; teachers and other staff based in or linked with schools; doctors, nurses and other health professionals; social workers, residential workers, day nursery workers; the police and probation officers. Since the death of Maria Colwell in 1973 (Colwell 1974), the importance of multidisciplinary work in the task of protecting children from abuse has been recognised. The structures, systems, procedures and practice guidelines evolved, first by the DHSS and then by the successor Department of Health, have increasingly been predicated on the need for inter-agency and interdisciplinary co-ordination. Public policy in this area is governed by a system of 'mandatory coordination', expressed in circulars and guidance. *Working Together* (1991), the guidance on child protection issued by the Home Office, the Department of Health, the Department of Education and Science and the Welsh Office in pursuance of the Children Act 1989 is unequivocal on this theme: 'interdisciplinary and inter-agency work is an essential process in the task of attempting to protect children from abuse' (para. 2.1), '...the protection of children...requires a concerted approach to interdisciplinary and inter-agency working' (para. 1.8) Joint or multidisciplinary training is seen as a key to the implementation of this policy.

This chapter aims to demonstrate some of the gains to be made from such training. But it will also explore some of the obstacles – political, organizational, professional and personal – that can get in the way of interdisciplinary training and point to how they might be overcome. Commitment to this philosophy is not unanimous and the policy system contains some mixed messages.

Conflict between child protection professionals can arise because of different perspectives on human problems. In the public welfare domain the problems that need to be tackled can either be broken down into small individual tasks or be considered in all their complexity. Each problem involves an individual or a group of individuals but there are also issues that spread out to involve others – family members, the local community and the wider community: it is analagous to the series of concentric circles that appear when a stone is dropped into a pond. If there is a restricted focus, for example, on an individual child and a particular difficulty, the outer circles can be ignored; but if the total phenomenon is to be addressed in all its complexity they must be considered. The child can only be fully assessed and understood if a range of skills and perspectives are drawn upon. If he or she is to receive the most effective service possible, then professionals from all the different agencies need at the least to coordinate their interventions and at best to decide together what needs to be done, and how it will be done. Agreement has to be reached as to which professionals will undertake which task and how they will share information and decision making (Hallett and Stevenson 1980, Huntingdon 1981, Taylor 1986).

Welfare problems can be understood as jigsaws, each agency holding certain information, skills and knowledge which must be pieced together to provide the best possible understanding so that good decisions lead to the most effective interventions. Whilst the value of coordination is accepted widely by Central Government and by senior and middle management in welfare agencies in principle, when it comes to the particular case the pressures of money and the use of time become powerful constraints.

Whilst *Working Together* endorses multi-agency work, the National Health Service and Community Care Act and the Education Reform Act have inadvertently increased the pressures working against it. Multidisciplinary, multi-agency work requires time; time to meet together, to discuss, to plan. Individual budget holders struggle to provide what they can, in a context of endless demands and limited resources, but there are inevitably questions about the need for and the costs of collaborative work. Interdisciplinary rivalry, always an issue, appears to be increasing to the detriment of patients and users. With the heightened emphasis on the quasi-market in the NHS and the separation of purchaser and provider units, which involves competition among providers to win contracts, each discipline is struggling to justify its existence, to survive. Other structural factors accentuate the difficulties. Health, education, social services and the police have experienced major reorganisation. This has exacerbated long-standing problems, rooted in differing management systems and lines of accountability. How decisions are made, the priorities for each agency and the way resources are used varies between agencies. Professionals trying to work together can suddenly find they have been moved, the agency decides some other area of work is more important, or a decision is made to close down a particular service.

It must be questioned whether multidisciplinary, multi-agency work can survive, particularly in the light of community care policy which requires the cost of collaboration to be made explicit. Professionals certainly need to become more active in demonstrating the benefits to patients/clients/users of multidisciplinary assessments in decision making, planning and service delivery.   .

Forms of Multidisciplinary Work

Multidisciplinary services in child protection can be delivered in different ways. The Area Child Protection Committee provides a multi-agency framework and lays down policies and procedures to be followed in its geographical area. There is a general expectation that information will be shared and that professionals will work co-operatively, although multidisciplinary work may take a number of forms:

(1) *Ad hoc* networks of professionals which come together because they are all involved with a particular case. They meet to discuss the case, share information, and decide together what needs to be done and who will be the lead workers. They may meet again to review progress and to decide how to take the work forward. But their *raison d'être* is the single case.

(2) Regular networks which come together when there are numbers of shared cases. These regular networks are able to build on their knowledge of each other and their particular skills, and so function in a more flexible and creative way to the benefit of the patients or users. For example, where a school or day nursery serves a local population with many family problems, then the local patch social worker, the general practitioner, health visitor, and police officer will meet regularly and build up a knowledge of each other's skills. They will discuss worries and concerns and together may well be able to

intervene appropriately or support a vulnerable child or family. They are unlikely all to meet together systematically to discuss cases. More often there is a phone call or a meeting between two of the professionals but they build on a shared knowledge of and commitment to the locality.

(3) Multidisciplinary teams which work together regularly, often weekly, and have a regular meeting time. They discuss and share a range of cases. Over time they change and develop, learning from each other, particularly where there is joint working face to face with the patients/users. The teams can accommodate more argument and disagreement because of the commitment to regular team meetings: different views can be debated with more rigour and this advances knowledge and understanding. This level of debate is rarely possible in informal networks where the need is to find common ground and where there is pressure to compromise and agree what is mutually acceptable so as not to waste time.

Most of the literature on inter-professional working deals with the last of these, the multidisciplinary team of an established kind. There is little research on informal professional networks in child care, how they operate, and to what effect, though this is central to the implementation of government policy. In general, coordination and collaboration are portrayed as problematic (Stevenson 1989), though the important work of Hallett and Birchall (Birchall 1992, Hallett 1993) gives a different and altogether more positive emphasis, revealing that professionals generally place a high value on working together, and believe it to be working well in their own area.

Multidisciplinary Training

If professionals are really to work well together then it appears obvious that they need to train together. This chapter draws on experience of short courses in many localities, including those held under the auspices of the local (Camden) Area Child Protection Committee and the long post-qualification MA in Child Protection based at the Tavistock Clinic. The examples are drawn from child protection but the issues discussed are applicable to other areas of welfare activity.

Throughout the 1980s there has been a steady growth of knowledge, understanding and skills in the field of child protection. The whole area has expanded and developed. Trainings began as short courses, half a day or a day for members of the different disciplines who were already qualified. During the 1980s these lengthened and became more specialised, to focus, for example, on indications of abuse, assessment, legal issues, management of cases, sexual abuse, offenders' treatment, research findings and updating. By the late 1980s, the need for additional longer specialist courses became apparent.

In my view, multidisciplinary training has to be built on the premise that each discipline takes responsibility for the basic, core training of its members. Considerable problems arise if professionals lack a grasp of the role and tasks of their own discipline, since multi-disciplinary training builds on a person's existing professional identity, skills and knowledge base. Short courses may last from half a day to two weeks, but more frequently one or two days are used to teach particular topics to a multi-disciplinary group. This provides opportunities for discussion of the issues and how best to tackle them jointly. These courses are most effective when supported by the ACPC; they encourage the development of local networks, which can build upon shared knowledge and experience of training.

More advanced and longer courses, for example, for a day a week for one or two years, incorporating practice and theoretical work, have developed to meet the needs of workers specialising in this area of work. This is the model adopted by the Tavistock Child Protection Course.

Problems and Issues in Multi-Professional Training

What are the issues that arise in such trainings? In 1990, the problems identified on the Tavistock course were salary differences, status and power, interdisciplinary rivalry, personality clashes, membership of different systems with different priorities, the building itself, and policies and procedures (Trowell 1990). Current issues, identified within current groups of students, are similar but the emphasis seems to have changed.

Salary differentials remain, with doctors and lawyers as the best paid, and nurses and day nursery workers the least well paid, but the conflicts around them seem to have lessened and issues of status and power now emerge as more important. Stereotypes pervade any course and have to be constantly addressed. For example, social workers hold considerable power and authority, but feel attacked and denigrated; nurses are valued by the public but feel they lack status and authority; teachers and police are the focus of mixed feelings; and doctors are idealised, feared and denigrated. Closely linked is the question of personality. It is easy to blame personality clashes for the problems in multidisciplinary work and at times that is indeed the issue. But often the personality is blamed when the problem is money, or power, or status, or (more problematic possibly) leadership. In any group of professionals leadership is a key issue. In welfare and legal aspects of child protection social workers and the police respectively have lead roles, and a leadership role in interdisciplinary work may be assumed by one of their number with the necessary personal qualities. But in practice it is often a doctor, a psychologist, a therapist who takes the lead. This can work well but at times creates problems if the energy and creativity of the leadership is out of step with, for example, social work's practice, constrained and shaped as it is by statutory requirements.

Such difficulties arise year after year in training but others have emerged more recently. As trainings have lengthened and deepened there has been a recognition that the style of learning, the training techniques and assessment methods of the individual disciplines are very different. This has led to problems in assessed work where trainees and staff have found that there are considerable differences in approach to what appears to be a straightforward task. Linked with this is the question of language: each discipline's jargon needs explanation, particularly when words have been taken over and ascribed particular meanings. But it is not just at a verbal level; there are also problems at the level of thinking and conceptualising where the differences are less obvious and yet profound. They seem to arise from differences in background and occupational culture (Huntingdon 1981) as well as learning and assessment styles. The educational level of entrants to each discipline is very different. Graduate entry professions have learnt to think and function in a way that is at variance with trainings modelled on apprenticeship. These differences are played out, particularly between nurses and social workers, although it could as easily be teachers and the police. Doctors occupy the middle ground, as they are a graduate profession that also has a large apprenticeship element in its training. Doctors can therefore relate easily both to nurses and social workers. Mutual identifications are possible with both and this perhaps explains why they are often to be found in leadership positions.

Differences in management structures and practices are further fertile sources of professional conflict. The deluge of guidelines, policies and procedures makes it difficult for individual professionals to retain the flexibility and time that is needed to work together. In the important area of equal opportunities each agency has its own policy, its own attitude and expectations. Professionals feel passionately about aspects of equal opportunities practice, and in areas such as child protection where issues of race, gender and disability are often central, personal and professional differences in attitude can be explosive. It is extremely important to struggle with these issues. In the Tavistock Clinic course a predominantly white female staff group, all able-bodied, needed to find ways of increasing their awareness of and means of facing these issues in themselves, and to be able to think with the trainees. Staff development meetings with an external facilitator proved an important way to help staff to think creatively and develop their teaching in these areas.

Other contested issues are linked with variations and differences in models of practice. Simple things like length of involvement can be problematic, the social work 'task and finish' style of work contrasting with the teaching profession's expectation of 'involvement over a number of years', and the general practitioner's view of the person as a patient of theirs indefinitely. More substantive clinical issues such as assessment and supervision have needed considerable exploration. What does each discipline mean by assessment? How can they complement each other, rather than duplicate, and agree what is to be assessed, and how it is to be done? What is supervision? Who supervises? What skills do supervisors need? The distinctions between management, supervision, training, consultation and therapy are muddled and differently understood by each profession.

The biggest issue of all is that of role – whose role is what? How flexible can professionals be without eliminating themselves? Does one discipline de-skill and marginalise another whilst possibly idealising a third? Currently there is pressure to use nurses much more, as case workers, therapists, community workers, counsellors, health educators, and for the social work role to become more narrowly defined as care management buying packages of care, or 'social policing', paralleling the work of the police in the civil domain.

Underlying Dynamics

Working in any area of welfare stirs up powerful and primitive feelings in all professionals. Confronting difference and being reminded of the needy aspects of ourselves is very painful. Children reflect our own vulnerable selves. Disability points to our own mortality, and racial and gender differences confront us with envy, rage, hatred and our need of others. We all deal with these early, very deep feelings and conflicts by mechanisms such as splitting, denial, projection and projective identification. All too often these mechanisms are re-evoked, re-aroused by the powerful feelings stimulated by welfare patients/users. Issues of dependency, aggression and sexuality are particularly powerful and touch these deeper areas (Furniss 1991). In child protection, where children are predominantly abused by men and where disabled children are particularly vulnerable, the feelings provoked by the work can be so intense that they sweep through the trainee group and the staff group. Splitting can occur on gender lines – the women attacking the men, the men perhaps denying their masculinity; or there are splits along racial groups, with stereotypes and prejudices about certain racial groups carrying the 'bad', 'out of control' aspects of aggression and sexuality for the whole group. Abuse of disabled children is often even more unthinkable and workers in this field can be ostracized, their existence effectively denied, unseen, as the client group is frequently unseen. In a multidisciplinary training it can be all too easy for the process of splitting, denial and projection to use the discipline differences as a means of dealing with unbearable feelings. All too often one discipline group can carry the 'bad' or 'unthinkable' or 'unthinking' aspects for the group. Nurses seem particularly vulnerable to being dumped with these projected negative aspects.

The role of phantasy, conscious and unconscious, is even more complex and difficult to make sense of. Envy, destructiveness, rage, self-destructiveness, sexual feelings, all forms of sexual deviation, sado-masochism, and infantile needs and longings lead to phantasies. Conscious and unconscious guilt can be provoked as well as shame and despair. These can influence how the person thinks, feels, behaves, but may well be unacknowledged because they are unthinkable by the person's conscious mind. One of the most important aspects of the training is therefore to find ways of developing in trainees the capacity to think, to be able to tolerate their own thoughts because it is all too easy for thinking to be attacked, destroyed, fragmented, and for the possibility of making links to be eliminated. Professionals can be stirred up by the degree of violence, perversion, or corruption involved, and this can resonate with their own inner feelings and phantasies so that, without recognising why, the professional reacts, makes decisions, or does things, and the capacity to reflect and arrive at a decision which is as objective as possible, is lost. If a multidisciplinary group can recognise this process they can use their differences, which all too easily lead to splitting, projections and irrational decision making, to enable them as a group to arrive at a capacity to think together so they can together make rational objective decisions. However, to use the feelings of rage, aggression and fear of death, madness and dependency arising from the patient/user group requires considerable maturity and inner resources in both the trainee and the staff groups. This is a key issue in selecting trainees.

More obvious and therefore perhaps easier to recognise and handle are the issues to do with trainees' own past history. Where similar issues emerge in the training there may be acting out, or elements of repetition compulsion, as their own unresolved conflicts surface. The obvious unconscious phantasy that is also conscious is the Oedipal conflict. This seems so old hat and cliché'd that it is hard to mention, but nonetheless it continues to exert its power. Where professionals do not have in their internal world a creative parental couple, it can be very hard to resolve some of the issues and accept being left out and to deal with the need to find one's own partner that must follow. The risk is that a professional makes an alliance with one family member or another professional, and someone else has to carry the role of the one left out: for example a worker makes an alliance with a single mother, and the child is forgotten.

In addition to all the individual conscious and unconscious processes there are continuing and inevitable group processes. It can be very hard to sustain a working group and keep it on task. All too easily a multidisciplinary training course becomes, in Bion's terms, a basic assumption group where there is dependence, pairing or fight and flight (Bion 1961). Members take on different roles but the whole becomes anti-work, anti the task of learning.

The Multidisciplinary Staff Team

The subject of child protection causes problems in the staff group similar to those that affect the trainees, with splitting, denial and projection. To hold and use these tensions, opening them up to exploration rather than closing them off, a multidisciplinary course needs a multidisciplinary staff group capable of self-reflection. The unconscious conflictual material can reveal itself in the staff group in different ways. The few male staff (unconsciously perceived as abusers) are easily blamed for any problems or they can be ignored, cease to exist, be forgotten so that the tensions in the staff group (representing child and mother) can be dealt with in an 'all women together' group with the men extruded. But then the trainee who presents the topic of the role of women in abuse, who has to discuss women who knowingly or unknowingly allow men to abuse, or women who themselves abuse, becomes the one who needs to be extruded and is blamed for all the problems. Perhaps more difficult to handle than these, however, are the inter-professional tensions. Nurses, despite their staff status, all too easily see themselves as inferior and incompetent and they find it hard to have a voice. The social workers and mental health professionals can easily collude with this acceptance of blame and fail to notice what is being enacted. Certainly there have been moments when the nurses (the child?) have accepted difficulties as their fault and the social workers (the abusers?) have confirmed that it is their fault and the mental health professionals (the mothers?) have ignored or looked on or failed to protect.

Organisational Issues

Particular problems on the Tavistock Clinic course derive from variations in approach to training, that is, teaching style, language, the level of experience of different staff, and rivalry and competitiveness. This raises questions about ownership of the course. Where different institutions are releasing staff to teach, this still causes problems, despite very careful thought and acknowledgment. Leadership is a problem in training as well as in practice and much is left unsaid: how much, for example, is leadership due to power, status, position, professional discipline, and how much to personality, skill and competence? It is not easy honestly to discuss this nor to acknowledge that other aspect of leadership, responsibility. Who is responsible for the trainees? Is it the lead person for each discipline, or the course conveners? Clarity in course leadership and management is often absent and issues of course organisation require time for thought and reflection.

For trainees the overwhelming issue is to do with money – money to pay fees, money to enable them to be released. Time and money are interwoven, money providing time to attend, time to do the course work, time to do the emotional work provoked by the course. Who pays for this time? Is it personal time or agency work time? The pain of the envy of colleagues in the work place or their denial of newly acquired knowledge and skills has also to be faced by the course participant. In addition there is massive uncertainty caused by changes and reorganisation which have left most professionals in the welfare systems anxious about employment. Trainees have to struggle with trying to learn and develop whilst waiting to see if they will be made redundant or offered a post they do not want; little wonder it is so hard to think.

Wherever such trainings are based there are complex issues for the organisation offering them. Feelings, rational and irrational, are provoked by courses which address painful and difficult areas. The course can be seen as a good thing and yet at the same time there can be a desire for it to go away. This ambivalence can lead to repeated conflicts internal to the organisation which can threaten the viability of a course and victimise the trainees and staff within the host institution.

The Benefits of Multidisciplinary Training

The literature contains strongly contradictory findings on the effectiveness and the benefits of multidisciplinary training. There is work pointing to shared value systems between nurses and social workers (Dingwall 1979) which suggests that differences in orientation between professionals have been exaggerated and that organisational structures and impediments may be greater obstacles to effective coordination than professional differences. However, in general it is strongly geared either to exhortation (*Working Together*) or to the difficulties of working multi-professionally (Stevenson 1989).

If there are so many problems, are there advantages that justify the struggle to train and work together? (Hey, Minty and Trowell 1991). The understanding, trust and appreciation of each other's skills are important, and should lead to a better and more appropriate use of each other in the field. It also results in better coordinated service delivery, and the decision-making and review process becomes more patient/user focussed and less a power struggle based on interdisciplinary rivalry. These putative gains are supported by a recent evaluation of shared learning in child protection (Stanford and Yelloly 1994) but they are to some extent articles of faith and more research is needed into the effectiveness of multi-professional training and its impact on organisational and professional practices.

There are also considerable long-term benefits for all professionals. Staff develop and grow professionally and their skill base expands as they learn from each other. They find their jobs more satisfying and rewarding and this can reduce dissatisfaction, time off, and frequent changes of post. Where professionals feel valued, differences between them are useful because there is a full range of skills available to help patients/users; this increases their sense of value and usefulness. Career pathways also frequently involve linking and liaison with other agencies so that upward progress is facilitated for all the disciplines within their own management structures. Like the trainees, all the staff on the Tavistock Clinic's course, however senior, are part of the welfare systems and are struggling with the uncertainty created by restructuring, redundancy and the changing ethos, value systems and expectations of their employing organisations. It is unclear which agencies will survive and in what form. To hold on to the capacity to think, to be in touch and to have hope for the patients/users and for the future of multidisciplinary work and training requires strength, courage and not a little foolhardiness.

References

Bion, W.R. (1961) *Experiences in Groups*. London: Tavistock Publications.

Birchall, E. (1992) *Working Together in Child Protection: Report of Phase Two*. Stirling: University of Stirling.

Colwell Report (1974) *Report of the Committee of Inquiry into the care and supervision provided in relation to Maria Colwell*. London: HMSO.

Department of Health (1991) *Working Together under the Children Act 1989.* London: HMSO.

Dingwall, R. (1979) Problems of teamwork in primary care. In A.W. Clare and R. Corney (eds) (1982) *Social Work and Primary Health Care.* London: Academic Press.

DHSS (1977) *Working Together for Children and their Families.* London: HMSO.

Furniss, T. (1991) The Professional Network. In *The Multiprofessional Handbook of Child Sexual Abuse.* London: Routledge.

Hallett, C. and Stevenson, O. (1980) *Child Abuse: Aspects of interprofessional co-operation.* London: Allen and Unwin.

Hallett, C. (1993) *Working Together in Child Protection: Report of Phase Three.* Stirling: University of Stirling.

Hey, A., Minty, B. and Trowell, J. (1991) Interprofessional and Inter-agency Work: Theory, Practice and Training for the Nineties. In M. Pietroni (ed) *Right or Privilege.* London: CCETSW.

Huntingdon, J. (1981) *Social Work and General Medical Practice.* London: Allen and Unwin.

Stanford, R. and Yelloly, M. (1994) *Shared Learning in Child Protection.* London: ENB/CCETSW.

Stevenson, O. (1989) Multidisciplinary work. In O. Stevenson (ed) *Child Abuse: Public Policy and Professional Practice.* London: Harvester Wheatsheaf.

Taylor, J. (1986) Mental Handicap: Partnership in the Community. (unpublished).

Trowell, J. (1990) Sustaining Multidisciplinary Work. Royal College of Psychiatry OP8.

Chapter 12

Great Expectations?
Personal, Professional and Institutional
Agendas in Advanced Training

Penny Youll and Clare Walker

Introduction

This paper is concerned with advanced level programmes in social work education, that is, those which are assessed 'at the equivalent academic standard of a master's degree' (CCETSW 1990) and which prepare workers 'to provide clear leadership and expertise in their area of work' (CCETSW 1990). Such programmes are geared to experienced practitioners and people in management posts – those who are likely to be influential in policy-making, planning and management of services and in the way agencies respond to new demands and challenges.

In looking at advanced programmes, therefore, we are concerned not only with the aims, purposes and structures of higher level education in social work but also with its relationship to the development of knowledge, practice and management in social service agencies.

The aspects we highlight emerged from the experience of students taking a part-time higher degree – the M.Phil. in Social Work – from 1988 to the present time. The course comprised a taught programme and students' own empirical research presented in the form of a thesis. It was devised and taught jointly by the Tavistock Clinic and Brunel University.

We live in a period of growing recognition, and acceptance, that personal and social care services will be shaped as much by those who utilise them – direct service users, carers and purchasers – as by the professional practitioners, agency policy-makers, planners or managers who provide them. The nature and form of services will, increasingly, be the result of a negotiated order involving a number of stakeholders and this will present challenges to management and social work traditions. It is timely to ask questions about who sets the agenda for advanced programmes. Some years ago, Goodlad pointed out that 'education for the professions must involve some conscious attention not only to the technical components of the professional's service…but also to the fundamentally moral issue of who is controlling what knowledge for whose benefit' (1984), an observation that still has considerable relevance.

Professional social work education and training is structured on a national basis: new frameworks set in place structures and standards for post-qualifying levels. As regional consortia of educational institutions and health and social service agencies begin to gear up for the validation of existing and new courses, we note that, so far, the main concerns have been about the structures, guidelines, criteria and mechanisms for course approval. What about the intent, content and coverage of higher level programmes? Ensuring that 'opportunities for education and training at post-qualifying and advanced levels are available on a UK basis' is to remain a function of CCETSW (CCETSW 1990 section 7.1 ii). But it is likely that course aims and content will be more strongly shaped by local markets and, therefore, agency-led objectives.

The basic question we are examining is: who wants advanced programmes and for what purposes? Those who take advanced level courses are usually employees of middle tier or senior status. Notionally, they also belong to the peer community of professional social work practitioners with a set of norms and values independent of employing agencies. What kind of investment do individuals make and why? How is advanced education and research viewed by social service agencies? Are students having to effect some compromise between workplace, professional, course and personal principles and goals? Who designs and offers courses, who supervises students' research projects and what are their motivations? Should service users contribute to setting the agenda for professional education and if so how?

We can, then, identify a number of stakeholders and interest groups involved in the provision and uptake of advanced education and recognise that their objectives and values do not necessarily coincide:

- the peer community of professional social workers

- the individual student

- agencies providing social care services

- educational institutions providing advanced programmes

- academic and research staff who design and run courses
- users of personal social services.

These interests may display a degree of congruence but equally there may be significant tensions between any or all of them. The listing helps to outline the complexity of the learning environment which students enter and to identify questions about the relationship between the different stakeholders.

What emerges from the experience of the M.Phil. students is that the burden of managing the tensions and complexities involved in advanced study and in its utilisation is shouldered by the individual student. Although there may be a number of potential beneficiaries, the extent to which purchaser or provider agencies, educational institutions or those vitally concerned about the relevance and standard of services – users, carers, quality inspectors – become involved or make an investment in education is limited or non-existent.

The Aims and Purposes of Advanced Study in Social Work

At present there are two distinct levels at which education and training in social work can be pursued after basic qualification: post-qualifying and advanced. A basic justification for both post-qualifying and advanced training for professionals is to achieve 'better outcomes for recipients of (their) services' (Rushton and Martyn 1993). There is a general assumption that opportunities for structured academic study or empirical research add to the store of social work knowledge and expertise. However, the connection between such individually-led and often narrowly focused endeavours and *service* development – as distinct from personal, professional or career development – has been largely unexplored by employers and rarely exploited in any systematic way by service providers.

Advanced level study in social work encompasses a qualitative shift (Hey 1991) from knowledge acquisition to the development of analytic and conceptual skills, critical appraisal and the production of knowledge through independent enquiry (CCETSW 1990). Rushton and Martyn refer to '"higher order" professional skills' (1993) but do not define these. We suggest that the hallmarks of advanced practice – whether as social work manager, practitioner, educator or researcher – are the capacity for reflection, systematic review and critical analysis used in the development of responsive and innovative services. The bases of these skills lie in the development of *professional authority*, based in knowledge, experience and expertise, and *personal autonomy*, based in a capacity for independent thought and action. Together they represent the ability to act in ones own judgement.

Post-qualifying (PQ)level courses are primarily concerned with providing opportunities for the consolidation of social work practice skills and extending specialist knowledge. They are strongly shaped by agency demands, which are, in turn, determined by the requirements of legislative and service changes. PQ courses tend to be instrumental, providing the specialist with additional knowledge and skills required to maintain existing expertise or to implement new policies and organisational arrangements. Courses typically lay emphasis on the acquisition of knowledge, skills and information.

While it is the instrumental nature of PQ courses that is attractive to employers and justifies their expenditure, we believe that it is the opportunity to take a general and critical appraisal of social work practice and provision that attracts students to advanced courses. PQ level can be seen as having a more or less immediate pay-off for employers whereas the value of advanced study may be ambiguous. Critical appraisal or new knowledge are likely to be a source of innovation and to stimulate service development but may also challenge or disrupt existing arrangements.

The modularisation of education and training will allow students and those who fund their studies a greater freedom to 'pick and mix'. In this context it is important to know more about who selects which courses, on what bases and for what ends in order to understand how the agenda for advanced education is set and controlled. Course offerings are diverse at both PQ and advanced level and cover a wide range of contemporary concerns reflecting the interests of the various stakeholders we referred to earlier. On the whole they address specific areas of social care provision: the extent to which they also consider generic aspects or locate learning within the wider contexts of policy and practice in personal social services may vary. The following is a rough and ready categorisation of higher level programmes but it helps to illustrate the diversity:

Organisations and agency management:

- organisation studies
- organisation and management of services
- financial management

Quality assurance, service monitoring and evaluation:

- inspection and service monitoring
- quality assurance
- evaluation studies

Professional practice development:

- advancement of practice and specialist knowledge
- multidisciplinary and inter-professional studies
- assessment and care management

Socio-political studies:

- social and political contexts
- policy formulation and implementation
- studies of changing social and political trends
- gender, race, cultural and anti-discrimination studies

Consumer and user interests:

- studies of user and consumer involvement
- care group interests.

Many topics overlap and the list is not complete. However, it shows how different courses serve potentially divergent areas of interest. The complex interplay of interests in the market for advanced courses is well illustrated by the fact that the Tavistock/Brunel M.Phil. recruited four intakes of six to ten students but then closed. It was not able to meet the University's economic requirement for a larger intake. There was some reduction in demand from suitable individuals and the number of candidates able to obtain agency backing also fell: a trend also noted by other advanced programmes.

Motivations and Expectations

Several questions help to focus the discussion on who pursues advanced study and why. Who takes the lead in deciding on the take up of advanced programme offerings? To what extent is motivation linked to academic, professional or agency objectives? How and why are courses developed?

Student motivation

The experience of the Tavistock/Brunel course suggests that candidates applied for the course on personal initiative – rarely as part of a staff development plan resulting from discussion within their agency. They had a number of formal reasons for doing so which fell into three broad categories:

- Service or agency related aspirations, such as acquiring particular experience or knowledge in order to promote better services

   within their agency, examining links between services, aspects of
   multidisciplinary practice;

- Career advancement, such as enhancing prospects for promotion,
  gaining specialist knowledge, making a career change;

- Personal/professional development: time for personal reflection
  and reappraisal of priorities and aspirations. Motivation here
  related to issues beyond the practice of social work and the
  provision of services within a particular agency.

However, in the course of tutorial discussions more complex motivations
were usually revealed. Several students were aware that they had given
reasons for workplace consumption while actually pursuing other, more
personal (and not necessarily well formulated) goals. It was as if personal or
professional reasons for pursuing a research degree had to be re-formulated
or justified in relation to agency norms or priorities. Professional development was highly valued not only as a benefit for the individual but also as
a means of improving the quality and relevance of services. In this respect,
students showed a high level of commitment to the needs and interests of
service users and many were critical of their agency's management of staff
or service development.

   A strong element for many, if not all, students was to find a legitimate
way of carrying out a critical appraisal of the workplace or employing agency,
its values, principles, provisions, priorities. Students wanted a more powerful
voice within their organisation and thought they could gain authority by
taking a higher degree and by using research findings to back their views.
A rough indication of their concerns comes from an analysis of the research
topics pursued. The 25 studies which have been done or which are in
progress focus on (with some overlaps):

- users' views and experience of services   9

- approaches to professional practice including
  studies of multidisciplinary or inter-agency work   8

- aspects of professional and career developmen t   5

- in-house studies of the organisation, service
  development or evaluation   5

Although the majority of studies were conducted within the student's own
agency, they mainly explored generic questions rather than specific, local
concerns. The figures suggest that students were motivated to take a grassroots look at quality of service and conditions for professional practice.
Strategic issues relating to the implementation of community care were

analysed as they affected their research area but surprisingly few took this as a central interest. About half were concerned with aspects of child care but again the topics reflected students' individual interests – for example, gender based influences on practice, the experience of black children leaving care, values and principles underpinning practice – many of which had little direct link with stated agency priorities.

In general it appeared that students were taking an independent line on how they wished to use the course. Research topics were selected to explore areas of particular interest rather than necessarily to enhance career prospects. Students came with personal, professional or, in some cases, political questions: the research topics they chose provided a legitimate means of exploring them.

Agency motivation

The thinking of service agencies is less clear. Few of the M.Phil. students, for example, were financed or mandated to follow the course in order to gain knowledge and experience which could be utilised by their employing agency. There was little recognition that a higher degree course – with or without a research element or, indeed, any advanced programme – might be an investment and exploited for service development or evaluation, or wider staff development, in a systematic way. Typically, training and educational opportunities were seen as benefiting the individual: a luxury which the employee might be allowed to pursue as long as mainstream work was not hampered.

As a recent evaluation of training for care workers commented 'the personal social services, in independent and public sectors, have had little tradition of developing services through job enhancement or investment in staff development' and practice development has not been seen as 'an inherent part of service provision' (Youll and McCourt-Perring 1993 p.119).

Students, on the other hand, saw the M.Phil. course as providing professional renewal, intellectual refreshment, new knowledge and skills in enquiry and analysis and opportunities for personal growth. These were not provided within the working context and it was interesting to note that these were not seen as necessarily appropriate expectations to have of an employing organisation. However, all students considered professional and self development to be essential in ensuring that those planning and managing services are informed, have the ability to understand and the capacity to respond to changing demands. Students' dominant point of reference appeared to be a core set of values and principles for practice as represented in the notion of a peer professional community rather than the aims and values of their employing agency.

The general message was that agencies were preoccupied with organisational and managerial changes and taking financial decisions about community care. Employers were keen to promote businesslike ways and managerial approaches concerned with, for example, service specification, monitoring and control. It seemed that agencies found it difficult to see how any advanced course which took personnel away from base or rested on students pursuing their own research interests might be of benefit. However, some of the basics of management are to know customer needs, understand the market, analyse the threats, strengths, opportunities and weakness of the environment and to respond to changing demands. New management theory is placing more emphasis on human resource development.

Course staff motivation

The M.Phil. was set up by a group of staff from the two institutions – Tavistock and Brunel – all of whom were social workers and who encompassed between them clinical practice, management, teaching, research and academic experience. The intention was to offer a course which was attractive to senior professionals partly by offering a research degree but also by challenging people to draw on and integrate the rather different theoretical backgrounds and traditions of the two institutions. The staff believed that advanced practice could be enhanced through bringing into conjunction the theories and frameworks of social policy analysis and organisational studies and those of psychodynamic approaches to understanding individual, group and organisational processes and relationships. It was considered important that employing agencies were involved by actively supporting the student as well as (passively) agreeing study time and that, in turn, the research element should be of relevance to the agency.

The staff group had evidence (from students following other courses in both institutions and a small research exercise) that individual practitioners and managers might find such an course attractive: it was less clear how it might be viewed by agencies. The course was based on a series of assumptions, shared by the staff group, concerning the value and relevance of:

- research and systematic enquiry in planning and managing social care services

- understanding the processes and interpersonal dynamics involved in practice and management

- recognising different levels of experience and analysis

- a critical and analytic stance in relation to policy, practice and service development
- a connection between individual and agency benefits.

We are not in a position to comment on how typical the experience of the M.Phil. staff group is but it provides an example of course innovation led by a particular set of values congruent with, but not led by, academic objectives and distinct from agency-led concerns. The expectation was that staff and students would learn together about the value of particular frameworks and theories for research and practice. Staff were not concerned with enhancing their personal academic reputation although it was hoped that the course would exemplify good practice in teaching and professional education and be innovative.

What Advanced Study Entails

We commented earlier that it is the individual student who takes on most of the responsibility for managing the educational experience and that this involves a complex set of tasks. Most students are simultaneously engaged in educational, research, professional and agency work. It means that they are continually moving between organisations and work environments which have different value bases, objectives, work methods and approaches to assessing competence and so on.

We outline briefly the kind of tasks that study at this level entails and the significant accommodations and transitions which students have to manage:

- joining the course, identifying as a student and learner
- entering an academic environment, making sense of a new institution
- carrying out course work: reading, conducting literature searches, seminar presentations, writing essays
- defining and designing a research study – becoming a researcher
- writing the thesis – presenting research findings with accuracy and authority
- applying new ideas and knowledge.

In the case of the M.Phil., students had also to encompass a move of learning base in year two from the University to the Tavistock clinic: this was a discontinuity and was disruptive. Although unusual, this may foreshadow the experience of students building up credits by taking modules in different institutions.

During the two year course students faced intellectual challenges as they revisited familiar knowledge bases and were introduced to new theoretical and analytic frames. Research methods and practice were new areas for most but the research was a central part of the programme and the main rationale for taking an advanced course. All of these transitions are experienced by anyone embarking on a course of advanced study but the two dimensions we highlight from the M.Phil. experience are the dynamics of part-time study and the impact of undertaking one's own research.

The dynamics of part-time study

To find physical, emotional and intellectual space to think in a systematic way is a challenge to most people whose lives are already full of competing demands, personal and professional. The pressures of home and work mean that part-time students have fragmented opportunities to concentrate.

But a key feature of part-time study is that of changing mode between student, researcher, manager and individual and doing so on a day-by-day basis. Each of these states involves particular psychological, social, emotional and intellectual skills, value bases and sets of expectations and may take place in specific settings, institutions or agencies. How far are these compatible roles, able to be undertaken concurrently? Or do they require a clear separation in time and space?

The experience of most M.Phil. students was that they had to fight hard to preserve not only the time but also physical and mental space for study. Although most had secured agency agreement to take the amount of study time advised by the course, this was easily and constantly subject to erosion: pursuit of advanced education was rarely seen as part of the work, as of direct benefit to the service or as having potential value for colleagues. Even where there was wider agency interest in the research and support in principle, this rarely resulted in strategic or practical backing from the agency.

The issue of finding mental space for study was also important. It seemed that students needed to establish a physical space for their study – free from work or family invasions – and this helped to create a mental space. The issue may be one of negotiating legitimate time out from other responsibilities and expectations which then helps to free psychological energies for study.

In identifying these experiences we are asking about the kind of boundaries that students have first to recognise and then be able to move across, if all roles are to be successfully sustained during the course. The transitions are complex: they involve not only physical moves but also cognitive, emotional and psychological adjustments and over an extended period.

Walker has shown how there were considerable personal and professional tensions involved in social workers moving to become first line managers and that the processes of adjustment might take up to two years (Walker 1992). It is interesting to consider what pressures are involved in a two or more year period of moving between different, if familiar, contexts. As far as we are aware, existing writing in this area is based on full-time education (for example Salzberger-Wittenberg 1983, Youll 1985) and there is little systematic information about the impacts of part-time high level courses.

The research role

Some of these questions relate to how research and its associated activities – the examination of events, obtaining and handling data, the production of knowledge, the formulation of new theories and ideas – are valued.

For the student, the research role brings together personal, professional and academic activities. In taking on this role most students have first to convince themselves that they can sustain interest in their subject over a period of time, that it will be of worth to others, that it is possible to achieve and will be sufficiently systematic and rigorous to gain academic recognition.

The M.Phil. provided academic input and seminar support for students' research. However the shift between social work and research modes was, for many, difficult. Some felt that the only way to achieve authority was to use quantitative methods: others pursued qualitative approaches for the same reasons. All were concerned that their study should be valued by their peers and within their agencies as well as earning them a higher degree.

For students researching in their own field of work there were added complications. For example, experience suggests that it is neither desirable nor possible to act as a manager or practitioner and as researcher within the agency at the same time. It was important that the methods and design of the research and the way access was negotiated enabled students to separate these roles. Research in the student's own area of practice also led to tensions. For example, it was easy for the student-as-researcher to respond to an interviewee as if in a social work practitioner role. There were circumstances where students decided that it was unethical not to respond as a social worker even if this compromised their research approach. Or they began to question their own practice with the same critical analysis applied to their research data – a potentially painful emotional experience which could be disabling to both work and research.

The effects and impact of being a researcher can seldom be fully appreciated prior to undertaking a study: the personal process whereby the research affects the researcher and vice-versa has been little considered in the literature. Feminist approaches are looking at the significance of the connections, interactions and emotional dynamics involved in the research process (Stanley and Wise 1983) but most texts assume an objective researcher able to remain as if hermetically sealed from the impact of their actions. Part of the intention of the M.Phil. course was, however, to understand and analyse processes, relationships and interactions. This was applied to the research activity as well as the work of organisations. Research seminars frequently considered, for example, the impact of emotionally charged and difficult material generated by data gathering. Respondents in research into social care agencies and services are often commenting on highly personal and painful experiences. The emotional impact of this can be transferred to the person carrying out the research and may resonate with their own experience. It is clear that, unless this can be recognised and worked with at a conscious level, it can affect the way the data is viewed. If the researcher also holds a full-time post the impact may also affect their paid occupation.

We suggested earlier that capacity for independent thought and action were hallmarks of the advanced practitioner. Research helps to develop professional authority since students gain unique knowledge of and expertise in their selected field of study. The loneliness of research – standing alone in obtaining, interpreting and presenting the findings – is also formative. It is a means by which students gain experience of acting with autonomy based on their own judgements.

In carrying out their research students faced four differing kinds of expectation: academic achievement, peer recognition, working within a research ethic that did not compromise social work values and managing the emotional impact of the research experience.

Responsibilities and Investment in Learning

What this analysis highlights is that it is primarily course members who manage the complex activities entailed in taking an advanced course. They have to encompass a series of role switches on an almost daily basis, work across personal, professional and institutional boundaries and maintain the integrity of their different areas of work in the process.

Should this, in the interests of attaining professional autonomy, be such an individual responsibility and investment? What is the proper stance of the different stakeholders in relation to educational and research undertakings? Much hinges on how the purposes of advanced programmes, the ownership of learning and the benefits of study and research are viewed.

However these questions are answered there are three cases which can be made:

- for greater collaboration between stakeholders in clarifying the aims and purposes of advanced programmes,

- for more exploration of how advanced study and empirical research can be utilised and

- for greater understanding of what is involved in following advanced courses and more support for the individual learner.

First, the rhetoric of community care and commentaries on its implementation point to the need for service agencies that are flexible, responsive, able to work in collaboration with others, to forge new relationships and to maintain links with providers, purchasers and users. Many of these characteristics require the capacity for vision and innovation – the kind of skills that can be developed through advanced level study and research. The case for agencies to invest in staff development and job enhancement, as happens in other service industries, must be a strong one on these grounds. To date the tendency has been to see post-qualifying courses as providing education and training that is of immediate relevance and application in the workplace. Approaches to staff development at this level are, typically, of a bolt-on and instrumental nature which falls far short of a coherent or developmental agency policy for staff training. However, the growing recognition of the value of staff development suggests that service agencies will have to take a more active part in shaping the educational resources which promote this.

There is also a strong case for involving service users in social work education. Alongside the emphasis on enabling individual user participation in services there is an increasing demand from agencies for user organisations to help in service planning, review and development. A report on a recent consultation exercise (Beresford 1994) offers guidance on, and raises issues about, policy and practice for increased user involvement in basic qualifying courses. This work (together with the growing number of studies on user participation such as, for example, Beresford and Harding 1993, Ellis 1993, Morris and Lindow 1993, Smale and Tuson 1993) helps to legitimate the place of lay views and experience alongside academic and professional sources of knowledge in social work education and training. In relation to courses at all levels, user perspectives are a key source of critical commentary. What kind of direct representation or research is required to make these authoritative rather than anecdotal and available for debate at advanced levels?

But there may also be a case for seeing professional development as the responsibility of the individual. If part of the value of the advanced practitioner or manager is their capacity for reflection, analysis and independent judgement, tying them into an agency-led programme of staff development may not help to promote or preserve these qualities. Again there is a tension between using advanced educational opportunities instrumentally, in the service of agency objectives, and speculatively or idiosyncratically, in the service of individual, professional aspirations.

There is, we believe, a strong case for those who provide, pursue, utilise and potentially benefit from higher level programmes to collaborate in discussion about their aims and purposes. Those who offer advanced courses have a responsibility to demonstrate how academic and research teaching link with and promote agency and other interests. The wider responsibility is to ensure that the value of advanced study is recognised, or debated, in the interests of preserving an independent and critical voice in social work – the peer professional community.

Second, we have touched on a number of issues about how advanced study and research are viewed and utilised. A central issue seems to be that agencies are more likely to assess relevance or value by looking at the substantive content or focus of study rather than at the training, skills, discipline or tools the experience provides. The assessment tends to relate to the specific rather than the generic educational value of courses. There have been few incentives for service agencies to invest in intellectual capital but this may already be changing. Purchasers and providers are having to respond to new demands and expectations and to include lay and user views in the way services are reviewed and developed and this requires a climate of openness and the capacity to change. It is innovative rather than prescribed responses established patterns and traditions of service which are more likely to meet these demands while preserving essential continuities. Utilising the experience of staff on advanced training and education programmes in a systematic and planned way is one route by which agencies can access such knowledge and skills.

A third set of issues relates to the experience of the students who take advanced programmes and the kind of support they need. Our discussion highlights how students face complex tasks which require considerable emotional and mental effort as well as time and money resources.

The M.Phil. students were not unusual in investing a high level of personal time and energy in their course. Although employers gave permission, the agency environment in which most students were pursuing their studies was disabling. The drop out rate from the M.Phil., strongly linked with increased work pressures or changes in the workplace – was about 25 per cent. Again, we do not know how typical this might be of advanced programmes but any drop-out represents an actual and potential wastage of time and effort on the part of students, academic staff and agencies. It raises questions about the way courses are designed and run, how candidates are recruited and the extent to which employers are, or are helped to become, active participants in, and beneficiaries of, the educational process.

Who should take a lead role in ensuring that students are well supported and that their study time is properly negotiated? Course staff have a primary responsibility to see that the design and demands of the course are congruent and realistic and that candidates have a full picture of what is entailed over the whole study period. How far should they be involved in discussions within agencies about staff development, about the links between course and agency objectives and about the application of academic studies and re-search? Should courses set requirements for employers which, if not met, would bar a student from entry in the interests of reducing wastage? The answers relate to the extent to which it is important that the course maintains both an independent space for learning and enquiry while, at the same time, being involved in dialogue with professional, agency or other external interests.

Conclusions

We are aware that we have posed more questions than we have attempted to answer. The central issues relate to how higher level training is viewed: as value added for the agency; for services and thereby users; for the advance-ment of professional knowledge and expertise or for students as individuals? The costs of advanced study – in time, money and personal resources – are high, requiring investment from individuals and from agencies. But compari-sons with other sectors would show that training for leadership and innovation is likely to be cost-effective in the longer term.

Services should be striving for excellence. Advanced study is an essential element in developing professional practice and the knowledge base of social work and social services. Although costly in financial and personal terms, the payoff is in creative, reflective, innovative and competent leaders in strategic and operational management, in policy making and planning and in practice. At the moment it seems that the burden of bridging the gaps between course and workplace is left with the student as if there were no other stakeholders or beneficiaries of advanced level study. While it is important that educational opportunities and research studies are inde-pendent of agency objectives, it is doubtful that education in the professions

– particularly at advanced level – should be decoupled from service and service user values and interests.

References

Beresford, P. (1984) *Changing the Culture: Involving Service Users in Social Work Education.* CCETSW Paper 32.2

Beresford, P. and Harding, T. (eds) (1993) *A Challenge to Change: Practical experience of building user-led services.* London: National Institute for Social Work.

CCETSW (1990) *The Requirements for Post Qualifying Education and Training in the Personal Social Services: A Framework for Continuing Professional Development.* Paper 31. London: CCETSW.

Ellis, K. (1993) *Squaring the Circle: User and Carer Participation in Needs Assessment.* Joseph Rowntree Foundation & Community Care.

Goodlad, S. (ed) (1984) *Education for the Professions. Quis Custodiet?* London: Nelson, SRHE & NFER.

Hey, A. (1991) *Post-Qualifying Education and Training: Towards a Methods Exemplar.* Study conducted for CCETSW.

Morris, J. and Lindow, V. (1993) *User Participation in Community Care Services.* Department of Health Community Care Task Force.

Rushton, A. and Martyn, H. (1993) *Learning for Advanced Practice. A study of away-based training.* Paper 31.1. London: CCETSW.

Salzberger-Wittenberg, I., Henry, G., and Osborne, E. (1983) *The Emotional Experience of Learning and Teaching.* London: Routledge and Kegan Paul.

Smale, G. and Tuson, G. (1993) *Empowerment, Assessment, Care Management and the Skilled Worker.* London: HMSO.

Stanley, L. and Wise, S. (1983) *Breaking Out: Feminist Consciousness and Feminist Research.* London: Routledge & Kegan Paul.

Walker, C. (1992) *Transition from Practitioner to Manager in Social Work.* M.Phil. thesis, Brunel University.

Youll, P. and McCourt-Perring, C. (1993) *Raising Voices: Ensuring Quality in Residential Care.* London: HMSO.

Youll, P. (1985) The learning community. In R. Harris (ed) *Educating Social Workers.* Leicester: Association of Teachers in Social Work Education.

List of Contributors

Stephen Briggs is Clinical Lecturer in Social Work in the Adolescent Department of the Tavistock Clinic where he is engaged in clinical work and is joint organising tutor of the M.A. in Child Care Practice, Policy and Research. He is completing Ph.D. research based on observational study. His current interests include consultation, group relations, and developing observational study on social work courses.

Gill Gorell Barnes is Senior Clinical Lecturer in Social Work at the Tavistock Clinic, Honorary Senior Lecturer at Birkbeck College, and Consultant for Training at the Institute of Family Therapy.

Mary Henkel is a Senior Lecturer in the Department of Government, Brunel University. She was a founder of the joint Brunel-Tavistock M.Phil. in Social Work course and her most recent research has been on graduate education in Britain.

Judy Hildebrand is a family therapist, Clinical Director at the Institute of Family Therapy, and Senior Clinical Lecturer at the Tavistock Clinic. She has published on bereavement, group work, sexual abuse and the effects of marital conflict on children.

Lynette Hughes is a Senior Marital Psychotherapist at the Tavistock Marital Studies Institute. Previously she was Principal Social Worker in the Department of Child and Adolescent Psychiatry at the Maudsley Hospital. Her interests include the impact of couple dynamics in child care work, and staff supervision.

Sandra Jones has completed major research studies on maximum security imprisonment, police-public relationships and equal opportunities in the police. She was a member of the Centre for the Study of Community and Race Relations at Brunel University, and has directed the Enterprise in

Higher Education programme for six years. She is currently Senior Research Fellow in the Centre for the Evaluation of Public Policy and Practice.

Richard Joss is a Principal Partner of IRM International, a management consultancy group specialising in human resource development, and a Senior Research Fellow in the Centre for the Evaluation of Public Policy and Practice at Brunel University.

Ilan Katz qualified as a social worker at the University of the Witwatersrand. He is now National Evaluation Officer for the NSPCC, currently seconded to the Centre for the Evaluation of Public Policy and Practice at Brunel University. His research interests include comprehensive risk assessment, user empowerment and Area Child protection Committees. His Ph.D. concerned the development of racial identity in infants of mixed parentage.

Paul Pengelly was a staff member of the Tavistock Marital Studies Institute from 1978 to 1994, after twelve years in the probation service, and now works freelance. He has published on interprofessional collaboration and on counselling in infertility treatment centres.

Marilyn Pietroni is Principal Lecturer in Primary Health and Community Care at the University of Westminster. Her practice base is Marylebone Health Centre. As a social worker and adult psychotherapist, she taught at the Tavistock Clinic for many years, including the joint M.Phil. in Social Work. She edited *Right or Privilege?*, a book on post-qualifying training, is a former editor of the *Journal of Social Work Practice*, and with Jill Spratly, co-authored a recent report on interprofessional training priorities, *Creative Collaboration*.

Rose Stanford is a research fellow at the Tavistock Clinic, and teaches at the Centre for Community and Primary Health, University of Westminster. Her particular interests include interdisciplinary learning and collaboration, and she has recently completed an evaluation of shared learning in child protection.

Judith Trowell is Consultant Child and Adolescent Psychiatrist in the Department of Children and Families at the Tavistock Clinic; Senior Lecturer in the Childrens Department, Maudsley Hospital, and the Institute of Psychiatry; and honorary Senior Lecturer at the Royal Free Hospital School of Medicine. She has a special interest in child protection and has been extensively engaged in interdisciplinary training and in post-qualifying education for social workers. She is Chair of Young Minds and her books include *Children's Welfare and the Law* (with Michael King).

Clare Walker is a group manager for children's services in Hertfordshire Social Care, and formerly managed services for older people for Westminster City Council. She studied for her M.Phil. in Social Work at Brunel University and has extensive management experience in field, day care and residential settings.

Penny Youll is a Senior Research Fellow in social policy at Brunel University with a particular experience in evaluative research in health and social services. She was a Lecturer in Social Work and Applied Social Studies and currently teaches part-time on the M.Phil. in Social Work and M.A. courses at Brunel.

Margaret Yelloly was until retirement Tavistock Clinic Professor of Social Work at Brunel University and is currently part-time Research Professor at Brunel University College. Recent publications include the *Contribution of Psychodynamics to Professional Education in Social Work* and *Shared Learning in Child Protection*.

Subject
Index

Author Index

WITHDRAWN